PRAISE

"[An] eye opening l[...]om to
the psychiatrist's co[...]worst
qualities of two pow[...]ritten
and of much interes[...]
—*Kirkus Reviews*

"Lucid and accessible, immensely informative and insightful. . . . One of
the most important books on the relationship between the United States
and China to be published in at least a decade."
—**Glenn C. Altschuler,** *Huffington Post*

"An important and fascinating book about the structural changes and evolving codependency of the world's two largest and most dynamic economies.
Unbalanced is an education in growth, stability, and postwar globalization,
full of deep insights and colorful personalities on both sides, and wonder-
fully well written. Very few people have the breadth of knowledge and experience to write such a book."
—**A. Michael Spence, Nobel laureate in economics**

"How the United States and China will transit from precarious codependency
to stable coexistence is one of the most crucial questions for the twenty-first
century. Stephen Roach, with his profound grasp of the economic and political systems in the United States and China, describes the challenges, opportunities, and necessary adjustments for both countries. This is a timely
must-read book for anyone concerned about the future of the world."
—**Justin Yifu Lin, former chief economist, the World Bank**

"*Unbalanced* is a compelling analysis of China's transition to a new model
of economic growth and the challenges this transition will create for the
United States."
—**Nicholas Lardy, Anthony M. Solomon Senior Fellow, Peterson Institute for
International Economics**

UNBALANCED

STEPHEN ROACH

Unbalanced

THE CODEPENDENCY OF AMERICA AND CHINA

Yale UNIVERSITY PRESS

NEW HAVEN & LONDON

Yale University Press books may be purchased in quantity for
educational, business, or promotional use. For information, please e-mail
sales.press@yale.edu (U.S. office) or sales@yaleup.co.uk (U.K. office).

Set in Scala type by Integrated Publishing Solutions.
Printed in the United States of America.

The Library of Congress has cataloged the hardcover edition as follows:
Roach, Stephen, 1945–. Unbalanced : the codependency of America and China /
Stephen Roach.
pages   cm
Includes bibliographical references and index.
ISBN 978-0-300-18717-5 (hardback)
1. United States—Commerce—China. 2. China—Commerce—United States. I. Title.
HF3128.R63 2014
337.73051—dc23   2013021900

ISBN 978-0-300-21265-5 (pbk.)

A catalogue record for this book is available from the British Library.

10 9 8 7 6 5 4 3 2 1

For Katie

CONTENTS

China and America—or is it China versus America? The distinction lies at the core of the most important bilateral relationship of the twenty-first century. With 5,000 years of Chinese history dwarfing only about 240 years of U.S. experience, it may seem audacious to contrast such an old civilization with a relatively youthful country. But there can be no mistaking the significance of the interplay between the world's two largest and most powerful economies. The relationship between the United States and China may hold the key to a global economy that is now in great flux.

Yet that relationship is afflicted by a unique pathology. Both nations are trapped in a web of codependency. China has turned increasingly to the United States as the sustenance of its economic development strategy. At the same time, the United States has become heavily reliant on China as a major source of its growth. Psychologists warn of the inherent instability of codependency—of a mutual pathology that only worsens over time. That warning applies equally to economies. Without treatment, codependency presents great risks to both the U.S. and Chinese economies, with enormous implications for the rest of the world.

But there is an important twist in assessing the shared pathology of the United States and China. There are no guarantees that both nations are equally afflicted. That raises the possibility of an asymmetrical coping mechanism, with one economy lapsing into more destructive behavior than the other, or even one that begins to heal before the other. Codependency does not assign equal guilt to the United States and China in perpetuating this pathology. It simply underscores the two-way character of an insidious feedback loop. How the United States responds to China bears critically on how China responds to the United States.

Two recent developments have been especially important for the codependent U.S.-Sino relationship: First came the Great Recession of 2008–9—spawned by a financial crisis unlike any other in modern times. Because it was made in America, it drew into question the strategies of many in the developing world who are tightly linked to U.S. markets. Questions arose not only because the United States was a major driver of the demand that supported most export-led economies but also because the crisis discredited America's status as a role model.

These developments came as an especially rude awakening for China. Rapidly expanding exports have long been the most dynamic aspect of the Chinese growth equation. The crisis and its aftermath—an aftermath now glaringly punctuated by Europe's sovereign debt crisis—are likely to have a lasting impact on the external underpinnings of the all-powerful Chinese export machine. Moreover, modern China's stunning evolution from Soviet-style central planning to market-based socialism was shaped to an important degree by the aspirational image of the American Dream. That dream is now badly faded.

The sustainability challenges facing China didn't arise just from its external linkages and the postcrisis dampening of external demand. There are also serious internal problems that arose from China's own miscalculations. After more than thirty years of spectacular growth, China is now plagued by worrisome imbalances in its domestic economy—from income inequality and excess resource consumption to environmental degradation and pollution. As the Great Recession exposed America's imbalances, it did the same for China's.

A second recent twist in the U.S.-China relationship reflects Washington's long-standing penchant for blaming others for problems of its own making, a deflection of responsibility that also fits the classic diagnostics of the psychologist. Twice in recent years, the U.S. Congress has come close to enacting trade sanctions against China to counter its alleged currency manipulation. Democrats and Republicans agree on very little these days, but in an era of historically high unemployment, they are united in blaming China for what ails America—namely an unprecedented shortfall of saving.

If such legislation were enacted, it would impose steep tariffs on all goods shipped from China into the United States. Not only would this deal a devastating blow to China and the rest of an increasingly China-centric Asian supply chain, it would backfire in the United States. It would do grave damage to hard-pressed American families by raising the costs of the goods that the United States imports from abroad. It could also send the dollar plunging, interest rates soaring, or both.

In a highly charged political climate, venting by the U.S. Congress is hardly unexpected. But there is no telling if or when political bluster becomes reality. If allowed to shape law, U.S.-Sino trade frictions have the potential to undo many of the most important benefits of international trade and globalization. Misdirected trade sanctions would be Washington's biggest economic policy blunder since the Smoot-Hawley tariffs of the early 1930s. At a minimum, the unthinkable Bad Dream has now become thinkable.

How did we get to this point? How could the United States have squandered its once unchallenged global economic leadership? Is China at risk of falling into the same trap? Why is it so easy for the United States to lash out at China as a scapegoat? Is it Washington's last gasp of hegemonic desperation? Is it a rite of passage, marking the decline of one great power and the ascendancy of another—the American century evolving into the China century? Is it the manifestation of a deep-rooted mutual misunderstanding?

These questions are part of a narrative that has been unfolding for many years. It's hard to put a finger on how and where it all started. But there can be no mistaking the critical role played by America's fixation on growth for the sake of growth—a mindset that ultimately became prescriptive and came to rely on asset and credit bubbles to sustain a false prosperity.

China's dependence on America's false prosperity is equally important. China took American growth for granted, only to ask questions later, and used the fruits of that growth as the basis of its own development strategy. Each of these trends fed the other. They allowed both nations to push the envelope on economic growth, but ultimately at great peril.

The days of false prosperity were always numbered. Underpinned by bubbles, outsize imbalances emerged. Imbalances aren't sustainable, and most knew the end would come someday, even if they thought it was not imminent. But the crisis of 2008–9 left little doubt that such a realization could not be deferred to some distant point in the future; it had finally arrived. The bubbles that supported America's spending binge have burst, bringing down China's artificial export boom as well.

Yet before the Great Recession, it all seemed so sustainable. China gave Americans a way to repeal the basic laws of economics. They could live beyond their means, and that enabled the Chinese to do the same. Or so they both thought. The severe recession of 2008–9 unmasked these fantasies for both nations. China and the United States, each caught up in false prosperity, now need new recipes for sustainable economic growth.

Both nations need to learn tough and possibly painful lessons. With America reeling from postcrisis aftershocks, China can't count on bruised and battered U.S. consumers to support its exports and sustain its seemingly invincible economic strength. Nor can America go back to its bubble economy for another fix. The crisis and its aftermath bring U.S.-China codependency into sharp focus. Each nation needs to take a hard look in its own mirror.

That won't be easy. Denial, consistent with the pathology of codependency, runs deep in both nations. Rather than embrace the hard tasks of rebalancing and structural change, each country finds it far easier to hope for a return to the way it once was. But that is hoping against hope in an era when the script of an interdependent world has been turned inside out.

Physics teaches us that momentum is a powerful force to arrest. Psychology tells us that it is hard to break old habits. And economic experience demonstrates that structural changes tend to be painful and glacial. But time and again, history has been altered by the unexpected—geopolitical developments, natural disasters, or technological breakthroughs. Impossible as it is to predict the unexpected, it is well worth the effort to ponder what might drive the coming realignment of the world's two largest economies.

China seems to get it. Since the days of Deng Xiaoping, one of modern China's greatest strengths has been strategy—especially when it comes to economic policy and macromanagement. And China has recently adopted a new strategy that entails a fundamental rebalancing of its economy, shifting away from its increasingly unsustainable manufacturing-led export model toward internal private consumption and more services-led growth. That will allow China to reduce its fixation on the sheer speed of economic growth and turn its attention instead to the quality dimension of the growth experience, which it has heretofore neglected. Rebalancing offers China the opportunity to aim for a lighter, cleaner, greener, and more sustainable economy.

America doesn't seem to get it. Strategy doesn't come easy for a nation whose economy sits on the bedrock of the Invisible Hand. Despite the obvious warning signs of massive imbalances and the bubbles they spawned, there is a strong predisposition in the United States to resurrect the timeworn recipe of consumer-led economic growth. That would be fine if America had a solid base of income generation and tended to its competitive strengths, investing in its people and infrastructure and funding those investments with internally generated saving. But America has done none of that in recent years, making it next to impossible to recapture the magic.

Codependency is about to call America's bluff. China is pushing ahead with rebalancing. That shift will have enormous implications for a tired U.S. growth model. As the Chinese consumer comes to life, China's saving will decline, reducing its international current account surplus and thereby diminishing its demand for U.S. Treasuries and other dollar-based assets. As the world's largest international borrower, a savings-short United States will have an exceedingly difficult time replacing its largest foreign lender. At a minimum, that should squeeze the terms on which America has been borrowing in international capital markets, yet another reason to underscore the potential for destabilizing risks to interest rates and the dollar. The feedback effects of such developments will only add to the stiff headwinds already constraining U.S. economic growth. Made in China, these pressures are coming—whether America likes them or not.

The United States needs to think hard about how it will respond to the Next China. Codependency frames America's choices in a stark light. Like China, it needs to set aside the false assumptions of a now antiquated recipe for growth, and it must embrace rebalancing. A rebalanced U.S. economy, one that saves more and draws much greater support from capital spending and exports, will be well positioned to sustain growth in the years ahead. But if the United States resists that rebalancing, failing to muster the political will to pull it off, it will suffer as the Next China emerges.

Looking at this challenge through the lens of codependency offers an important ray of hope for the U.S. growth dilemma. China's rebalancing should be seen as America's opportunity, a basis for its long-term resurgence. A growth-starved United States simply cannot rely on another consumption binge to solve its most daunting postcrisis problem: the enormous overhang of unemployed and underemployed workers. With unusually sluggish U.S. consumption likely to remain the postcrisis norm, exports and investment—investment in its people as well as in infrastructure and new productive capacity—are the only hopes for offsetting an otherwise chronic growth shortfall.

The potential export bonanza to China is an especially important aspect of this tale of codependency. China is America's third-largest and most rapidly growing export market. For that reason alone, any resurgence of U.S. exports depends on sharply expanded shipments of American-made goods to China. The United States offers a product line that would sell very well in the Next China—especially motor vehicles, aircraft, appliances, pharmaceuticals, and sophisticated machinery.

As with China, the trick for America lies in implementation—in this case, a competitive revitalization of hollowed-out export industries as well as negotiations that focus on enhanced access to domestic Chinese markets. Polarized domestic politics only complicate this equation, especially Washington's recent penchant for threatening China with trade sanctions. If the United States chooses that option, it is bound to evoke reciprocal actions from Beijing that would effectively foreclose American exporters' chances to participate in the coming surge of Chinese consumption.

In the end, the psychologists probably have it right: Codependency is not a stable condition for either human beings or economies. It tends to feed on itself. While China and the United States have benefited in the past from their seemingly symbiotic relationship, they have now crossed the line of a sustainable codependency. America's excesses have become the sustenance of China's unsustainable development, and vice versa. This poses enormous challenges for both.

Rebalancing is the only lasting solution for unstable codependency. It will take enormous effort, self-discipline, and time. It will also require a coherent framework of action—what might even be called a strategy. China excels at that—America abhors anything that even hints of a plan. While the stakes are obviously high, this should not be seen as a race between the world's two largest economies. The question is *not* how America can win against China but how it can best improve itself. The question is the same for China.

If it occurs, the coming rebalancing of the United States and China is not a big deal just for the two nations. It could be a transformational event for the world at large. At critical moments in history, a realignment of economic power has often been associated with major shifts in military might and geopolitical stability. Historian Paul Kennedy, in *The Rise and Fall of the Great Powers,* has argued that the ascendancy and ultimate demise of great powers reflects such tectonic shifts. Does a similar fate await a U.S.-Chinese rebalancing?

Such a possibility can hardly be taken lightly. The United States, in many respects, is a good fit with the classic Kennedy example of a declining power. The imbalance between America's unparalleled projection of its vast military power and the erosion of its domestic economic base is, in fact, quite consistent with the pattern of "geostrategic overreach" that Kennedy traces back to the crumbling of dynastic power in Europe in the early sixteenth century. Juxtaposed against the backdrop of a rising China and the aspirational, indeed nationalistic, imagery of the "China Dream" being espoused by its new leader, Xi Jinping, the two nations could well be entering an increasingly precarious phase of their codependency.

The endgame is anyone's guess. The possibility of a major power realignment—at first economic, eventually military—can hardly be ruled out. It is safe to say that the strategic thinking and economic management skills of both the United States and China could ultimately determine whether this transition is both stable and peaceful.

While few would dispute the imperatives of a seamless rebalancing, it is naïve to take that for granted. Leaders of both nations must take the risks of economic and geopolitical instability seriously. The diagnosis of codependency prescribes its own cure—coalescing around a new identity that comes from economic realignment and rebalancing. While the U.S. and Chinese economies should emerge stronger and eventually less dependent on each other, improving the all-important relationship between them is vital to any such cure.

Yet there are grounds for serious concern on this count. The Great Recession and escalating trade tensions leave both countries on the brink of a very slippery slope. The same can be said for the confluence of the China Dream and the mounting perils of America's savings-short economy. It will require leadership, political will, shared values, and mutual trust to establish a more sustainable relationship. Long haunted by increasingly precarious imbalances, the United States and China are now at critical junctures in their economic journeys. Can they make the leap from false prosperity to something more sustainable?

PART I

IN THE BEGINNING

ECONOMIC GROWTH DEFINES the road to prosperity. But that road can have many twists and turns. The rise and fall of nations speak to its unexpected detours. In the early nineteenth century, China was the world's dominant economy. Courtesy of forensic accounting metrics, we know that the Chinese economy in 1820 accounted for about one-third of world gross domestic product (GDP)—more than fifteen times the share of the United States, which accounted for less than 2 percent. By 1950 there had been a stunning reversal: the U.S. share had risen to 27 percent, whereas China's slice had shriveled to 4.5 percent.

China's economic collapse in the late nineteenth century and in the first half of the twentieth—especially when juxtaposed against the extraordinary ascendancy of the United States—turned the global economic map inside out. The United States was reaping the rewards of a spectacular industrialization. China not only failed to industrialize, it had suffered a dynastic implosion followed by chaos, fragmentation, and ultimately revolution.

But now there is the potential for another role reversal. On the heels of a stunning thirty-year resurgence, China has already surpassed Japan as the second-largest economy in the world. The debate is over when—not whether—it will surpass the United States.

Yet the growth sweepstakes can be misleading, especially in light of huge population disparities between nations. What matters most is per capita incomes—spreading and raising the income for as large a cross section of a country's population as possible. This is the ultimate challenge for the economic development of poor nations—just as steady growth in per capita incomes is the arbiter of sustained prosperity for rich economies.

China's 1.3 billion citizens have average per capita income levels that are still less than 13 percent of those in America. While China will undoubtedly close the aggregate GDP gap with the United States at some point in the next ten to twenty years, the disparity in individual living standards will remain large for decades.

In contrast to China's spectacular growth in output and income, the United States has been struggling on both counts over the past forty years. But that has not arrested America's infatuation with the self-gratification of excess consumption. Washington stopped at nothing—including reckless financial engineering and the delusions of self-regulation—to encourage American citizens to live beyond their means. China, meanwhile, seized the moment, building a low-cost production platform that catered to better-off consumers elsewhere, especially those in the United States. This strategy played a key role in rejuvenating a Chinese economy that was in shambles after the Cultural Revolution in the late 1970s.

The United States and China have been especially tenacious in their search for growth. For China, it was about the survival of a vulnerable nation, whereas for the U.S. hegemon it was more about sustaining prosperity and power. Irrespective of the motives, the countries were united in their fixation on growth and entered into a new and powerful collaboration aimed at achieving that objective. The United States provided China with something very important: the world's largest base of external demand that could support China's export-led production model. China, for its part, offered the United States a broad menu of cheap goods to satisfy its hard-pressed consumers as well as a vast source of foreign capital that could enable it to enjoy sustained economic growth despite a lack of domestic saving.

Scale was a key aspect of this compact—two large economies had large gaps to fill. They quickly became hooked on what each could offer the other in their collective quest for economic growth. Out of that addiction came a codependency that eventually took on a life of its own.

Initially, economic collaboration between the United States and China was beneficial. It allowed each nation to draw on the other's strengths in supporting their collective growth agendas. But in the end, this marriage of convenience morphed into a destabilizing codependency.

America took its consumption model to excess and squandered its savings on asset and credit bubbles. China's low-cost production platform and cheap supply of surplus financial capital enabled this increasingly unstable U.S. model. China, for its part, pushed its export-led growth model to excess. That led to serious imbalances in its economy and an increasingly destabilizing surplus in its international current account balance. This couldn't have happened without support from the United States. America's seemingly endless demand for Chinese products helped perpetuate an increasingly unstable Chinese model.

And so, as collaboration went from benign to malign, two unstable and unbalanced economies ran faster and faster on the treadmill of economic growth. And they needed each other more and more to pull it off. Sustainability was the ultimate constraint. The mirror images of codependency ultimately played a key role in spawning the massive global imbalances that came to a head with the Great Recession of 2008–9.

The Political Economy
of False Prosperity

I n 1933, one out of every four Americans was out of work. Karl Marx appeared to be right—the capitalist model was on the brink of failure. Forty years later, China was in the throes of the Cultural Revolution and its economy was in shambles. Famines had killed thirty million of its citizens, poverty was rampant, and joblessness was soaring. Socialism wasn't the answer either.

Both nations were determined to find that ever-elusive answer. Seared by these wrenching experiences, the United States and China vowed never again to allow their economies to go to the brink. The U.S. Congress formalized this commitment with the Full Employment Act of 1946, forever enshrining maximal growth and full employment as overarching goals of public policy.[1] In China, the pledge was implemented through an extraordinary leadership transition—the post-Mao ascendancy of Deng Xiaoping, who drove the "reforms and opening up" of the modern Chinese economy.

Two systems, two ideologies, two political frameworks. Yet out of their dissimilar origins and experiences came remarkably similar commitments: Pro-growth policies were consecrated as the elixir of prosperity.

This simple but powerful belief eventually turned seductive. When the fundamental underpinnings of growth come under pressure, as they inevitably do, social and political backlash invariably demands a new recipe for growth. That's where well-intentioned nations often get into trouble. Pressured into what can be called the political economy of false prosperity, nations are tempted to cut corners. They begin to chart perilous shortcuts to economic growth. Perhaps unwittingly at first, the United States and China both succumbed to those very temptations. Over time, as increasingly codependent economies, they relied heavily on each other to pull it off.

The Ultimate Consumer

Personal consumption is the essence of the American Dream. It has long defined the ultimate in success for the world's most powerful economy. Most of the time during the past century, that dream came true. But there were times when it didn't. And that's where our story starts. During the 1930s and 1940s, most U.S. families were forced to do without—first by the Great Depression, then by wartime mobilization and rationing. Citizens of the Land of Plenty became steeped in hardship and sacrifice.

During those two decades, purchases of cars, furniture, appliances, and even clothing were put on hold—first out of necessity, due to soaring joblessness and near economic collapse, and then out of a purposeful and noble focus on military victory. It took everything a great nation could muster to endure these pressures, and the American consumer shouldered the bulk of the burden. For twenty years, a long and steady improvement of American lifestyles was put aside. The era of sacrifice became an age of pent-up demand.

With victory came economic recovery. Factories shifted from tanks back to cars, from armaments to consumer goods. The boys came home and went to college, or back to work. The great American job machine shifted into gear, sparking a regeneration of household incomes and purchasing power that allowed consumers to start chipping away, at last, at all that pent-up demand that had been deferred during Depression and wartime.

The resurgence of jobs and consumption fed on itself—just as the new Keynesian economic analysis promised.[2] The recovery in consumer demand pushed manufacturing plants back to full capacity—sparking an investment boom aimed at modernizing and expanding America's production platform. The powerful combination of consumer demand and business investment gave further impetus to employment and labor income—long the sustenance of vigorous growth in personal consumption. The American Dream was back.

There seemed to be no stopping the United States. There were certainly no serious threats from foreign competition. The United States was the only major industrial power to emerge largely unscathed from the war; Europe and Japan were focused on rebuilding and reconstruction. Nor were the poor developing economies a factor. The United States prospered largely as an autonomous or "closed" economic system, making most of what it consumed. Merchandise imports averaged just 3.5 percent of gross domestic product in the 1950s and 1960s. America and its workers had their home markets largely to themselves. In many respects, it was an era of sheltered innocence.

Things started to sour in the late 1960s. The war in Vietnam shattered the nation's newfound tranquility—on social, political, and economic grounds. At the same time, Washington took on the weighty responsibility of the Great Society: civil rights, poverty reduction, medical care, and retirement security. From the standpoint of macroeconomic policy, this should have been a classic "guns and butter" tradeoff—in essence, weighing a sacrifice by the private sector against extraordinary new responsibilities being taken on by the public sector.[3] But with memories of the 1930s and 1940s still vivid, America was not in the mood for another sacrifice.

So Washington finessed the choice, funding massive new domestic programs such as Medicare while also escalating a costly war in Asia. The federal government embarked on both of these commitments without tightening its purse strings—either in fiscal or in monetary terms. This was the first in a long line of efforts to "kick the can down the road." But the economy knew better. Slack capacity vanished in both labor and product markets, and inflationary pressures started to mount.

In the early 1970s, complications intensified. The accomplishments of the first two decades of the post–World War II era instilled a false confidence in the art and practice of economic management. Inflation was incorrectly diagnosed as an administrative problem that could be addressed by a peacetime version of the wartime wage and price controls that were so successfully deployed in the 1940s. At the same time that U.S. President Richard Nixon put these controls back in place, in August 1971, he also responded to international pressures on the dollar by severing America's commitment to the gold standard—in effect, depriving U.S. economic policy of its anchor to history's most deeply entrenched store of value.[4]

Meanwhile, America's boom was matched by comparable trends elsewhere in the global economy. A synchronous surge in worldwide economic activity in the early 1970s only intensified the inflationary pressures. Then came the Yom Kippur War of late 1973, the first oil embargo, and soaring energy prices. The kindling wood of the Great Inflation was lit, and the era of innocence became unhinged.[5]

One policy mistake followed another. Notwithstanding soaring prices, long gas lines, and mounting wage pressures, Washington deepened its resolve in one key aspect of economic stewardship: Despite a worrisome buildup of inflationary pressures, both fiscal and monetary authorities resisted the temptation to tighten their policies. True to the Employment Act of 1946, they were unflinching in their pro-growth commitment.

This single commitment unlocks much of the story that lies ahead—not just for the United States but also for China. By erring on the side of policy accommodation, U.S. authorities thought they were protecting the American consumer as the mainstay of the modern U.S. growth miracle. Tax incentives such as the deductibility of interest paid on home mortgages and other forms of consumer credit left little doubt of Washington's pro-consumption bias. A notable lack of savings incentives, like interest rate ceilings on consumer saving accounts, only reinforced this tendency.[6] It was all about maximizing current consumption. And it seemed to work. The U.S. economy's share of personal consumption expenditures, which had fluctuated in a tight range of 59–61 percent of gross domestic product in the 1950s and 1960s, started to drift up by the mid-1970s.

This is where the plot thickens. Beginning in the early 1980s, the traditional sources of U.S. consumer demand came under increasing pressure. Job growth slackened, as did gains in inflation-adjusted, or real, wages. Overall growth in labor incomes started to falter. The noose was tightening on the American consumer.

Even with the benefit of hindsight, it is not altogether clear what caused the squeeze on the U.S. economy's ability to boost labor income. Techno-logical change, by substituting machines for people, and globalization, by drawing low-wage offshore labor into integrated production platforms, are high on the list of likely suspects.[7] So, too, are demographics, especially an aging population, as well as the entry into the workforce of relatively inexperienced and low-paid female and younger workers. The demise of labor unions and the wage rigidity they stood for also squeezed worker compensation.

But the result was surprising. The squeeze in labor income did not stop the American consumer, and personal consumption continued to rise as a share of the U.S. economy. By the late 1980s the share was nearly 64 per-cent. This seemingly incongruous development—weak income growth and strong consumption—holds the key to America's deepest macroeconomic imbalances, such as low saving, balance of payments and international trade deficits, and a steady buildup of debt.

Unsurprisingly, the deeper the hole American families found them-selves in, the more the body politic was willing to cut corners to keep the consumption miracle alive. It was less a set of specific new policies that were enacted to boost consumption than it was an overarching mindset. Monetary and fiscal policies were locked in pro-growth settings, and per-sonal consumption was to be stimulated at all costs. And so the seeds were sown of what turned out to be a false prosperity.

It was not until the mid-1990s, however, that those seeds started to sprout and U.S. consumers figured out how to live well beyond their means, as those means were delineated by their wage incomes. Asset-based wealth creation held the key as a new source of purchasing power. First, there was the so-called wealth effect of a surging stock market.[8] There was noth-ing wrong with spending stock market wealth, went the argument. It was a proxy for long-term savings generated directly through portfolio invest-ments and indirectly via retirement funds invested in equity markets. As the stock market took off in the late 1990s, the ever-rising value of these in-vestments was widely presumed to rest on the solid fundamentals of Amer-ica's productivity resurgence stemming from miraculous breakthroughs in information technology.[9]

The only problem was that it was a pipe dream. In 2000, the stock market

surge of the late 1990s was unmasked as a bubble. Led by speculative buying in dotcom stocks, the NASDAQ composite index essentially doubled in
the twelve months ending March 2000 before plunging by more than 60
percent in the following ten months. Other broader indexes, such as the
S&P 500 and the Dow Jones Industrials, also surged, then suffered dramatic declines. When the equity bubble burst, the seemingly impeccable
logic of the wealth effect was quickly turned inside out. Many individual
investors believed that the stock market surge of the late 1990s was sustainable. The resulting wealth destruction shattered those expectations and
dealt increasingly equity-dependent families a devastating blow.

After some delay, consumption growth slowed briefly in 2001, before the
American consumer got a second wind from another round of even bigger
bubbles—in this case, both property and credit. Courtesy of an unprecedented surge in home prices, together with the new financial technology of
home equity loans and mortgage refinancing that enabled homeowners to
extract unrealized capital gains from their personal residences, America's
consumer spending binge resumed, stronger than ever. Excessively easy
monetary policy played a key role in this phase of America's consumption
binge; low interest rates fueled bubbles in property prices and mortgage
credit that enabled U.S. homeowners to keep consuming well in excess of
their wage incomes.

A transition from income-dependent to asset- and ultimately bubble-
dependent consumption had occurred. It played a decisive role in America's reckless journey down the road of false prosperity. The blame for this
detour will long be debated. But there can be no mistaking its visible manifestations.

For starters, the consumer-led tilt of the U.S. economy spiraled into rar-
efied territory. Personal consumption soared from 64 percent of gross domestic product in 1990 to 69 percent by 2011—a record for America and, in
fact, for any nation. As before, this spending binge came against a backdrop of unusually anemic growth in labor income. Inflation-adjusted compensation paid to workers increased a cumulative total of just 8 percent
over the 2002–11 period—one-fourth the average gains over comparable
periods of the four earlier business cycle expansions.[10]

This confluence of a record surge of consumption growth juxtaposed against a severe shortfall of labor income generation delineates the broad parameters of America's lapse into a false prosperity. The disturbing consequences of this mismatch were dismissed by many as benign manifestations of a New Economy.[11] The personal savings rate fell to a post–World War II low of 2.3 percent of disposable personal income in 2005—well below the 9.3 percent norm in the final three decades of the twentieth century. Household sector indebtedness surged to a record 132 percent of disposable personal income in early 2008—well above the 43 percent average over the 1970–2000 period. And a savings-short U.S. economy, aggressively borrowing surplus savings from abroad in order to grow, ran massive current account and foreign trade deficits.

American consumers were in a league of their own. The United States, with only 4.5 percent of the world's population, spent $10.7 trillion on personal consumption in 2011, accounting for 17 percent of global consumer demand. U.S. consumption is nearly 35 percent larger than pan-European consumption, even though Europe's population is slightly larger than that of the United States. It is four times that of China and India combined, even though those countries account for close to 40 percent of the world's population, nearly nine times that of the United States.

Yet the ultimate consumer was in serious trouble. The more American families labored under mounting pressures, the greater became the temptation to uncover new—and eventually fleeting—sources of purchasing power. First the equity market, then the home—U.S. consumers became overaggressive in converting their asset holdings into purchasing power. Never mind that those sources rested on a shaky foundation of asset and credit bubbles. The political economy of false prosperity deluded a generation of Americans into believing they could pull it off. Sadly, that became an irresistible siren song for many other economies around the world, including China's.

The Ultimate Producer

On the surface, a very different story seemed to be playing out in China. The contrasts are obvious and noteworthy—a poor country versus a rich country, as well as the juxtaposition of one of the world's oldest civilizations with one of the newest. But there are also some striking parallels that connect the respective journeys taken by the United States and China since the late 1940s.

For America, the Second World War ended in a rush of victory. For China, it brought another, equally wrenching war—the civil war of the Communist Revolution—followed by the birth of a new nation. America found itself picking up the pieces as the world's strongest economy and a victorious military power. China, meanwhile, was essentially starting from scratch from the standpoints of governance, poverty reduction, economic development, and social harmony.

The first thirty years of China's journey, under the volatile and messianic leadership of Mao Zedong, were filled with chaos and turmoil. In the early years after the founding of the People's Republic of China, Mao borrowed heavily from the Stalinist economic policy template of the Soviet Union— drawing up a series of complex five-year plans that provided detailed, yet often inconsistent, sector-by-sector and industry-by-industry targets for production, investment, employment, and prices.[12]

The plans of the 1950s and 1960s were unmitigated disasters. That was especially true of China's Second Five-Year Plan (1958–62), which featured the "Great Leap Forward." Intended to modernize China's backward and long-fragmented agricultural sector, the plan focused on the consolidation of 740,000 farm cooperatives into 26,000 communes. This was sold as a recipe for efficiency and sustenance for a Chinese population that, at the time, included some 500 million peasants.

The leap was anything but forward. The efficiency dividends of the economies of scale were undermined by Mao's fanatical emphasis on self-reliance. Peasants were scattered to the countryside in search of natural resources, and production was localized into misadventures such as "backyard steel furnaces." Unwieldy large-scale communes began to fragment back into their earlier form of smaller cooperatives, and unrealistically ambitious agricultural production targets became a major source of embarrassment and hardship.[13] Output of grains, pork, and cotton plunged, leading to famines on an unprecedented scale. The human toll will never be known with precision. Estimates range from twenty million to forty million deaths by starvation in the late 1950s and early 1960s—unprecedented in the annals of modern history.[14]

At the same time, a major falling out with the Soviet Union severed China's most important link to the rest of the world. Out of this chaos, isolation, and sheer human tragedy, Mao unleashed modern China's most destructive force—the Cultural Revolution of 1967 to 1976. Jonathan Spence puts it best in depicting this tumultuous period as a "movement [that] defies simple classification."[15] At its core, it reflected Mao's attempt to repudiate emerging conservative elements in the Party and return to the more radical roots of the Communist Revolution. This entailed a massive disruption to work lives and education, to say nothing of a near complete breakdown of social cohesion. By the end of the Cultural Revolution, the Chinese economy was in shambles. From the standpoint of faltering economic growth, the first thirty years after the founding of the People's Republic of China had become lost decades for the Chinese economy—not all that dissimilar from the U.S. growth experience of the 1930s and 1940s, and a precursor of what was to await Japan, Asia's first postwar economic miracle. China was in desperate need of a new answer for an economy that was on the brink of outright collapse and a society that was torn by upheaval and distress.

The answer came only after the death of Mao Zedong in 1976. This was in a sense ironic. Historically, leadership transitions in China have frequently ushered in periods of great instability. That was certainly the case in the aftermath of the collapse of the Ming and Qing dynasties in the early seventeenth and early twentieth centuries, respectively, and the pattern seemed to repeat itself in the early years following Mao's death. At first, radical leaders of the Cultural Revolution—the notorious Gang of Four—made a grab for power, rushing in to fill the vacuum left by Mao's death and the subsequent leadership struggle between Hua Guofeng and Deng Xiaoping. But once Hua got the upper hand, the four aspiring leaders were arrested and the focus quickly returned to the fate of a struggling economy that was now desperate for recovery in the aftermath of the Cultural Revolution.

The twin perils of a shaky economy and persistent social instability weighed heavily on modern China's first major leadership transition. With the economy going from bad to worse, Hua's hold on power turned out to be far more tenuous than it initially appeared. Deng's fact-based pragmatism had much greater appeal, especially after he refocused attention on the "Four Modernizations," a new approach to Chinese economic development that stressed a balanced emphasis on agriculture, industry, national defense, and science and technology.[16]

He brought this approach to life in December 1978 at the Third Plenum of the 11th Central Committee of the Chinese Communist Party, with a forceful speech whose tone of ideological moderation came as welcome relief from the turmoil of the Cultural Revolution and the post-Mao power struggle. Deng focused on implementation—what it would take to bring the Four Modernizations to life as a pragmatic and viable development strategy. He recognized that growth was the only antidote to what ailed China. His recipe was simple but daunting: "reforms and opening up."

Implicit in Deng's strategy was the critical recognition that the "closed" model of economic development—one that relied on the self-sufficiency of Chinese producers and consumers—was incapable of sparking meaningful progress on the road to economic development. This was a stunning realization for a nation that had been steeped in the Maoist ideological convictions that the combination of massive state-owned enterprises (SOEs), agricultural collectives, and fragmented light industries could provide for the basic needs of its people. Deng Xiaoping's ploy was that China needed far more if it was to address mounting social instability and the wrenching poverty of its still largely rural citizenry. Deng's genius came in recognizing the potential of a more "open" model to satisfy those aspirations. For a Chinese economy on the brink of collapse in the aftermath of the Cultural Revolution, this was a make-or-break growth gambit.

Like America's commitment to the U.S. consumer, Deng's strategy became a mindset for modern China. But unlike Washington's reinforcement of that mindset with broad fiscal and monetary policies, China turned to a specific agenda of initiatives. Over the next twenty-plus years, the catchphrase "reforms and opening up" gave rise to decisive policy actions in the rural, urban, and trade areas. Sequencing was key. Rural reforms came first, in 1980, centered on the highly successful township village enterprises (TVEs). TVEs offered an alternative to China's large state-owned enterprises—spawning a new and vibrant collection of small and medium-sized enterprises that, as the meticulous research of MIT professor Yasheng Huang shows, were modern China's first example of successful private entrepreneurialism.[17] In many respects, they spearheaded the development of China's dynamic market-based sector of economic activity.

Urban reforms, launched in 1994, entailed a dramatic rethinking of industrial ownership and led to the listing of shares of newly restructured SOEs in international capital markets. Trade reforms, especially tariff reductions, concessions on agricultural subsidies, the opening up of services (financial and nonfinancial alike), and even agreement to abide by international intellectual property rights conventions were driven by China's admission to the World Trade Organization in 2001.[18] Equally important was Deng's focus in the early 1990s on the establishment of export-oriented special economic zones, which in conjunction with aggressive incentives for foreign direct investment provided added impetus to a then nascent Chinese export machine.

While all of these reforms were crucial to the development miracle that was about to unfold, the opening up to international trade appears to have been the most decisive. For a closed Chinese economy that had failed to attain the critical mass of economic development, the bet on foreign trade was an especially stunning about-face. The timing of this initiative was close to perfect. Beginning in the late 1990s, it added a critically important external dimension to China's growth just as a new and powerful surge of global trade was about to take off.

The reforms' effects were monumental. Over the thirty years from 1980 to 2010, China's growth rate in real GDP averaged 10 percent per annum. Of course, it is much easier for poor, undeveloped economies to record rapid growth rates. That was certainly true of China in the late 1970s and early 1980s. But catching up doesn't last forever. At some point for most developing economies, the law of large numbers usually kicks in and prompts the inevitable slowing. That hasn't happened in China—at least not yet.

Yet aggregate GDP growth does not tell the full story for a vast nation like China. With a population that now totals slightly more than 1.3 billion—four times that of the United States—the scale of China's economy should be large. What matters most, however, is how the rewards are parceled out on a per capita basis—a far more accurate gauge of any nation's standard of living. China's GDP per capita in U.S. dollars was estimated at $6,629 in 2013.[19] While that is about thirty times the level in 1980, when Chinese development took off, it is far short of the $51,200 per person in the United States. The Chinese economy may be large, but, on average, its people remain relatively poor.

If current trends continue, the United States and China will probably have about the same levels of aggregate gross domestic product at some point in the 2025–30 time frame.[20] Parity on a per capita basis is a different matter. Even if we heroically extrapolate the two nations' trends in per capita GDP growth at their recent pace—10 percent average annual growth in China versus 4 percent in the United States—the lines would not converge until 2050, at the very soonest.

But the history of economic development urges great caution in such open-ended extrapolation. Unexpected detours can, and often do, happen. Financial crises, political upheavals, natural disasters, and policy blunders can render such exercises meaningless for any economy. Moreover, research shows that growth of low-income economies eventually risks falling into what has been called the middle-income trap, meaning that they stall out when per capita incomes reach $17,000 (in 2005 constant international prices),[21] as should happen for the Chinese economy around 2015.[22] No one can say for certain whether China will be an exception to this time-honored trend. The one thing we can say is that, based on history, developing economies are typically ensnared in the middle-income trap when they stick with old growth models for too long. As I stress repeatedly in the chapters that follow, Chinese leaders seem determined to avoid that tendency by changing the model. That provides grounds for optimism, but certainly no guarantee that China will be one of the rare counterexamples in the annals of economic development.

But that's getting ahead of our story. The point is that China has seen an unprecedented economic growth and development performance since 1980, when Deng Xiaoping seized the moment and lit the fuse on reforms and opening up. China's formula for success was unique. Two sectors, exports and fixed investment—namely, infrastructure, residential, and commercial building activity, manufacturing capacity, and a wide range of capital equipment—accounted for the bulk of the increase. Collectively, their shares of the Chinese economy more than doubled during the three decades of China's development sprint—rising from 31 percent of gross domestic product in 1979 to 75 percent in 2007.

Of the two sectors, exports provided by far the greatest source of uplift. Exports went from 5 percent of GDP in 1979 to 36 percent in 2007—a more than sevenfold increase. The investment sector went from 28 percent of GDP to 39 percent over this same period. While fixed investment has long been the largest segment of the modern Chinese economy, its impetus to economic growth since the late 1970s, as measured by the increase of its share of GDP, pales next to that of exports.

The combination of export- and investment-led growth leaves little doubt as to the most salient feature of the Chinese development miracle: It was largely about supply and not demand. Most especially, it was not about internal private consumption. The consumption share fell from about 50 percent to 35 percent from 1980 to 2008, underscoring one of the great ironies of the People's Republic of China. In contrast to the ideologically inspired paradigm of Mao Zedong, the people remained on the outside as major drivers of the modern Chinese economy. Instead, a state-of-the-art low-cost production platform was largely geared toward supplying goods that satisfied people elsewhere in the world.

Putting it another way, in contrast to the self-sufficiency aspirations of Mao, the impetus to China's spectacular development was a direct outgrowth of Deng Xiaoping's commitment to shift China's focus from a closed to an open economy. The main difference was that Deng's pragmatic approach worked. Just as the world has never seen a consumer like the American consumer, it has never seen a producer like China. In just thirty years, China went from the bottom of the heap, in terms of its share of global exports, to the world's number one exporter in 2010.

Simple metrics of global progress don't begin to capture the full ramifications of this surge. While China's GDP surpassed Japan's as number two in the world in 2009, that is a U.S. dollar–based comparison subject to the whims of often volatile foreign exchange markets. "Purchasing power parity," as calculated by the International Monetary Fund, is less prone to such market volatility and adjusts for international disparities in pricing structures. By that more accurate measure, the Chinese economy is now more than twice the size of Japan's and basically as large as the entire euro area's.[23]

In short, in just three decades, China's production, as measured by purchasing power parity, has come from practically nowhere to roughly three-quarters that of the United States. Such a phenomenal surge in economic output, unparalleled in history, has reverberated throughout the world economy. China has emerged as the world's number one consumer of a wide range of natural resources and industrial materials, ranging from copper and zinc to cement and iron ore. To claim that China "shakes the world," as James Kynge argued in a celebrated book under the same title in 2007, actually understates the impact.[24] The world's ultimate producer has turned the global resource supply chain inside out.

The ultimate producer has also redefined the development sweepstakes for other emerging economies. The scope of Chinese poverty reduction—estimated by the United Nations to have lifted between 300 million and 400 million out of poverty since 1980—is without precedent.[25] Yet there is an enduring and profound paradox: Despite the thirty-fold increase in per capita incomes since the late 1970s, a massive imbalance has opened up between the lack of China's internal impetus to economic development and its reliance on the external underpinnings of its thirty-year growth formula. Resolving that imbalance poses one of China's greatest challenges to sustained economic development.

The Growth Trap

The social and political imperatives of growth have long ensnared policy makers around the world. In the post–World War II era, this tendency first emerged in the 1980s. Back then, the trap was set when economic growth came under pressure in the advanced economies for a variety of reasons—ranging from globalization and rapid technological change to the demography of aging and the entry of some 2.5 billion new workers from China, India, and the former Soviet Union into the global production arena. Whatever the cause—and it was different for different countries—in a tough economic environment, the temptations to sidestep the pressures on growth only became more compelling.

The fixation on growth for the sake of growth has long been fraught with peril. Japan, with its political and social commitment to lifetime employment, was the first victim in modern times. In the early 1980s, its mercantilist growth model was putting pressure on manufacturing companies and factory workers in the United States and Europe. The world's major industrial countries, coming together in September 1985, forced Japan to accept the so-called Plaza Accord, which "solved" the problem by bringing Japanese currency suppression to an end. But that created a new problem for Japan. The significant appreciation of the yen that then ensued instilled great fear in Japanese political and policy circles that it would lose its export competitiveness—the pillar of the "developmental state"—and the lifetime employment it fostered.[26]

Japan's response to these pressures is in many respects a template for subsequent misguided policy actions that were taken by many of the other so-called advanced economies.[27] With the yen appreciating sharply in the immediate aftermath of the Plaza Accord, Japanese authorities attempted to compensate for the feared shortfall of export-led growth by turning to the lower interest rates of an aggressive monetary stimulus. Policy instruments were, in effect, transformed into tools of financial engineering—aimed, in Japan's case, to offset a threat to its yen-sensitive manufacturing sector, the engine of the nation's economy.

By embracing the easy money "remedy," Japanese authorities created a bubble-intensive strain of false prosperity. By late 1989, Japan's equity and property markets had ballooned in value, and Corporate Japan felt this justified a massive boost to capital spending.[28] But then Japanese asset prices collapsed in the early 1990s, unmasking the market surge as a bubble. The subsequent collapse in business capital spending pushed the Japanese economy into the first of its multiple lost decades. The case of Japan will forever go down in history as a telling example of the high price of false prosperity.

Steeped in denial and unwilling to learn the lessons of Japan, the United States and Europe followed with risky bets on their own strains of false prosperity. As in Japan, underlying growth in both economies had come under mounting pressures in the 1980s and early 1990s. And like their Japanese counterparts, politicians in the United States and Europe leaned hard on policy makers and regulators to find ways to compensate for these pressures.

Authorities in both economies responded with even more creative strategies than those adopted in Japan. Each embraced exceedingly complex tactics of financial engineering to turbocharge their economies. In America, this took the form of a massive property bubble that was turbocharged by an equally large credit bubble. In Europe, it was a manifestation of a deeply flawed currency union.

In both the United States and Europe, as in Japan, the corrosive signs of false prosperity were not immediately evident. Growth in the U.S. and European economies initially surged. Believing, or at least wanting to believe, in the legitimacy of the growth gambits, the authorities took the bait and actually upped the ante on their grand experiments. Washington basked in the warm glow of low inflation and the self-proclaimed Great Moderation it purportedly spawned.[29] The Federal Reserve took this characterization to heart and kept interest rates too low for too long and ended up running an excessively accommodative, bubble-inducing monetary policy. Europe expanded its malformed currency union from seventeen to twenty-seven countries (twenty-eight with the addition of Croatia in mid-2013). The bubbles went from manageable to unmanageable, and the rest is now a very painful history.

Most important, this history is an indictment of the political economy of false prosperity. The resulting bubbles ended up fostering huge distortions in real economies and excess leverage in financial systems. In an era of low inflation, policy makers deluded themselves into thinking those risks were worth taking as a price to pay for satisfying the goals of price stability and full employment set by their political overseers. Those were major miscalculations. These were all epic policy blunders.

No nation has a monopoly on the cravings or the temptations of false prosperity. They stem critically from the political economy of growth—the self-imposed pressures that the body politic of a nation-state puts on the perceived ability of economic growth to achieve the noble objectives of absorbing surplus labor, reducing poverty, tempering unemployment, and narrowing inequalities of the income distribution.[30] In multiparty democracies like the United States, where election or reelection often hinges on short-term trends in growth and unemployment, these pressures can be intense. But they are equally intense in one-party nations like China, whose leaders have deep and painful memories of social instability and chaos seared into their consciousness—memories that can easily be triggered by shortfalls in economic growth. The political economy of growth is just as powerful in China as it is in the United States. It is blind to ideology.

The Codependency Trap

In personal relationships, there is a distinct affinity between codependency and the so-called marriage of convenience. The former pertains to the mutual pathology of shared needs, whereas the latter depicts a formal union derived from those needs—essentially a "loveless" partnership based largely on financial, professional, or other strategic considerations.[31] While the marriage of convenience can start out innocently enough, risks arise from the mutual addiction to the gratification it offers. That's when codependency comes into play. In the case of the economic relationship between China and the United States, strains of both are at work.

Modern China, with all its historical baggage, was hardly an innocent bystander in this relationship. While it has an entirely different political system from the West's, it shares one important priority: It has had its own wrenching problems with labor absorption and social stability. In the aftermath of the Cultural Revolution, China's economy was on the brink of failure and its social fabric was in shreds. It was desperate for an antidote. Just as economic growth was the palliative in the West, it became the cure for China as well. Ever mindful of the perils of a relapse, modern China's leaders, from the time of Deng Xiaoping forward, would stop at nothing to encourage rapid economic growth and the social stability it would presumably foster.

But there was an important difference between China's strategy and those of the more advanced economies. Unlike Japan, the United States, and Europe, China did not have the wherewithal to regenerate growth from within. Its economic and social structure had been decimated, and its impoverished masses were incapable of sparking a revival of internal demand. This is where Deng Xiaoping stepped in and provided a very different answer for China than that offered by Mao Zedong. In focusing on export- and investment-led growth, China took what it believed to be the only pragmatic path open to it: It became the ultimate producer to satisfy the demands of the ultimate consumers in the West.

In doing so, China, perhaps unwittingly, set a policy trap of its own—not all that dissimilar from the traps set by the more advanced economies. It enrolled willingly as a participant in the era of excess—not as a consumer but as a producer. That meant it effectively condoned its role as a leveraged play on the political economy of false prosperity that was sweeping the advanced economies of the world. To the extent that China's craving for growth framed its social stability and development imperatives, that leverage factor has only intensified over the course of the past thirty years.

Therein lie the roots of the powerful codependency between the U.S. and Chinese economies. For different but equally compelling reasons, growth models emphasizing closed economies came under pressure in both nations. Mao's dream of a self-sufficient China was replaced by Deng's gambit of externally led development. At the same time, Washington came to realize that the insatiable appetite of the American consumer—the mainstay of its grassroots political support—could be satisfied only by drawing on the external support of low-cost foreign producers and cheap capital from abroad.

And so the marriage of convenience was consummated. The United States had just what China needed—a huge and rapidly expanding reservoir of consumer demand. And China had just what America needed—an open-ended supply of inexpensive goods and surplus saving. The ultimate supplier fed off the world's biggest consumer, just as the ultimate consumer thrived on the basis of what the nascent Chinese producer was able to offer. The more China prospered, the harder it became to wean itself from this arrangement. The same was true of the United States—the more its consumers drew sustenance from China, the greater the addiction to excess consumption.

The ultimate consumer and the ultimate producer share many important characteristics. The most obvious is that each needs the other as the sustenance of economic growth. But that invites the toughest question of all: Why did the United States and China both embrace unbalanced and ultimately unsustainable growth models as the means toward that end?

The answer is central to the remainder of this book. It hinges on what can be called *the growth trap of codependency*, a construct we will explore from the standpoints of leadership, institutions, technology, and the connectivity and frictions that a new globalization offers through trade and capital flows. The interplay among these factors, and the responses of both the United States and China to recent challenging developments in the global economy, takes us to the heart of the great dilemma of economic codependency: crisis or opportunity?

The genesis of this dilemma, how the United States and China became ensnared in the growth trap of codependency, is especially important. As stressed above, the two nations had one critical experience in common in the first half of the twentieth century: a tough history of near failures of their economies. Determined never to risk their systems again, political leaders, policy makers, and regulatory authorities in both countries became overzealous in their search for the antidote, economic growth. They would stop at nothing in this search, including the willingness to gamble with the shortcuts of a false prosperity.

For a while they got away with it, especially in the 1990s and early 2000s. And the longer they did, the deeper the conviction that it could last[32]—the classic belief in a "new paradigm" that invariably occurs at the end of a period of excess.[33] The toughest complication eventually arose out of sustainability. In their quest for growth and prosperity, each economy ended up embracing unbalanced growth models. Their imbalances were serious, both internal and external—saving, trade deficits, and debt in the case of the United States, and excess resource demand, income inequality, and environmental degradation and pollution in the case of China.

But the most precarious imbalance was the insidious codependency between the producer and the consumer. America's voracious consumer demand rested on the quicksand of asset and credit bubbles. Similarly, the outward-facing Chinese production model drew great sustenance from illusory gains in U.S. consumer demand. The United States and China were both hooked on different strains of the same false prosperity. The seduction of codependency was complete—that is, until 2008, when the music finally stopped.

2

Who Depends on Whom?

Relationships between economies are difficult to disentangle. They can be both constructive and contentious, comforting and prickly. It is often arguable who has the upper hand. That said, there is a natural tendency to simplify complex relationships between economies. In part, that's to make them understandable, but it's often done to drive home an agenda. The finger-pointing of recent years is a case in point—especially when it comes to the relationship between the United States and China.

The U.S. Congress blames China and its undervalued currency for many of the problems facing hard-pressed American workers. Senior officials at America's Federal Reserve also blame China and its so-called glut of surplus saving for much of the instability in financial markets. China argues that the United States is simply looking to deflect blame for self-inflicted wounds. This disagreement raises two specific questions for these co-dependent economies: What role has China played in shaping the macro-climate of the American economy? And what role has the United States played in supporting the Chinese development model?

In an increasingly globalized world, the causality behind economic relationships is usually more elusive than the context. In the case of the U.S.-

Sino relationship, the recent context has been critically conditioned by a very tough economic climate—the worst multiyear global crisis since the 1930s. But the Great Crisis and the equally Great Recession it spawned have not occurred in a vacuum. They have unfolded in an interconnected era of globalization, where all economies depend to some extent on one another.

There is a deeper issue here. As will be detailed in the chapters that follow, cross-border connectivity, the fabric of globalization, has many threads —trade flows, capital flows, information flows, and labor flows. By binding real economies and financial markets together, these flows underscore the different dimensions of the codependency between the United States and China. In many respects, they are the metrics of codependency. As the two economies evolve over time, the metrics should capture these shifts, signaling stresses and strains, as well as mutual benefits, that shape the world's most important economic relationship.

Codependency has yet another important dimension—China's role in the rapid expansion of multinational corporations. In recent years, China has been the world's second-favorite destination of surging foreign direct investment in offshore manufacturing and assembly facilities—second only to the United States. And with good reasons: Production and assembly in China provides an immediate and important efficiency solution for high-cost producers in the West. Down the road, it also positions multinationals to tap domestic demand in the world's most populous market.

The explosive growth in the activity of multinational corporations also blurs the distinctions between the United States and China. It turns out that a vast network of Chinese subsidiaries of U.S. and other Western multinationals plays an increasingly important role in driving China's export machine. Over the past decade, these subsidiaries accounted for more than 60 percent of the cumulative growth in Chinese exports. It therefore makes little sense to blame China for the conscious efforts of U.S.-headquartered companies like Apple, General Electric, and Ford to reduce production costs for goods sold in America by relying on low-cost offshore production and assembly platforms.

Codependency permeates many layers of the U.S.-China economic relationship, but this relationship cannot be assessed in isolation. There is a broad macroeconomic framework that provides an overarching context for the economic connectivity between countries. It is not just a simple matter of trade between nation-states. It is also a tale of the balancing act between savings and trade flows—and the multilateral imbalances that arise from any disconnect between these flows. All are central to the discussion that follows.

The Trade Connection

Trade flows represent an obvious and important starting point. As noted in Chapter 1, China has rewritten the script of economic development by its reliance on trade as an engine to power economic growth. By IMF estimates, China currently accounts for fully 25 percent of total exports from emerging and developing economies, and 9.4 percent of the world's total exports.[1] In 2010, it surpassed the United States as the largest exporter in the world.

This represents an enormous leap in a very short period of time. Ten years ago, China's shares in global trade were about half what they are today. But then its trade took off, with exports and imports combined growing by 25 percent per year between 2001 and 2011.

Sometimes timing is everything. In China's case, it was. China's export-led growth came during a period of unprecedented global trade liberalization. World exports went from 24 percent of global GDP in 2002 to a record 32 percent in 2008. China alone accounted for half of that increase. That put it in the enviable position of becoming the most powerful engine of global trade at precisely the time when trade itself was exploding as never before.

The relationship between trade and economic development is nothing new. The two have long gone hand in hand, especially in Asia. But China has been far more aggressive than other Asian economies in parlaying this strategy into unparalleled success. This shows up very clearly in the differential impetus from foreign trade experienced by Asia's other developing economies. In the twenty-five years following its economic takeoff in 1982, China increased its share of world trade by a factor of eight. In contrast, the increase was fivefold for the broad collection of Asia's so-called newly industrialized economies of South Korea, Taiwan, Hong Kong, and Singapore over comparable phases of their development. The ASEAN-4 economies (Association of Southeast Asian Nations, the four being Thailand, Indonesia, Malaysia, and the Philippines) saw only a threefold increase in their share of global trade in their first twenty-five years of development. India was the laggard, with only a twofold increase—underscoring its pursuit of a much more closed (that is, domestically focused) development model.[2]

China's two largest export markets today, Europe and the United States, collectively accounted for 38 percent of total Chinese export demand in 2010. For most of recent history, the United States was the larger of China's two major export markets. But once the euro was launched in 2001, China's exports to Europe started to rise sharply. Its shipments to the European Union surpassed those to America in 2008; as of 2010, the share going to Europe was 20 percent versus 18 percent going to the United States.[3]

The mix of Chinese export products to the United States has changed considerably. In the 1980s, they mostly consisted of relatively low-valued consumer nondurables—especially apparel and toys—as well as electronic components like semiconductor chips. But Chinese exporters have been moving up the value and quality chain. That progress has imparted ever-greater sophistication to its manufacturing sector, but in doing so, as we will argue later, has sown the seeds for some of modern China's most serious imbalances.

Beginning in the mid-1990s, China's exports to the United States shifted increasingly into motor vehicles and parts, as well as information technology products and capital equipment. As a result, China went from a small source of American demand to being its largest foreign supplier, accounting for fully 19 percent of total U.S. imports in 2012. That even surpasses the import shares coming from America's nearby NAFTA partners, Canada (14 percent) and Mexico (12 percent).

There is reason to believe, however, that at least two key distortions in these numbers may be overstating U.S. dependence on Chinese producers. The most obvious distortion is that China's role in the global production chain has changed: It is now less of a global factory and more of an assembly line drawing on inputs from other nations. As will be discussed in Chapter 7, foreign produced components and parts account for about 40 percent of the value added of Chinese exports, meaning that domestic value added by indigenous Chinese production accounts for the balance, or 60 percent. The U.S. trade data, which fail to make this distinction and simply allocate 100 percent of the value of the imports to the country of embarkation, end up exaggerating the bilateral U.S.-China trade deficit by a wide margin.[4]

A different distortion comes from an important ownership distinction that never makes it into either the Chinese export data or America's portrayal of the Chinese import data. About 60 percent of total Chinese exports come from foreign-funded enterprises, or FFEs.[5] These are basically Chinese subsidiaries of Western multinational corporations—offshore production platforms that take advantage of cost arbitrage and other efficiency solutions that are not available in their home markets. That paints a very different picture of the widely feared Chinese export colossus. Contrary to general perceptions of rapidly growing indigenous Chinese producers enjoying state subsidies in the form of cut-rate financing, a cheap currency, and other forms of nontariff protection, the bulk of China's export impetus has come from subsidiaries of Western-owned companies.

In sum, the China trade threat is not what the published statistics make it out to be. If the U.S.-Chinese trade deficit were adjusted for both of the biases noted above—value added by non-Chinese producers as well as the foreign ownership dimension of Chinese export activities—the imbalance between the two nations would look a lot less lopsided. Why Washington continues to vilify China's purported trade aggression in the face of these obvious distortions in the public data is a subject we will take up later.[6]

Overlooked in the debate over bilateral imbalances is a trade connection between these two codependent economies that has increasingly become a two-way street. China is now America's third-largest export market, exceeded only by its NAFTA partners, Canada and Mexico. Moreover, U.S. exports to China rose, on average, at 16 percent per year from 2005 to 2012, more than double the eight-year growth rate of U.S. exports to Canada and Mexico.[7]

But in this case, the past only hints at what lies ahead. U.S. export growth to China may be on the brink of a major acceleration that could transform

America's trade connection to China from a liability into a growth- and jobs-enhancing asset. And that, in turn, could tip the codependency balance between the two nations. Three factors are at work:

First, China has long been an open economy, with a natural bias toward the consumption of foreign-made goods. This contrasts sharply with Japan, modern Asia's first growth miracle. In China, the import share of GDP has been around 28 percent since 2002—nearly three times Japan's 10 percent import ratio during its high-growth era (1960–89). That means that for a given increment of domestic demand, China is far more predisposed to draw on foreign producers than Japan was.

Second, as I will describe in detail later, China is on the cusp of important structural shifts in its economy that could prove to be a windfall for its overseas trading partners. As it rebalances away from exports and external demand toward consumption and internal demand, its appetite for foreign-made consumer products—from personal technology devices to luxury goods—is likely to expand sharply. Additionally, as Chinese consumers grow wealthier, they will acquire a taste for a wide range of increasingly sophisticated foreign-made products—from new-generation information technology and biotech to motor vehicles and pharmaceuticals.

Third, as will be discussed in Chapter 12, there are enormous opportunities in the Chinese services sector, where the country is starting from an extremely low base. At just 43 percent of GDP, the services slice of the Chinese economy is the smallest of any major economy in the world. China's latest economic plan—the pro-consumption Twelfth Five-Year Plan—targets an aggressive expansion in services in the years ahead. America is the world's leading services economy. Its multinational services companies are particularly well positioned to participate in China's coming push into services.

These paybacks from coming shifts in the mix of Chinese growth will not be instantaneous—a services sector, for example, can hardly spring to life overnight. It takes time to bear fruit, especially in the more knowledge-intensive professional services occupations, such as accounting, law, and consulting. In large part, that's because development in these areas requires initiatives in educational reform and other forms of investment in human capital where payoffs are usually measured in decades. But there are plenty of opportunities for quick paybacks at the lower end of the services value chain, especially in the distribution (wholesale and retail trade, domestic transportation, and supply chain logistics) and transactions processing segments (healthcare and finance). In these areas, staffing is more a short-term training challenge than something that requires more advanced schooling and, by inference, a multigenerational commitment to educational reform.

In short, notwithstanding the data distortions noted above, the West in general, and America in particular, continue to fixate on the threat from Chinese imports. In doing so, they lose sight of the considerable opportunities on the export side of the trade equation that should arise as China shifts to more of a consumer-led development strategy in the years ahead.

Capital Flows

While cross-border trade flows bind real economies together in an increasingly globalized world, cross-border capital flows do the same for international financial markets. This also shapes a key aspect of the U.S.-Chinese codependency.

Like trade in goods and services, bilateral capital flows between the two nations cut both ways. On one hand, China's demand for dollar-denominated securities anchors the currency policy that underpins its export competitiveness. This aspect of the story first began to crystallize during the Asian financial crisis in 1997–98. The so-called East Asian miracle was at risk of disintegration.[8] The reasons were many, but large current account deficits, a lack of foreign exchange reserves, excess exposure to short-term ("hot-money") foreign lending, and sharply weakening currencies were at the top of the list.[9]

As that crisis unfolded, China moved quickly to differentiate itself from the rest of Asia and vowed never to fall into the same trap. It embarked on the biggest binge of foreign exchange reserve accumulation in history. It wasn't hard to pull off. China's export-led growth model generated outsize trade surpluses, which, together with speculative bets on the appreciation of an undervalued currency, set the massive buildup in motion. Its foreign exchange reserves, less than $100 billion in the late 1990s, surged to $3.5 trillion by mid-2013, pushing China well past Japan as the largest holder of foreign exchange reserves in the world.[10]

The disposition of these reserves presented China with an important strategic choice: It could either convert them into its own currency, which would push up the value of the renminbi and undermine Chinese export competitiveness, or it could recycle them into dollar-based assets in order to prevent sharp currency appreciation relative to the U.S. dollar, its benchmark for international financial stability and export competitiveness.

In July 2005, China chose the latter when it abandoned a fixed peg to the dollar. Since then, it has carefully managed its purchases of dollar-denominated assets so as to allow a gradual appreciation of the renminbi relative to the dollar. In doing so, it resisted pressures in the West for a large one-off shift. China's leaders were especially mindful of the destabilizing experience of Japan, where, as noted in Chapter 1, a sharp yen revaluation, compressed into a relatively short period in 1985–86, had disastrous results. But Chinese authorities have also been mindful of the risks of exposing their embryonic and vulnerable financial system to the potentially disruptive impacts of sharp currency swings.

Still, a confluence of domestic and international pressures convinced Chinese authorities that a carefully managed renminbi revaluation was in China's best interest. The domestic considerations reflected a desire to contain inflation and boost consumer purchasing power of foreign-made goods; the international considerations were China's desire to contain its burgeoning trade and current account surpluses as well as avoid trade tensions and protectionism.

By sticking with its commitment to a gradual and steady increase in the value of the renminbi, the impacts became significant over time. By mid-2013, the renminbi had appreciated 35 percent relative to the U.S. dollar since mid-2005. That averages out to a revaluation of about 4 percent a year—actually a significantly faster pace of currency realignment than the 2 percent average rate of dollar depreciation that the United States has experienced since early 2002.[11]

China's currency path has also had important implications for the management of the mix of its foreign exchange reserves. Chinese ownership of long-term Treasury securities soared from less than $100 billion in 1998 to more than $1.3 trillion by mid-2013. It owns approximately another $700 billion in other dollar-based fixed income instruments, mainly the so-called agency debt of Fannie Mae and Freddie Mac. That boosted China's ownership share in mid-2013 to about 16 percent of all long-term government and quasi-government securities, making it the leading foreign owner of official U.S. debt.[12]

That takes us to a key aspect of America's dependence on China. Surging capital flows from China to the United States, an outgrowth of the unbalanced character of the Chinese growth model, also played an important role in supporting America's consumption binge. It did that by boosting demand for Treasuries, one of several factors that prevented long-term U.S. interest rates from rising in the years before the 2008 crisis.[13] That, in turn, ended up supporting the value of America's equity market while suppressing mortgage interest rates. This only added to the froth of the enormous U.S. housing and credit bubbles—the sustenance of America's excess consumption in the early 2000s, as noted in Chapter 1. In that sense, a significant portion of bubble-induced U.S. consumer demand was indeed made in China.

For a long time, it all appeared to be the ultimate sweet spot for the United States and China. Chinese inflows into U.S. capital markets helped American families use the housing market to fund surging consumption. And courtesy of an undervalued currency that persisted in the face of those flows, the Chinese producer maintained its competitive edge as an increasingly important supplier for the world's ultimate consumer.

Codependency became coindulgence. And the cross-border flows of codependency became a central part of the mechanism spawning unstable excesses in both economies. Yet that didn't seem to matter—at least not for a long while. China was more than happy to support an era of excess U.S. consumption and ride the coattails of America's false prosperity. And there were few complaints in the United States. It was a happy marriage of convenience, with both partners steeped in denial.

Europe's Role

The United States hardly had a monopoly on the false prosperity that drove its codependency with China to excess. The European strain of this story is different from what we saw in the U.S.-China interplay. But it has many of the same characteristics in fueling the Chinese export boom.

The European outbreak of false prosperity can largely be attributed to the excesses that followed the launching of a new common currency on January 1, 1999. Greece, Ireland, Spain, Portugal, and Italy had only to sign up for the European Monetary Union (EMU) in order to be blessed with German interest rates on their sovereign debt. Never mind that they did next to nothing to improve their underlying economic fundamentals, like productivity, competitiveness, and fiscal discipline, in order to justify receiving such low borrowing rates. The temporary gains from financially engineered lower interest rates that came with EMU membership provided benefits that were far more attractive than the heavy lifting of structural change. At least, so that appeared to be at the time.

The mismatch between financial and economic convergence only deepened during 2001–7, when there was tight uniformity of interest rates across Europe. This set the stage for Europe's binge of false prosperity. Low interest rates, coming like manna from heaven, led to outsize property bubbles in Ireland and Spain and fostered a complacency that led to reduced competitiveness in Italy and Spain and a lack of fiscal discipline in Greece and Portugal.

Despite the damage that was being done in Europe during the false prosperity of 2001–7, few paid attention to the excesses. It was analogous to the same complacency that prevailed in the United States under the guise of the so-called Great Moderation. The euphoria over the interest rate convergence bubble diminished any concern and only deepened the denial. Growth was just the right medicine for the peripheral economies of Europe, as well as for their major suppliers—namely, exporters in Germany and France, who benefited enormously from artificially supported demand in Spain, Italy, Portugal, Ireland, and Greece. Another house of cards had been built, just as precarious as the one in America.

Collapse was soon to follow. Starting with the Great Recession of late 2008, convergence gave way to divergence, and by early 2012, yields for all the so-called peripheral economies had widened back to their pre-euro levels of the early 1990s. And the windfalls associated with interest rate convergence quickly became headwinds that sent Europe's peripheral economies into sharp recessions.

China was hardly an innocent bystander. It had benefited significantly from sharply rising exports to all of Europe—to core as well as peripheral economies. Europe's boom, taken well to excess by the artificial support provided by the region's common currency and interest rate profile, became increasingly important to the surge in Chinese exports. When Europe surpassed the United States as China's largest export market in 2008, the Chinese strain of false prosperity took on an added fragility.

Postcrisis recessions in both the United States and Europe reveal how risky China's bet on the West's false prosperity had become. The great Chinese export machine had long been oriented toward supplying external demand from the West. Yet seduced by its own growth bonanza, which paid handsome dividends in output growth, labor absorption, and poverty reduction, China never questioned whether that external demand was sustainable. But deep recessions experienced by its two largest foreign customers, both of which have been followed by unusually weak recoveries, reveal with painful clarity the complacency that underpinned the unbalanced Chinese economy. That complacency ultimately was no different from that which afflicted the West.

With hindsight—especially in light of two wrenching crises in a four-year time frame—it is evident that Chinese export demand was built on an intrinsically weak foundation of external demand. In the United States, bubble-dependent consumers produced a froth of demand for foreign-made goods that Chinese exporters were more than happy to satisfy. The same was true of the transitory windfall of European demand artificially created by euro-led interest rate convergence.

Globalization and the cross-border connectivity that defines it are the glue that binds these stories together. As a poor developing economy, China bought into the same false prosperity that drew in the richest of the developed world, the United States and Europe. They all made the same fundamental mistake: They gave in to the foolish belief that there could be a magical shortcut to economic growth. Who depends on whom? The Great Crisis and its aftermath assign blame to the world's major developed economies. Codependency implicates China, as well.

Multinationals and a Seamless World

The role of multinational corporations sheds light on another critical dimension of the codependency between the United States and China. The multinational corporation has long been recognized as one of the core institutions of the increasingly borderless era of globalization.[14] According to the consulting firm McKinsey, multinationals now account for 30 percent of worldwide business revenues—up dramatically from 10 percent in the 1980s. Not surprisingly, connectivity to China has become a central focus. Fully 65 percent of the companies in the Fortune Global 500 now have operations in China.[15]

Multinationals provide the organizational and logistical infrastructure, as well as the financial capital and corporate strategies, behind many of the modern linkages between China and the rest of the world. U.S.-headquartered corporations have played an especially pivotal role. Chinese statistics indicate that nearly 131,000 subsidiaries of U.S. companies were operating in China in 2010. The U.S. Commerce Department valued the direct investment position of American companies in China in 2012 at $51.4 billion.[16]

Like most aspects of globalization, the export connection via multinationals has grown tighter over time. As recently as 1997, just 41 percent of Chinese exports came from subsidiaries of multinational corporations. Over the next decade the ratio surged to nearly 60 percent. That means that close to two-thirds of the growth in overall Chinese exports over the decade ending in 2010 has come from what Chinese statisticians label "foreign-funded enterprises."

The sharply increasing production and export activity of corporate America's Chinese subsidiaries offers a glimpse into the laboratory of codependency between the two economies. Most obviously, multinationals provide important benefits to Chinese workers employed by their subsidiaries.[17] They also make an important contribution to overall Chinese economic growth. Up to 2 percentage points of China's annual 10 percent GDP growth between 2000 and 2010 came from FFEs. The U.S. piece would represent only a portion of that—probably around half a percentage point each year over the past decade.

But in a globalized world, the direct gains from multinational activity in China cut both ways. The U.S. economy enjoys two benefits: First, American companies are able to prune their operating costs by taking advantage of relatively low-cost Chinese production platforms. The benefits of such "labor-cost arbitrage" are considerable. According to the U.S. Bureau of Labor Statistics, compensation in Chinese manufacturing averaged just $1.36 per hour in 2008—or only about 4 percent of the hourly rate of $34 paid by manufacturing companies in the United States.[18] While Chinese workers' productivity is well below that of their American counterparts—thereby justifying a significant portion of the pay differential—considerable saving can still be achieved by arbitraging productivity-adjusted gaps in worker pay. In today's highly competitive climate, the cost-saving benefits of Chinese "offshoring" strategies can hardly be minimized.

Second, and this is where the rubber meets the road for globalization, the broad population of American consumers is a direct beneficiary of cheaper goods that come in from China. The low-cost China-centered Asian supply chain has enabled U.S. families to stretch their purchasing power. The U.S. Commerce Department has calculated that import prices of nonauto consumer goods rose just 5 percent from 2000 to 2011—less than half the cumulative 11.4 percent increase of prices for all consumer goods over the same period. With U.S. imports surging and low-cost Chinese imports accounting for a disproportionate share of foreign buying over this same time frame, China's role as a significant brake on U.S. inflation was an important factor enabling Americans to buy more with otherwise depressed gains in inflation-adjusted consumer purchasing power.[19]

The disinflationary benefits of China-centric globalization strategies by America's leading multinationals are best illustrated by the case of Walmart. The world's largest retailer, Walmart has more than ten thousand suppliers in China that provide some 70 percent of all the merchandise it sells. It is one of the most powerful cogs in the Chinese export machine.[20] In 2010, Walmart was responsible for more than $40 billion of exports from China, most of which went to stock store shelves in the United States. Many have pointed out that if Walmart were a nation, it would be China's sixth-largest export market.[21] Putting it another way, Walmart alone accounts for more than 10 percent of all Chinese exports to the United States. By inference, that also means that value-conscious American shoppers owe much to China for the bargains they find at Walmart.

In an increasingly seamless world, with multinational corporations sitting atop massive networks of cross-border supply chains, there is an intense debate over whether the benefits of globalization outweigh the costs. As multinationals outsource production and jobs to cheaper overseas platforms, jobs and labor income in the home market of the outsourcer are certainly displaced. Meanwhile, the "outsourcee" on the other side of the exchange benefits from newfound demand for its low-cost production.

But this is only the tip of the iceberg: There is good reason to believe that the indirect effects of the multinational connection far outweigh its direct effects. As the output of China-centric offshore production gets recycled back into higher-cost economies such as the United States, many consumers benefit. The cruel calculus of globalization suggests that the potential number of beneficiaries—namely, more than 310 million American consumers—vastly exceeds the 12 million manufacturing workers who may feel the pressures of outsourcing head-on. That's not to minimize the total impact of job loss stemming from trade-related pressures—economic and social repercussions that also include the so-called multiplier effects of those who provide goods and services to displaced workers. But it is important to put the first-round effects of job losses due to globalization in a broader context.

The multinationals' ultimate hope is, of course, to convert the toehold of the outsourcer's China platform into that of an "insourcer," present for the dawn of what many have long felt would someday become the world's largest consumer market.[22] For most, this has been the dream that has yet to come true. But as the producer society at last becomes a consumer-led economy, such a possibility no longer seems remote.

Shifting Codependency

Codependency, as it applies to our assessment of the United States and China, is agnostic on the concept of parity in the economic relationship between the two nations. Of course, as in any relationship, parity is in the eyes of the beholder. Both China and the United States find comforting aspects to their relationship, as well as tensions. As I argued in Chapter 1, China certainly depends on the United States—not just as a source of external demand for its export machine and an anchor to its currency regime but also as an inspiration for its ultimate goal of an innovations- and knowledge-based model of economic prosperity. And the United States certainly depends on China—not just as a source of foreign capital to fund its savings-short economy but also a provider of low-cost consumer goods for American families. The metrics of codependency confirm the role that each economy plays in satisfying the needs of the other.

But fulfilling these needs has not always been healthy for the individual parties in this codependent relationship. While China's export-led growth model has delivered unprecedented prosperity for a developing nation in a remarkably short time, as detailed in the chapters that follow, the intrinsic imbalances that have arisen from this rapid transition have also led to excess resource demand, soaring commodity prices, environmental degradation, pollution, and mounting income inequalities. While the United States has benefited from China's ample supply of low-cost goods and cheap capital, it also condoned China's role in fueling America's biggest source of instability—hugely destabilizing asset and credit bubbles and a monstrous binge of excess consumption.

It has been a delicate balancing act for both nations. And it is hard to judge who did what to whom and who now needs the other more. Maybe that's the point of codependency—it blurs the distinction between needs. But the forces of codependency are not set in stone. Just as they have changed dramatically since the early 1980s, it is likely that the balance will tilt yet again in the years immediately ahead—perhaps decisively.

In large part, that's because both the United States and China are on the cusp of important transformations in the structure of their economies. Both economies are currently in states of unsustainable disequilibrium, in which they face mounting pressures for rebalancing. As will be detailed below, China must temper the excesses of surplus saving and export- and investment-led growth. Conversely, the United States must rebuild saving and wean itself from the excesses of hyperconsumption and massive budget deficits. The degree to which each nation addresses its rebalancing imperatives will bear critically on their codependency in the future.

While that future is, of course, unknown, educated guesses are possible and certainly desirable, especially if they shed light on the tensions and opportunities that will shape the U.S.-China relationship. That assessment hinges critically on one key consideration—the outlook for saving in both China and the United States. Saving is the most robust metric of codependency. Surpluses or deficits in a nation's saving position drive the capital and trade flows that delineate macro imbalances between economies.

Significantly, China has recently made much more progress in paring its surplus saving than America has made in reducing its saving deficit. These trends, if they continue, may have important consequences for how the savings arbitrage between the two nations unfolds in the future. In particular, Chinese rebalancing, and the further reductions in saving it implies, could have great significance for deficit-prone America, who still saves too little and depends heavily on Chinese saving to plug the gap.

If the recent divergence in saving trends persists, an asymmetrical rebalancing might begin, which would subject codependency to new stresses. Deficit-prone America would still have a considerable need for external financing, while China's role as the buyer of Treasury and other dollar-denominated debt would probably diminish. Who will fund America's deficits if the Chinese don't? And on what terms? We address these questions explicitly later on, but the basic thrust of the answers is to underscore the possibility of a Chinese rebalancing leading to mounting pressures on the United States if it doesn't begin to save more.

The point here is to underscore how quickly codependency can become destabilizing. For the past thirty years, both China and the United States have framed their bilateral economic policies under the presumption that self-interest equates with mutual interest. To the extent that rebalancing implies a rethinking of self-interest, the mutual pathology of codependency will most assuredly change as well—and there are no guarantees it will be a healthier outcome for either party. Who depends on whom? It's a trick question. In a codependent relationship the answer, of course, is, both.

PART II

LEADERSHIP AND POWER

WAS IT STRATEGY THAT primarily drove America and China on their recent journeys? Vision or leadership? Strong or weak institutions?

Or is the how just as important as the why? Strategies are fine on paper, but they are vacuous intellectual exercises if they don't meet the tests of commitment and implementation. It takes both leadership and power to make the leap between goals, the framework for achieving those goals, and execution. For China and the United States over the past few decades, there have been both strengths and weaknesses in leadership and power. Contrasts on both counts explain an important aspect of the codependency between these two economies—how it came into being and how it has become a source of tension and potential instability.

In the next three chapters we look inside the power structures of the United States and China. The focus is on the key personalities and institutions that have led the world's two most powerful economies to different ends of the spectrum of imbalances. The emphasis is mainly on the past twenty-five years—the period when America's hegemonic role in the world economy started to fray while China became ascendant.

How much of this divergence reflects organic differences in the inherent dynamism of each of these economies? How much can be attributed to leadership and how that leadership was exercised through ideological conviction, determination, and political and administrative skills?

In both the United States and China, strong personalities played key roles in driving their respective economies down paths of unbalanced growth. That was certainly true of Zhu Rongji and Alan Greenspan—powerful economic policy makers who left sharp imprints on their nations in the pivotal decade of the 1990s. While Zhu pushed for reforms that led to an increasingly modernized Chinese economy, Greenspan embraced financial engineering as a new and sustainable source of U.S. economic growth. The results speak for themselves: Zhu's China ended up on far more solid footing than Greenspan's America—perhaps temporarily, but that remains to be seen.

The leadership imperative was at least as challenging for their successors, Wen Jiabao and Ben Bernanke. They too had very different takes on economic stability. Wen believed that stability risks were not worth taking under any circumstances and did everything in his power to dampen any destabilizing tendencies in the Chinese economy. Bernanke didn't worry that much about stability but believed, instead, that market-based systems were strong enough to cope with the inevitable disturbances, and that countercyclical stabilization policies were more than capable of offsetting short-term vicissitudes in markets and the real economy. Both sets of beliefs were subjected to the ultimate test: a crisis that in many respects was an outgrowth of the failures of an earlier generation of leaders.

Wen and Bernanke also played key roles in articulating the challenges of macroeconomic management that each country faced. Premier Wen's famous critique of the Four Uns forced China to confront the mounting risks of an economy that was increasingly "unstable, unbalanced, uncoordinated, and ultimately unsustainable." Chairman Bernanke, on the other hand, had to venture into the uncharted territory of experimental monetary policies to save the system he thought could take care of itself. The jury is still out on whose vision will prevail.

Leadership, of course, does not exist in a vacuum. We must understand its context when assessing the recent direction of either the Chinese or the U.S. economy. China has placed an unmistakable emphasis on strategy and stability for the past thirty-three years. The results have been extraordinary, but they grew out of a blended model of resource allocation guided by the heavy hand of the state, operating through the National Development and Reform Commission (NDRC), the modern incarnation of its old central planning agency. China describes its development model as reflecting the fundamentals of a market-based socialism, combining ideology with incentives that are grounded in market mechanisms. But there was an important catch: The two architects of the model, Zhu Rongji and Wen Jiabao, didn't seem to grasp some of the inherent contradictions of the blended approach they championed.

Strategy has never been the United States' strength. That's especially the case when compared with Chinese-style state-directed planning. Macro strategy in the United States has been largely an afterthought, almost an oxymoron. This hasn't worked out well in recent years. It's not that planning would have shielded the system against the Great Crisis. But the absence of strategy allowed, if not encouraged, the United States to ignore stability risks in its search for growth. With an increasingly myopic and polarized political leadership, the U.S. economy has suffered from the recklessness of a precrisis strategy vacuum as well as from the lack of a postcrisis macro strategy. Now it languishes in an anemic recovery.

China and the United States both face extraordinary challenges. The question is whether either nation has the vision and leadership capacity to seize the moment and redirect, or in the case of the United States resurrect, its economic strategy.

3

The Boss and the Maestro

GREENSPAN AND ZHU

Each man grew up without a strong father figure. Zhu Rongji's father died before he was born, and Alan Greenspan lived with his mother after his parents divorced when he was five years old. Coming of age in the 1930s, each developed a keen sense of self-reliance and intellectual curiosity. These qualities defined their tenures as leading architects of economic policy for China and the United States in the 1990s.

Seared by the Cultural Revolution in his forties, Zhu Rongji eventually emerged as the tough guy. Known as "the Boss," he was the incorruptible reformer who led the marketization of modern China. Greenspan, having grown up during the Great Depression, bore personal witness to the fickle state of economic prosperity.

They differed on the role that ideology should play in the formulation of economic policy. Notwithstanding the Maoist ideological roots of modern China, Zhu Rongji's focus was pragmatic: He implemented the "reforms and opening up" that framed Deng Xiaoping's "fact-based" economic vision. Greenspan, as America's dominant central banker, was actually more blatant than Zhu in injecting ideology into the economic policy debate. He leaned heavily on the laissez-faire objectivist philosophy of Ayn Rand as the intellectual anchor to his free-market approach.

Each was a hero during the go-go 1990s. The Asian financial crisis of 1997–98 showed Zhu what could go very wrong on the path to economic development. As modern China's fifth premier, he advanced two key policies: dismantling the state's corporate ownership structure and formalizing China's global linkages through accession to the World Trade Organization. China emerged and thrived as the new economic leader of postcrisis Asia, while the former leader, Japan, lapsed into a series of "lost decades."

On the other side of the world, Alan Greenspan became enamored of a New Paradigm of economic growth, a vision framed by the productivity-enhancing virtues of new information technologies and seemingly spectacular financial innovation. The U.S. economy could do no wrong in the 1990s, and Greenspan was the Maestro.[1] As the world's leading example of economic dynamism, America defined the benchmark that others, including China, could only dream of.

Yet by the time they left power, Zhu and Greenspan had something else in common: Fixated on growth, each pushed his economy too far. Asset and credit bubbles sent America's economic miracle careening toward instability, with risks that Greenspan failed to appreciate. Meanwhile, an unbalanced Chinese economy was veering down an increasingly treacherous path. Zhu failed to see this problem.

As the risks mounted in both economies, and in effect reinforced one another, the codependency between the two nations started to deepen. The legacies of Greenspan and Zhu are inextricably linked as a result. It fell to the next generation of economic leaders in both countries to face the consequences.

"One Assurance, Three Implementations, and Five Reforms"

Zhu Rongji had no formal education in economics. Born in Hunan province in 1928, he earned a college degree in electrical engineering from Tsinghua University, the so-called MIT of China and one of the nation's most prestigious educational institutions. He was one of only three of modern China's senior leaders to have enrolled in Tsinghua before the Communist Revolution of 1949.[2]

This background provided Zhu with two important benefits: a rigorous analytical approach to problem solving, and a Tsinghua-based connection to a powerful political network. His maiden voyage into politics came toward the end of his university career as chair of the Student Union in the early 1950s. This was a tumultuous time, the first days of the People's Republic, and Zhu's role as a student leader at a major university doubtless drew the attention of the nation's new leaders.

Following graduation from Tsinghua in 1951, Zhu immediately got his hands dirty in the management of the Chinese economy. His knowledge of economics came not from the classroom but from the trenches of a floundering central planning process. After a first assignment as deputy chief of the Production Planning Section of Industrial Development for the Northeast Government, he was quickly promoted to deputy division chief for the nationwide State Planning Commission.

During that time, 1951–57, China began to emulate Soviet planning models and developed its own variants of the USSR's five-year plans. Zhu was both a witness to and a participant in these disasters. Driven by Mao's revolutionary fervor, state-directed resource allocation led to spectacular misadventures such as the rural mobilization and centralization of the Great Leap Forward. As stressed in Chapter 1, the economy struggled badly during that period and the combination of horrific weather and upheaval in the agricultural sector led to severe shortages of food and devastating famines. Zhu Rongji learned a critical lesson from this experience: The pragmatic translation of ideology into workable economic policies was far more important than blind adherence to the ideology itself.

Zhu's strength in practical analytics would eventually serve him well. But like most in China, he was sidetracked by political turmoil. His candor—an indelible characteristic of his future leadership style—got him into trouble early in his career. His "misstep" can be traced to a speech he gave in 1957, while still employed by the State Planning Commission, in which he questioned the wisdom of China's poorly designed economic policies.

That criticism made Zhu Rongji one of more than 300,000 victims of the "Anti-Rightist Campaign" of 1957.[3] He was dismissed from the planning agency and stripped of his membership in the Chinese Communist Party for twenty years. When the Cultural Revolution gained full force in the 1960s, he was assigned to two separate five-year stints of reeducation and work programs, tending livestock and doing menial work in the countryside. It was a painful experience that time didn't heal. The otherwise affable Zhu was never willing to speak about it in public.[4]

With the death of Mao, the end of the Cultural Revolution in 1976, and the ascendancy of Deng Xiaoping as China's new supreme leader, Zhu Rongji was rehabilitated. Then in his late forties, he seized the moment by parlaying his practical analytics into a successful stint as an economic manager. In doing so, he got Deng's attention just when China's new supreme leader was focusing on the "reforms and opening up" of a severely weakened economy.

Having returned to the planning bureaucracy, first as deputy bureau chief at the Ministry of Petroleum and then as vice chairman of the State Planning Commission, Zhu stumbled into an extraordinary opportunity. In the early 1980s, the World Bank sent a major study mission to China to explore the potential of Deng's transformation. Zhu volunteered to head up the collaboration from the Chinese side. This mission was a great success—it essentially put modern China on the map. The 1985 publication of a three-volume report by the World Bank on the transition potential of the Chinese economy was the first official endorsement of China's new economic strategy coming from the world's foremost development institution.[5] It also served as the basis for the World Bank's first loan to China. Deng was ecstatic over the outcome and at the pivotal role that Zhu had played.[6]

As the Chinese economy came to life in the early 1980s, Deng's attention turned to local development issues. He favored the "special economic zone" concept as an experimental means to drive rapid development in southern China, especially in Shenzhen and Zhuhai, and felt strongly that this approach needed broader application—particularly in Shanghai, long China's leading commercial center. And he believed that Zhu Rongji could make that happen.

In 1983, Zhu was transferred to Shanghai as deputy Party secretary under Jiang Zemin. When Jiang was elevated to central Party leadership in 1988, Deng turned to Zhu as the logical replacement, appointing him Shanghai Party secretary and mayor and charging him with taking reforms and opening up to the next level.

Zhu delivered beyond Deng's wildest expectations. As a hands-on mayor, he plunged immediately into some of Shanghai's most intractable issues—corruption, a bloated bureaucracy, resource shortages, inadequate housing, water pollution—and made solid progress on all counts. He was a micro-manager with a macro vision. He trimmed official banquets from twelve dishes to four and rang the first opening bell for the Shanghai stock exchange in 1990. He also had to deal with some of China's toughest issues. Early in his tenure as mayor, in June 1988, he was confronted with democracy demonstrations. He avoided the martial law and violence that eventually erupted in Beijing in 1989 and was able to defuse the Shanghai protests relatively peacefully.

But Zhu's singular accomplishment in Shanghai was his vision of its future as China's leading city. Under Zhu's leadership, city planners saw that future in Shanghai's Pudong Development Zone—an urban development project on a scale the world had never seen. Rising up from the rice fields across the Huangpu River from old Shanghai (Puxi), Pudong was very different from the manufacturing-intensive special economic zones farther south, in the Pearl River Delta area. It had a much broader economic base that, in addition to manufacturing, included finance, trade, and infrastructure.[7] Zhu's creativity and drive in promoting the urban reforms that gave rise to Pudong further solidified his role in Deng's inner circle.

Advancement came quickly. In 1991, Zhu was elevated to central government leadership with an appointment as vice premier in charge of finance and banking. He chafed at the label "economic czar," but his expertise and responsibilities went well beyond the financial sector.[8] As Deng put it at the time, "Zhu Rongji is the only one who understands economics."[9] He managed China's economic policy portfolio with great skill—tackling the inflationary surge of 1993–94 through a judicious coordination of monetary tightening and administrative actions aimed largely at agricultural prices, streamlining and reorganizing the central bank into a multidistrict Federal Reserve–like structure (Zhu assumed the added role of governor of the People's Bank of China from 1993 to 1995), and pushing through a dramatic program of state-owned enterprise reforms. For all that and more, he was appointed premier of the State Council in 1998.

It was inauguration under fire. The Asian financial crisis was raging when Zhu Rongji took the reins of the Chinese government and economy. As a leader, he was transparent, blunt, aggressive, and strategic. On the occasion of his first press conference as premier in March 1998, the slogan-prone Zhu spelled out his agenda as "one assurance, three implementations, and five reforms."[10]

The assurance was that China could cope with the Asian financial crisis by growing its way out of it. The Chinese government, Zhu maintained, would avoid the collapse in economic growth and currencies that was infecting other Asian economies. The three implementations, later to become known as Zhu's three promises, referred to a restoration of profitability for state-owned enterprises (SOEs), financial system reforms—especially cleaning up nonperforming bank loans—and central government streamlining and reorganization. And the five reforms pertained to grain distribution, investment financing, residential housing, healthcare, and the tax system. Zhu delivered on the first of two promises through SOE ownership reforms directed at share sales in international capital markets and a reduction of bad debts in the banking system, but he could not clean up a bloated and corrupt government bureaucracy.

Premier Zhu proved especially adept in steering China through the Asian financial crisis. He put the nation's huge reservoir of surplus savings to work in funding an aggressive fiscal stimulus aimed largely at accelerated infrastructure spending on roads, rail, port facilities, and power. At the same time, while other Asian economies were being advised by the IMF to devalue their currencies, he was adamant in holding the line on the renminbi. Largely as a result, the Chinese economy was relatively unscathed by the devastating regional crisis. By the early 2000s, when the dust had settled after this tumultuous disruption, China was well on its way to supplanting Japan as the dominant economy in Asia. Delivering on the growth assurance was key—not just in avoiding the downside of the Asian financial crisis but also in providing Chinese leaders with confidence in a new strategy, the growth gambit, which was to come in quite handy many times in the years ahead. As we shall see, the Boss had borrowed a page right out of the Maestro's script. And like the Maestro, Zhu focused on the short-term benefits and failed to appreciate the long-term costs.

Zhu also took calculated risks, of which state-owned enterprise reform was the best example. He knew there were inherent conflicts of interest in the transition from state ownership of Chinese enterprises to a blended system in which a large minority of a company's shares are listed in international capital markets while the central government retains a controlling stake. Notwithstanding these tensions between international investors and Party officials charged with operational management of SOEs, Zhu pushed ahead. He believed that market discipline was essential to reduce the bloat and the concentration of power that hobbled the efficiency of state-owned enterprises.

At the same time, the government had certain strategic interests that it felt needed to remain under state control: telecommunications, transportation, and power (fuels and electricity). Premier Zhu reconciled these opposing considerations—market-based efficiencies versus state-directed strategy—under the mantra of "grasp the big, let go of the small." The result was a unique blended system—"with Chinese characteristics," as they like to say in Beijing—that has since become known as the socialist market economy.

China's long-delayed accession to the World Trade Organization was another important example of Zhu Rongji's aggressive risk taking. The WTO application, initiated in 1986, had become stalled over U.S. concerns about job security in the face of surging Chinese imports, and Zhu was determined to break the logjam. He invested enormous political capital in bringing this issue to a head in 1999. In a celebrated trip to the United States in April of that year, Zhu Rongji became as adept as President Bill Clinton in playing the U.S. political game by appealing directly to corporate America in order to forestall an apparent last-minute rejection of China's application by Washington. A deal was finally signed in November 1999.[11]

Entry into the WTO in 2001 cost Zhu considerable political capital at home. Many of China's traditional Party factions did not want to face the challenges of foreign competition, and they believed Zhu had gone too far in making concessions to the United States. Some dissenters went so far as to label him a "traitor."[12] But Zhu believed strongly that the WTO trading system would force Chinese companies to restructure and reform. Market-based competitive pressures, he argued, could accomplish far more than the administrative directives of central planners. And he was right. The tariff reductions implemented ahead of China's WTO membership sparked a major push for efficiencies by bloated state-owned enterprises, positioning them well to drive an increasingly powerful export machine.[13]

Nor was Zhu Rongji afraid of debate. Starting in 2000, he convened the annual China Development Forum—a high-level exchange between senior government officials and an invited assemblage of domestic and foreign experts, held the weekend after the closing of the annual National People's Congress. It was his way of putting the ministers of the State Council on notice that their accountability as policy makers needed to be taken seriously. The China Development Forum quickly became a high-profile venue for raising and considering alternatives to China's orthodox policy strategies.[14]

In setting his nation's economic policy, Zhu Rongji gave China something very special. He took the spark lit by Deng Xiaoping and turned it into an operative and highly successful model of economic development. But beneath the surface, trouble was brewing. The transformation over which Zhu presided placed growing stress on China's role as the ultimate producer. All that seemed to matter was economic growth—and at a speed that large economies rarely experienced. Little attention was paid to emerging imbalances of the producer-centric growth strategy that would ultimately pose serious challenges to sustained development of the Chinese economy.

"To Exist, You Need an Ideology"

Born in 1926, two years before Zhu Rongji, Alan Greenspan would eventually be known as the Maestro.[15] For most of his eighteen-and-a-half-year tenure as chairman of the Board of Governors of the Federal Reserve System, he held the second–most powerful job in America. When he spoke, markets around the world quaked.

Although his stewardship of the U.S. economy will be long debated, Greenspan was as much a creature as a creator of the system he inhabited. When America's postwar boom started to fade in the 1970s, the electorate clamored for new answers. The man who called himself nothing more than "the senior Republican economist" was more than happy to provide them.[16]

Greenspan cut his teeth as an economist on the now seemingly arcane art of industry analysis. His mentor was Arthur Burns. In the early 1950s, when a twenty-something Greenspan was in the Ph.D. program in economics at Columbia while simultaneously working as an entry-level economist at the Conference Board, Burns was the leading business analyst in the country; he would later become one of Greenspan's predecessors as Federal Reserve chairman. The two would remain close until Burns died in June 1987, two months before Greenspan moved into Burns's old office at the Fed.

Greenspan didn't get the Ph.D.—at least not then.[17] While he was splitting his time between the Conference Board and Columbia, he became fascinated with America's heavy industries and wrote reports and articles on steel, autos, copper, aircraft manufacturing, and aluminum. His timing was impeccable: The nation's postwar industrial renaissance was about to take off. Greenspan became too busy to continue his studies at Columbia. He had found his calling as a consultant to Smokestack America.

His consulting career was built mainly on micro industry analysis, not from macroeconomic insights. But he had great curiosity about the economic policy debate as it was raging in Washington and Wall Street in the 1950s and 1960s. He was also intrigued by the interplay between economics and politics, and in 1967 was invited by Martin Anderson, a former Columbia colleague and then Richard Nixon's chief domestic policy adviser, to join the presidential campaign staff. When Nixon won, Greenspan started spending more and more time in Washington. He was quickly bitten by the Beltway bug.

The appointment of his mentor, Arthur Burns, as Fed chairman in 1970 made a strong impression on Greenspan as to the higher calling of public service. A number of his other Republican friends, including Herbert Stein, as well as Donald Rumsfeld and Dick Cheney, had been elevated to senior economic policy positions in the Nixon administration, but the Burns connection was an especially big deal.[18] When Burns called him in 1974 and began pressing him about obligations to national service, Greenspan, then still working as a private consultant, was hardly disposed to say no. He accepted an appointment by President Nixon, only to be sworn in by President Ford, as the tenth chairman of the President's Council of Economic Advisers.[19]

This was the start of a long and prestigious career in the government. Determined to "return the Council to its advisory role," but initially facing a daunting inflation problem, the Republican economist had to learn quickly how to cope with ever-fickle political winds.[20] When Gerald Ford lost to Jimmy Carter in 1976, Greenspan returned to his still very successful consulting business. He spent the one-term Carter administration on the outside, and was only tangentially involved in the first Reagan administration as a member of the Economic Policy Board. But that all changed in August 1987, when he got the call to replace Paul Volcker as Fed chairman.

Like Zhu Rongji, who was thrown immediately into the Asian financial crisis on being made China's premier, Greenspan went through inauguration by fire. On October 19, 1987, just sixty-nine days after he was sworn in as Fed chairman, the U.S. stock market plunged by 23 percent. The neophyte central banker had to rely less on experience and training than on gut instincts to quell a potential panic. The Fed quickly opened its borrowing window to securities firms and other financial institutions and moved aggressively to inject money into the markets by buying government securities. Within twenty-four hours markets began to stabilize. Greenspan and the Fed reaped financial market and political adulation. This was the first in what was to become a predictable pro-growth response pattern of "Greenspan puts"—Fed actions aimed at putting a floor on markets in distress.

Greenspan's gut reaction didn't come out of thin air. It was rooted in the ideological convictions that arose from his fascination with the teachings of Ayn Rand, author of *The Fountainhead* and high priest of objectivism. Starting in the early 1950s, he had been a regular participant in her weekly Collective, and he remained close to her and a member of her inner circle until she died in 1982. Ayn Rand was by his side, along with his mother, the day he was sworn in as the chairman of the Council of Economic Advisers in 1974.

Rand espoused a philosophical framework that "emphasized reason, individualism, and enlightened self-interest" as the pillars of laissez-faire capitalism—the system she considered mankind's optimal form of social organization.[21] Greenspan first came to her as a young empiricist in search of deeper meaning to the U.S. economy. Having rejected the new theories of John Maynard Keynes, he found in Rand something very different: a philosophy that brought markets to life and provided a framework for his data. When presented with a market failure on the scale of that of October 1987, Greenspan's reaction came from his deeply held ideological convictions as a laissez-faire objectivist. Nothing was more important to him than to restore the unfettered functionality of the world's most important stock market.

Greenspan was far from a one-dimensional ideologue. He brought to his trade as a central banker the analytical and empirical tools that he had developed during his twenty years as an economic consultant. But he had to make the difficult leap from micro to macro. In doing so, he drew on his strengths—especially his great curiosity about the forces that shape industrial activity, technological change, and productivity trends in the United States. True to his earlier form as a consultant, Greenspan was especially creative about bringing nontraditional data sources, like freight car loadings and cotton prices, into the Fed's analytical and forecasting functions.

But ideology proved to be a major stumbling block for the new Fed chairman. It ultimately distorted his analytics and prompted Greenspan to take his philosophy much too far in his role as the architect of U.S. monetary policy. At critical moments he allowed laissez-faire objectivism to overrule many of the time-honored axioms of macroeconomics.

That was very much the case when he famously reversed his view of the U.S. stock market in the late 1990s—arguing that "irrational exuberance," as he had called it in December 1996,[22] was actually rational in light of America's spectacular technology and productivity breakthroughs. Later, he denied the possibility of a nationwide housing bubble. The country, he argued, was not one single housing market but a vast collection of local and largely uncorrelated markets.[23] He also scoffed at credit bubbles, maintaining that financial innovations such as derivatives and so-called structured products—essentially packages of a broad spectrum of financial instruments—were outgrowths of the creative genius of the free-market system that were simply taking the risk out of the intermediation between borrowers and lenders.

Nor, Greenspan argued, was there anything wrong with the complexity of these new instruments. The same brilliant innovations that created them, he argued, also allowed the risks to be parceled out in tiny pieces to multitudes of free-market participants—who were presumed to provide a liquidity cushion that tempered the extremes of financial volatility.

Subprime mortgage lending, he famously maintained, was an example of how new technologies could be effectively deployed to achieve the lofty social goal of extending home ownership into the lower strata of the income distribution.[24]

In each of these cases, however, a dogmatic reliance on ideology led to serious policy blunders. There was nothing rational about the stock market in the late 1990s—the bubble burst in 2000, as did housing and credit bubbles several years later. Far from cushioning financial markets in distress, the derivatives markets brought the financial system to the brink of catastrophic failure in late 2008. And the subprime crisis, spawned by widespread defaults on home mortgages by low-income borrowers, turned out to be the harbinger of a nationwide housing market meltdown and an unprecedented wave of mortgage foreclosures.

The problem was not so much the bubbles themselves: Speculative bubbles are as old as markets. Think tulips in seventeenth-century Holland. The problems arose because the authorities had allowed bubbles to get so large, so pervasive, that they ended up creating severe distortions on the real side of the U.S. economy. It is the nature of bubbles that they burst. But when the reverberations cause contractions in major sectors of an already unbalanced economy, as was the case for homebuilding and personal consumption in 2008–9, the aftershocks invariably take a lasting toll.

Greenspan's failure to appreciate these risks came from his deep conviction that markets ultimately could do no wrong. With inflation low—and the Fed's easy monetary policy seemingly in compliance with its congressional mandate of price stability—Greenspan believed he could afford to take risks as a policy maker in order to achieve rapid growth and low unemployment. That conviction defined his core conclusion on monetary policy—to hold the Fed's short-term benchmark lending rate (the federal funds rate) much lower than frothy markets and a surging economy might have otherwise suggested. The magic of the Maestro became synonymous with easy money.

Why blame Alan Greenspan for the bubbles that burst and the havoc that sparked? He gave the American public exactly what it wanted. It was desperate for an antidote to slow underlying growth and eager to embrace the hopes and dreams of a New Economy. But Greenspan crossed the line when his ideological fervor turned him into a cheerleader for a supposedly bubble-proof U.S. economy. Congress and the White House—to say nothing of Wall Street and Main Street—took Alan Greenspan at his word that there was little risk that a free-market system could fail as it experimented with new and exciting forms of financial innovation. Nor was there concern that this was really financial engineering in disguise—tools that had little to do with innovation but, instead, fostered financial market excesses and serious imbalances in the real economy.

And so Washington, Wall Street, and Main Street collectively embraced a new formula for economic growth and prosperity. As long as inflation stayed low, the financial engineers had license to let it rip—and the Fed would not stand in the way of surging markets and the vigorous growth they spawned. The once cautious Greenspan who had warned of "irrational exuberance" now was the chief celebrant of America's rush to embrace the political economy of false prosperity. Former Fed Chairman William McChesney Martin famously quipped that his job was to take away the proverbial punch bowl "just as the party was really warming up."[25] Greenspan, instead, spiked the punch—and kept adding more of it to the bowl.

The repeated crises of the 1990s and 2000s cast Greenspan's grand ideological experiments in a very different light. In some respects it's less what he did than what he didn't do. He could have pricked bubbles, slowed the economy, and avoided crises and the systemic risks they unmasked. But he didn't. And the sad state of the U.S. economy in the aftermath of the Great Recession lays bare the costs of his policy mistakes.

The lesson is a tough one: Notwithstanding the virtues of innovation and technological change, there are no miraculous shortcuts to economic growth. There are certainly no grounds for allowing monetary and regulatory policy to be hijacked and held in an excessively accommodative position by an ideologically inspired search for growth. When called in front of the U.S. Congress to explain the role of the Fed under his chairmanship in the depths of the Great Crisis, Greenspan admitted his "shocked disbelief" at the failure of self-interest to guard against lending institutions' horrific mistakes.[26] The Maestro's mea culpa was more ideological than personal. He stopped well short of conceding any errors that were made by the Fed under his chairmanship.

Objectivism ultimately failed to provide the answers Greenspan thought it could. But he hadn't given up on his core value proposition. "To exist, you need an ideology," the Maestro maintained in front of the Congress as the Great Crisis intensified in late 2008. Nero couldn't have put it any better.

The Leap from Micro to Macro

The economic stewardships of Alan Greenspan and Zhu Rongji raise an important issue in the art and practice of economic policy. Each man came to his job well versed in the micro aspects of his respective economy. Greenspan was a consultant to heavy U.S. industry and Zhu was a central planner with a comparable portfolio of expertise. Neither had much experience as a macroeconomic practitioner. Yet that's exactly what the job descriptions of premier and Fed chairman called for.

The gulf between micro and macro has always made the economics profession uncomfortable. Microeconomics is more of a science, underpinned by elegant mathematical modeling. Macroeconomics is more of an art—using math as brushstrokes but often getting bogged down in dangerous aggregation assumptions. That latter point is key: Who's to say that what makes sense for one firm applies equally to all of them? Or that what makes sense for one consumer applies equally to a broad swath of a nation's population?[27]

The transition from micro to macro was rocky for both Zhu and Greenspan. The Chinese central planning bureaucracy was steeped in industry expertise and had good information on transactions and shipments between industries. But it was not well organized to address the challenges of an integrated national economy. Nor was China's data-gathering system designed to facilitate easy translation into the national income and product accounts, which summarize the structure and data collection of economies, important inputs to macro policy formulation. There was no central fiscal authority: Each ministry (education, defense, transportation, housing, and so on) was an island unto itself, and the tax collection function was divvied up between the central government (mainly consumption tax and customs duties) and provincial and local authorities (mainly real estate and property taxes). Similarly, the modern version of the central bank had just come into existence in 1998, as Zhu Rongji was preparing to assume the responsibilities as premier.

In other words, fiscal and monetary policy—the two pillars of macroeconomic management—barely existed in China when Zhu Rongji took over as the boss of its economy. That, coupled with inadequate monitoring of economy-wide performance, meant there was next to no understanding how the Chinese economy actually worked—to say nothing of how policy adjustments affected key sectors. This was especially problematic as the "blended" Chinese economy started to emerge—a rapidly growing collection of vibrant private businesses operating alongside the much larger state-owned enterprise sector. How this combination worked was anyone's guess. In the late 1990s, the Chinese authorities were effectively flying blind.

Fortunately, their instincts saved them. Their response to the Asian financial crisis—Zhu's first test as a macro practitioner—was an important case in point. Zhu quickly grasped how vulnerable China's export-led economy was to the sudden drop in external demand brought by the crisis in late 1998. He also grasped the risk of falling into a currency death spiral as the other Asian economies had done, where one devaluation begets another. Out of those realizations came a stimulus program that built needed new infrastructure and offset faltering external demand, and a strategy to defend the renminbi by maintaining its fixed relationship, or peg, against the U.S. dollar. These policies amounted to countercyclical economic improvisation by the Chinese leadership. But they worked. And they imparted significant lessons to Chinese authorities that were important in coping with future crises.

Greenspan, in making his own transition from a micro to a macro practitioner, had a different set of problems to contend with. He admits that early his career he was "far from comfortable in trying to comprehend the economy as a whole" and that he "understood more and more about its parts and how they connected."[28] But as Fed chairman he was quickly forced out of his comfort zone.

Unlike Zhu Rongji, the new Fed chairman could draw on a large and polished staff of Ph.D. economists, state-of-the-art macro forecasting models, and analytical tools that were linked to a comprehensive and well-developed database of the U.S. economy. But the Fed's analytical framework embraced long-standing conventions that ultimately created serious problems. The research staff was focused on current analysis—what the economy had been doing in the months before each policy meeting, and what that meant for an assessment of current-quarter economic activity. Fed economists were also wedded to cyclical analysis, pioneered by Greenspan's mentor Arthur Burns, that in essence tried to divine the future based largely on the business cycles of the past.[29] While that approach offered much in the way of comparative metrics, it made little allowance for major shifts in the structure and performance of a dynamic and rapidly changing U.S. economy.

Yet Greenspan was comfortable with the Fed's tool kit. As a longtime Burns disciple, he was naturally drawn to cyclical analysis. And the Fed staff's fixation on the processing of recent short-term data trends was right out of his own playbook as a consultant. Greenspan, to his credit, had a deep appreciation of the lessons of economic and financial history. But in the early days of his policy-making career, he framed those lessons largely in the Burnsian context of the recurring patterns of U.S. business cycles.

By viewing macroeconomics through the cyclical lens of the past, Greenspan missed many of the new and important challenges that were emerging in the 1990s. Globalization didn't fit neatly into his framework, and that created a real gap in his ability to appreciate the growing linkages between the U.S. and foreign economies, especially China's. For example, when pressed to account for low inflation, he dismissed the impact of China's inexpensive exports and attributed the Great Moderation of inflation to the successes of the Fed's monetary policy.[30]

That's not to say that Greenspan lacked intellectual curiosity. To the contrary, and consistent with his search for deeper meaning under Ayn Rand, he pondered many of the new developments in the U.S. economy— especially the impacts of new information technologies, shifting productivity trends, and the linkages between asset markets and Fed policy. But time and again he dismissed these developments as having actionable consequences for monetary policy. In doing so, he invoked his objectivist beliefs that unfettered markets were much better in discerning the impacts of these developments on economic growth, unemployment, and inflation than a group of central bankers sitting around a big table.

In the end, Greenspan as an economic manager relied more on ideology than facts. Zhu Rongji did exactly the opposite. Following the late 1970s credo of Deng Xiaoping, fact-based analytics became the essence of Zhu's macro framework. This critical distinction would come back to haunt the next generation of U.S. and Chinese policy makers.

No Exit

The comparison between Zhu Rongji and Alan Greenspan tells us a great deal about U.S.-Chinese codependency. The two nations' systems are obviously very different: America's quintessential free-market economy versus China's "market-based socialism." But they place very similar demands on their policy makers.

The United States and China obviously stood at sharply contrasting points on the development spectrum when Zhu and Greenspan took the reins of macro management. Yet both faced key strategic challenges. The new Chinese premier had to translate a strong but vague commitment to growth into action, while the new Fed chairman had to come to grips with the sustainability of economic growth in an ever–more complex world that had become increasingly competitive, increasingly interdependent. Growth was the challenge they had in common.

Zhu and Greenspan shared more in their approaches to economic management and policy design. Each cut his teeth on the empirics of industry analysis—Zhu as a central planner and Greenspan as a business consultant. Each was very analytical in assessing tough challenges and developed strategies that were well grounded in empirical evidence. Their main difference was ideology—but not in the way you might think. The miracle of modern China came from a powerful backlash against the ideological fervor of the Cultural Revolution. Deng Xiaoping converted that backlash into the Chinese development credo of "reforms and opening up." Zhu Rongji's contribution was the nuts-and-bolts implementation of this credo. In executing the strategy he was both pragmatic and nonideological—willing to use markets as well as state-directed planning to push ahead on the road to economic development.

Greenspan, by contrast, was far more the ideological purist. He was committed to finding a free-market answer to virtually every challenge. His laissez-faire ideology imparted an easy-money bias toward risk taking in the formulation of Fed policy that led to asset bubbles, subpar saving, excess debt, and postbubble aftershocks. In the end, the capitalist was far less pragmatic than the socialist.

The ideological contrasts between Greenspan and Zhu touch on another dimension of the relationship between the two economies—stability. The free-market champion in the United States was largely agnostic on matters of financial and economic stability. Greenspan believed that instability was a consequence of the choices the authorities made to adhere to the mandates of price stability and full employment as dictated by the Congress. Insisting that the authorities knew much less about bubbles than did market participants, he went on to argue that the central bank always had the tools to clean up after bubbles had burst.

Early on in his Fed tenure this was more of a hunch, grounded in his free-market objectivism. But in 2002 he invited onto the Fed's Board of Governors a professor from Princeton whose research on the role of monetary policy in addressing asset bubbles had come to similar conclusions. Ben Bernanke, as we shall see shortly, fit perfectly into Greenspan's ideological Fed. In a celebrated "mission accomplished" speech in 2004, the Maestro built on this collaboration and prematurely extolled the virtues of the "clean-up" approach to Fed strategy in the aftermath of the 2000 collapse of the equity bubble.[31]

For Zhu, stability was everything. Cognizant of China's long history of instability and turmoil, and seared by more recent memories of the Cultural Revolution and the Tiananmen Square events of June 1989, he made economic, social, and political stability the paramount objectives of Chinese policy. For example, mindful of the sharp slowdown in economic growth that hit the Chinese economy after an inflationary surge in the late 1980s—a "hard landing" that many believe contributed to the social disturbances of 1989—Zhu was quick to stress his desire for a more palatable "soft landing" in dealing with the inflation problem of 1993–94. Unlike Greenspan, who preferred to address postbubble carnage after the fact, Zhu believed in the preemptive strike in order to avoid damage before it occurred. China repeatedly deployed what it called proactive fiscal policy—first to address the Asian Crisis of the late 1990s, then in the postequity bubble climate of the early 2000s, and again in the face of the Great Crisis of 2008–9.

In the context of codependency, Zhu's successes ultimately became Greenspan's problems—and vice versa. By providing traction to "reforms and opening up," Zhu unleashed the most powerful export machine of the modern era. And the China-centric Asian supply chain that emerged from those efforts is one of several related forces that put pressure on jobs and incomes in the United States and other high-cost economies of the developed world.[32] Greenspan's response to those pressures—largely, his repeated and risky experiments with new recipes for growth—eventually got America into serious trouble.

But China's success added further complications. As its export-led growth gathered force in the 1990s and early 2000s, so too did its disinflationary impact on the economies of its major trading partners. Greenspan took the resulting low inflation as license to push even farther with his growth gambits and the easy-money accommodation they required. His ideological zeal left him steeped in denial—defending a scenario in which the so-called Great Moderation was underpinned by a productivity-led U.S. economy that had permanently tamed inflation. The alternative explanation—a Chinese export surge that had only temporarily restrained inflation—made no sense to him.

But Zhu Rongji should not be let off the hook in orchestrating the significant role that China played in contributing to ever-mounting global imbalances. While Deng Xiaoping rightly seized on a revival of economic growth as the antidote to a wobbly Chinese economy in the late 1970s and Zhu moved aggressively to frame and implement the reforms that allowed that growth to occur, this recipe was setting the stage for trouble ahead. Zhu, the micromanager whose experiences were originally formed in the era of central planning, failed to appreciate a major shift in the Chinese economy that was resulting from the business ownership transition he championed. Driven by profits and shareholder returns, the now marketized private sector focused more on cost control and the excess labor that could be pruned and replaced by machines.

This meant that China had to grow faster and faster to reduce poverty by absorbing surplus labor in the rural countryside. The breakneck speed of the Chinese economy that resulted was ultimately a major source of great instability inside of China and for the rest of the world. It led to excess energy and resource demand, widening inequalities, and environmental degradation and pollution. Notwithstanding the urgency of China's growth imperatives in the aftermath of the Cultural Revolution, the Boss failed to appreciate these mounting risks, risks that would come back to haunt the world's greatest development story in the years ahead.

On a personal basis, Alan Greenspan and Zhu Rongji were quite fond of each other. As with most of the world's leaders and senior policy makers, their paths crossed from time to time at various international conferences and forums. Greenspan writes, "I marveled at [Zhu's] detailed knowledge of China's economic shortfalls and the needed remedies."[33] And Zhu repeatedly refers to Greenspan as an "old friend," while noting that "whenever a crisis appears, he announces a lowering of interest rates."[34] Each appreciated the pro-growth agenda of the other and, in fact, began to count on that commitment in framing policies in his own economy. This personal side of codependency fit in well with the broader collaborative agenda of the United States and China.

That didn't last long. Zhu's approach took China down a path of unbalanced, export-dependent growth, while Greenspan's approach led the United States into bubble- and debt-dependent growth. The faster the treadmill went for both economies, the harder it became to jump off. Neither Zhu Rongji nor Alan Greenspan had any inkling of an exit strategy—the off-ramp to more sustainable growth and prosperity. Producers can't grow without consumers, they presumed, and consumers can't grow without producers. Growth was all that seemed to matter for both, irrespective of its consequences. Ultimately, the Boss and the Maestro became trapped in the same false prosperity.

4

The Great Stability Debate

WEN VS. BERNANKE

A ssessing economic policy is useless without understanding the context of its formulation. For most nation-states, irrespective of their systems of government, social and political considerations have long been critical in shaping economic policy choices. U.S. Federal Reserve Chairman Ben Bernanke and Chinese Premier Wen Jiabao, the successors to Alan Greenspan and Zhu Rongji, certainly had those considerations in common.

Wen Jiabao personified modern China's political balancing act. He was in many respects a transitional leader, positioned in the segue from reforms to sustainability. He brought a very human face to the leadership of the Chinese government, which during his tenure in office had to face much in the way of hardship and catastrophic experiences—from the SARS epidemic in 2003 to the devastating Sichuan earthquake in 2008, to ethnic unrest in Tibet and Xinjiang. He was also the chief celebrant of China's emergence as an economic powerhouse and as a showcase for athletic talent in the Beijing Olympics.

But Wen Jiabao's most important legacy as a policy maker may be his courageous willingness to question modern China's ability to stay the course.

In 2007, on the eve of the Great Crisis, he warned of an "unstable, unbalanced, uncoordinated, and ultimately unsustainable" economic growth model. In doing so he laid out the agenda for the next China—driven by a pro-consumption rebalancing. He also posed what could prove the toughest challenge of all—the imperative of political reform.

Wen Jiabao continued in the post-Mao tradition of letting the economic agenda take precedence over political reform. Ben Bernanke did the opposite; politics were critical in shaping his role as a central banker. A student of the Great Depression, he threw the full force of the Federal Reserve toward assuaging the deepest fear of the modern era: that a depression could happen again. In doing so, he turned to new and unconventional tools of monetary policy—especially so-called quantitative easing—in an effort to recapture the growth and jobs of yesteryear while avoiding a Japanese-style deflation. These actions blurred the distinction between monetary and fiscal policy and inserted the Bernanke Fed into the heart of the U.S. political debate. While America's central bank is politically independent on paper, Bernanke's actions spoke otherwise.

The interplay between politics and economics captures much of the recent tension between the United States and China. Yet Wen Jiabao and Ben Bernanke are offering strikingly different solutions—a China that opts for a new growth equation versus a United States that attempts to resurrect the old one. The odds are that one of them doesn't have it right—a conclusion that could have lasting and important consequences for these codependent economies and the world as a whole.

The People's Premier

Born in 1942, Wen Jiabao was a child of war and revolution. The first three years of his life were punctuated by the final stages of the Japanese occupation of China, followed by four years of civil war. Memories of those times never dimmed for Wen. Returning to his native Tianjin high school some sixty years later, he admitted, "My childhood was spent in war and hardship. The poverty, turmoil and famine left an indelible imprint on my young soul."[1]

Like Zhu Rongji, his predecessor as premier, Wen Jiabao received little formal economics training. He studied at the Beijing Institute of Geology, joining the Party after his graduation, in 1965. As was the case for many during this period, his graduate studies were interrupted in 1968 by the shuttering of universities during the Cultural Revolution. He was sent off to the desert town of Jiu Chuan in Gansu province, where he first met Hu Jintao, his future partner on the Chinese leadership team, who had also been banished.

Unlike Zhu Rongji, Wen received no menial farmwork assignments during the Cultural Revolution. Instead, he was initially tasked with low-level surveying duties in assessing the Gansu geological structure.[2] In the 1970s, he shifted his focus to Party work.[3] As the internal turmoil subsided late in the decade, his career as a senior geologist took off. He made an outstanding impression on the central government's Minister of Geology, and in 1983, at the age of forty-one, he was named vice minister of geology and mineral resources. At the time, he was one of the youngest Chinese officials holding ministerial rank.[4]

That appointment marked the end of Wen's career as a professional geologist. By 1985, he was serving as vice director in the Party's General Office—the administrative support organization for the central government's senior leadership team. Within a year he was the head of that office; a true political survivor, ultimately he served as chief of staff for a succession of three Party secretaries, two of whom were purged.[5] An affable *mishu* (secretary) with a reputation for coalition building and avoiding political cliques, Wen had an uncanny knack for dodging political bullets.[6]

An important case in point came during the democracy movement of the late 1980s, which embroiled Wen's boss, the liberal Party Secretary Hu Yaobang. When the popular Hu was forced out of power by Party backlash against student demonstrations in 1986, Wen's political survival hung in the balance and was saved only by a ritualistic self-criticism reminiscent of the Cultural Revolution. The word "self" was key. At no point did Wen cast any blame on other senior leaders, including the deposed Hu Yaobang.

Three years later, in the spring of 1989, Hu's unexpected death played an important role in sparking the massing of students in Tiananmen Square. Wen accompanied Hu's successor, Zhao Ziyang, who made a tearful plea to the demonstrators on May 19, a few weeks before they were forcibly dis-

persed. Sympathizing with the students, Zhao was later forced to resign
and then put under house arrest for the rest of his life (he died in 2005).
But Wen suffered no guilt by association. As chief administrative assistant
to the Party leadership, he received great credit for pulling off a delicate balancing act—accompanying the Party secretary at a moment of grave crisis
while appealing to the demonstrators for reason and calm. In contrast with
others associated with Zhao, Wen's ultimate loyalty to Deng Xiaoping was
never in question. That spared him from being tainted by the Tiananmen
tragedy.

Through a succession of Party alliances—especially with Jiang Zemin
and eventually with Zhu Rongji—Wen continued to move up the ranks. In
1998 he was appointed vice premier, working directly under China's most
brilliant economic tactician, the newly installed Premier Zhu. With that
came Wen's first real exposure to China's macroeconomic challenges in
the form of the Asian financial crisis. He was also given an important piece
of the national development agenda to manage—the long-discussed but
never fully implemented Western Development Strategy, aimed at a geographic broadening of Chinese development from the prosperous eastern
coastal region to more remote provinces in central and western China.

Wen didn't really shine as a problem solver during his tenure as vice
premier. But he didn't have to with Zhu in control. Wen's strengths were
more those of a hardworking and loyal team player, and that held him in
good stead with Deng Xiaoping and others in the Party hierarchy. And in
2003, in modern China's first smooth leadership transition, Wen Jiabao
was elected the sixth premier of the State Council.

He had big shoes to fill. Zhu Rongji's outspoken and decisive character,
his extraordinary analytics and strategic vision, stood in sharp contrast to
Wen's low-key, broad-brush, almost philosophical approach. Early in his premiership, Wen was not comfortable dealing with tough economic problems.
But eventually he found his way—choosing to focus more on principles
than on analytics in putting his unique stamp on China's policy portfolio.

Wen's perspective increasingly defined his leadership style. He had gotten to this stage in his career not just as a team player but also with a soft-
spoken, hardworking demeanor that lacked any sense of arrogance. He had
a sixth sense—a survival instinct—that came from his humble candor and

had been refined under fire during the tumultuous democracy demonstrations of the late 1980s. All this served him well in projecting an image of connecting the government to the Chinese people.

One of Wen's greatest strengths in reaching ordinary citizens was his knack for putting a human face on China's all-too-frequent national tragedies. In 1989, he shed tears for the students in Tiananmen Square, establishing a pattern to be repeated in the years to come, as Wen confronted a series of horrific natural disasters (floods and earthquakes), industrial accidents (mining collapses and train crashes), and health emergencies (diseases and food contamination). His emotional connection to the Chinese people was tested immediately after he became premier, when in April 2003, Wen took the lead in managing China's response to the SARS epidemic.[7] He also rushed to the scene in Sichuan province in the spring of 2008 to personally oversee rescue efforts after a devastating earthquake, and he grieved over the Wenzhou high-speed train crash of 2011. Wen Jiabao became the conscience of a nation that had longed for more compassion from its senior leaders.

Wen's emotional anchor as a sympathetic leader stood in sharp contrast to Zhu's analytical anchor as an aggressive reformer. Wen relied more on personal experience than on strategic calculations to shape his leadership style. He was also more eclectic in incorporating a broad range of input into his decision-making process, whereas Zhu could be more focused and at times dogmatic. In fact, in keeping with the challenges faced by a blended socialist market economy that rested on the foundations of both socialism and capitalism, Wen drew on the lessons of both Chinese and Western philosophy in grounding his leadership philosophy. He traveled with books by Adam Smith and Marcus Aurelius, hoping to learn from "ideas and thoughts of older generations [that] can offer food for thought for the current generation."[8]

This contemplative approach led him to ponder one of modern China's deepest economic dilemmas—the interplay between stability and growth. Wen worried about the tradeoff between China's rapid development and the need for economic, social, and political stability. As will be discussed in greater detail below, he famously pondered whether an increasingly unbalanced and unstable Chinese economy could stay its course. But he also worried about the social instability that had arisen from China's mounting income inequalities—ultimately the greatest threat to the socialist dream of what Chinese leaders call a Harmonious Society. And he was bold enough to push hard on one of China's toughest sustainability issues—political reform.

The internal politics of a one-party state like China are obviously quite different from those of a multiparty democracy. But they are no less vexing. With China on the ascent and memories dimming of a broken economy in the aftermath of the Cultural Revolution, a new sense of pride and nationalism bears on the nation's internal politics. External pressures also enter prominently into China's political calculus. Its response to those pressures can be especially prickly. Dating back to the Opium Wars of the mid-nineteenth century, the historical baggage of 150 years of perceived humiliation by the West has led to a strong resistance to foreign advice and a growing independence in shaping China's foreign policy, currency policy, and trade policy.

Contrary to accepted wisdom in the West, modern China has not entirely ducked the debate on democracy, elections, and other aspects of political reform. As discussed in Chapter 13, it has in fact made considerable progress in an experimental approach to local government elections. To be sure, this has been a hard issue for a one-party system to address—especially in the aftermath of the regime-threatening upheavals of the Cultural Revolution and the democracy uprisings of the late 1980s. But the debate has been active, to say the least.

Beijing's so-called Democracy Wall of the late 1970s sowed many of the early seeds of political liberalization. The now infamous "Fifth Modernization" wall poster of Wei Jingsheng argued that the Four Modernizations that formed the building blocks of Deng Xiaoping's reforms were not enough: China's modernization would not be complete without democracy and a freely elected representative government.[9] While uncomfortable with the Democracy Wall and the debate it spawned, Deng Xiaoping allowed it to continue for a while before clamping down. The political reform debate in China was on again and off again in the first half of the 1980s before mounting protests and the great tragedy of 1989 brought a sudden end to any public discourse on this subject for years to come.

Some twenty years later, Wen Jiabao felt that China's post-Tiananmen healing was more or less complete. In a series of articles and speeches in 2010, he courageously argued that it was time once again to begin contemplating one of the most important items of unfinished business on the Chinese reform agenda. In a lead op-ed in *People's Daily*, the official Party organ, Wen broke the ice and boldly praised his former mentor, the purged reformist Hu Yaobang, on the occasion of the twenty-first anniversary of Hu's death.[10] He also expressed concern over the growing concentration of power in the central government, cautioning that "without the safeguard of political reform, the fruits of economic reform will be lost and the goal of modernization will not materialize."[11]

This caused considerable stir in senior leadership circles and was ultimately countered by a hardline propaganda pushback strikingly reminiscent of tactics used in the Cultural Revolution. A strong response in *People's Daily*, written under an apparent pseudonym, argued instead for a consolidation of "the party's leadership so that the party commands the overall situation."[12] Wen took the hint and dropped the issue for a while.

His hand was finally forced by the extraordinary case of Bo Xilai, which came to a head in early 2012. A son of Bo Yibo, one of modern China's major revolutionary heroes, Bo Xilai was Chongqing Party secretary and a leading candidate for elevation to the Standing Committee of the Politburo in China's 2013 leadership transition. Yet he posed an immediate political and economic challenge to the Chinese leadership. He stood for a neo-Maoist populism that was garnering great attention in China, and his "Chongqing Development Model" favored a retrograde shift back to the 1980s and early 1990s, when economic growth was driven predominantly by state-owned enterprises.[13]

With Bo Xilai reaching for power and the fifth-generation leadership change looming, China's senior leaders decided to tackle the threat head-on, and Wen Jiabao took the lead. The circumstances that brought the issue to a head were reminiscent of the high intrigue of the Cold War—an attempted defection by his former ally, the Chongqing security chief, Wang Lijun, who also raised criminal charges of bribery and corruption against Bo.[14] On March 14, 2012, at a high-profile international press conference in the Great Hall of the People overlooking Tiananmen Square, Wen issued a stern warning:

"The current Party committee and government of Chongqing must reflect on the Wang Lijun incident and learn lessons from the incident." This was a thinly veiled threat targeted directly at the head of the Chongqing municipal government, Bo Xilai. It followed an equally severe warning that Wen had just issued a few minutes earlier at the same press conference when he cautioned of "new problems that have cropped up in China's society [that] cannot fundamentally be resolved and such historical tragedy as the Cultural Revolution may happen again."[15]

Cryptic, yes—but carefully chosen words expressed in the strongest possible fashion. They left little doubt as to the high stakes in this political battle. The translation: Bo Xilai, who posed a threat reminiscent of the Cultural Revolution, had to go. Notwithstanding his direct lineage to one of modern China's greatest revolutionary heroes, that, of course, is exactly what happened in the days and weeks that followed.[16] Delivered by Premier Wen Jiabao—the personification of modern China's conscience—this message underscored the Party's intolerance of the threats to political and economic stability that Bo stood for. It left Wen in a position of driving home the contrast between a forward-looking debate over political reform, which entertained the possibility of a freely elected representative government, versus a backward-looking return to the neo-Maoist principles of the Cultural Revolution. Moving into the final year of his tenure in office, the People's Premier was prepared to bet his legacy on this critical distinction.[17]

The Professor

Ben Bernanke has an entirely different take on stability. Like Wen Jiabao, he pays great attention to historical examples of instability—in his case as an academic who did careful research on the Great Depression, modern America's most serious threat of economic instability.[18] But ultimately, like his predecessor Alan Greenspan, he draws great comfort from the equilibrium tendency of a free-market system. Markets and the economies they support are presumed to be tough and resilient, and hardly ever are they thrown seriously out of kilter. Public policy, in Bernanke's world, should be aimed less at avoiding instability than at dealing with the consequences of rare destabilizing outcomes as they arise.

These principles lie at the core of the riskiest policy experiment in modern U.S. economic history. As noted previously, they provided justification for the monetary policy of Alan Greenspan, and they also shaped the strategy of his successor. But they originate in the academic work of Ben Bernanke, long before he came to the Federal Reserve.

If Zhu Rongji was educated at the Chinese equivalent of MIT, Bernanke is a product of the original. A Ph.D. from MIT in 1979—at the time it had arguably the leading economics department in the world—identified the bearer as a first-rate theorist. Bernanke's doctoral dissertation fit that script to a tee: three abstract essays examining the microeconomic foundations of macro business cycle fluctuations, with no real attempt to explore how these theories applied to any actual economic experience.[19] The future Fed chairman was hardly alone in embracing math and theory as a window into economics. It was the rage in the 1970s—especially at MIT.

To his credit, Bernanke quickly put his mathematical and theoretical skills to work on a variety of more practical empirical research topics. As a young assistant professor at Stanford University, he focused his early research on three aspects of applied macroeconomics: the credit cycle, the financial transmission mechanism (that is, the linkage between financial markets and the real economy), and financial crises. Unwittingly, he was laying down the intellectual foundation of the approach to monetary policy he would later adopt as a central banker.

After six years on the faculty at Stanford, Bernanke left for Princeton in 1985, where he stayed until 2002, when he was first appointed to the Fed as a governor. At Princeton his research agenda evolved into two major strains of investigation—how and why the Great Depression had occurred, and linkages between asset markets and the real economy. At the time, he surely had no idea how relevant those topics would become.

His work on the Great Depression was heavily influenced by the theory and historical insights of Milton Friedman.[20] Like Friedman, Bernanke came to the conclusion that the catastrophic collapse in the U.S. economy during the 1930s was largely man-made—and that the Fed was especially guilty in failing to erect a firewall around a crumbling banking system and in failing to provide enough monetary support for a U.S. economy in crisis.[21] These findings have long underlain the orthodox countercyclical strategy of modern central banks. Maximum monetary stimulus in terms of low interest rates and ample injection of liquidity into the banking system is now widely accepted as the most effective response to deep recessions, deflation, and depressions. In the depth of the Great Crisis of 2008, this approach was popularized as central to the "the big bazooka"—the heaviest artillery in the economic policy arsenal.[22]

Simple as it sounds, that approach is subject to great controversy. This is where the second strain of Bernanke's research was focused—the inter-play between the financial system and the real economy, and the role the central bank can play in shaping that interplay. Bernanke was a leading proponent of the idea that a "financial accelerator"—operating through the feedback loops between monetary policy and the credit cycle—can magnify the economic impact of sharp changes in financial conditions.[23] The more severely financial markets contract, goes the argument, the greater the neg-ative impacts on the real economy. It follows that only the full thrust of maximum monetary stimulus can neutralize and hopefully offset the con-tractionary power of the financial accelerator. This conclusion was central to Bernanke's prescription for the United States in the 2000s, and he also used it as an argument to criticize Japanese policy makers for their timid efforts to counter deflationary pressures during their "lost decades."[24] And, of course, it featured prominently in Bernanke's rationale for unusually aggressive Fed policy actions in the Great Crisis and the anemic postcrisis recovery.

The controversy arises on two counts: First, other academics have leveled a scathing attack on the financial accelerator mechanism as a purported major factor in accounting for sharp cyclical fluctuations during the Great Depression. The counterview pins most of the blame for the Depression on productivity and labor market frictions, rather than on financial frictions that could be magnified through an accelerator mechanism.[25]

Second, Bernanke and Mark Gertler of NYU, one of his closest academic collaborators in his pre-Fed days, went on to argue that monetary policy was more effective in cleaning up *after* the bursting of asset and credit bubbles rather than moving against bubbles *before* they did their damage.[26] This conclusion, which formed the basis of the Fed's postbubble cleanup campaigns of the 2000s,[27] rests on the notion that monetary policy is a blunt instrument whose impacts are likely to have a more severe impact on the broader economy than that caused by the bursting of bubbles. That would be especially the case if the amplification mechanism of the financial accelerator exacerbates the impacts of a bubble-pricking Fed policy initiative. Stressing this consideration, Bernanke and Gertler maintained that it was preferable to use monetary policy to deal with the carnage after the fact than to create a more serious problem out of thin air.

The wreckage of 2008–9, followed by an unusually weak economic recovery, draws this latter conclusion into sharp question. As blunt an instrument as monetary policy is, the bubble-related distortions to the real side of the U.S. economy were big enough—affecting personal consumption and homebuilding, which when combined accounted for about 74 percent of the GDP in 2005—that a so-called blunt Fed tightening was more than appropriate. When bubbles and their distortive impacts grow as large as they did in the United States in the 2000s, the nation loses less growth from a preemptive monetary tightening than it does from the postbubble carnage of a devastating crisis, recession, and a persistently anemic postcrisis recovery.

As contentious as this debate is, the professor–turned–Fed chairman was certainly well prepared to tackle these issues. That is rare in policy circles. Bernanke's academic research gave him tools, empirical metrics, and historical perspective in assessing the forces and problems that were about to bear down on the U.S. and global economy. But economics is a fickle discipline. It is a combination of art and science, instinct and models. The leap from academia to policy practitioner can be tricky. There is no guarantee that state-of-the-art research like Bernanke's will lead to optimal outcomes for the economies the experts are entrusted to manage. That is precisely the problem the United States is now confronting.

The Four Uns

There is no Ben Bernanke in the control room of the Chinese economy. Theory was not the answer to the policy challenges of China's rapidly developing blended economy. It required more in the way of instincts, principles, and priorities.

At least, that was the mindset that Premier Wen brought to the stage of the Great Hall of the People at his press conference on March 16, 2007, following the conclusion of the annual National People's Congress. It was a period of relative tranquility for the Chinese and global economy. There was no serious talk of the crisis that was about to erupt.[28] The world was in the fifth year of its most vigorous run of economic growth in the post–World War II era. It was a time for China to celebrate its newfound economic strength—not to worry about the lack of it.

Yet Wen warned of complacency. While conceding that all looked well on the surface, he went on to depict the Chinese economy as increasingly "unstable, unbalanced, uncoordinated, and ultimately unsustainable." This statement had a profound impact. The Four Uns, as they quickly became known, changed the conversation on the Chinese economy.[29]

In the months that followed, the premier embellished and clarified his critique. By *unstable,* he meant he was worried about overheated investment, excess liquidity, and the country's outsized current account surplus. By *unbalanced,* he meant the urban-rural divide as well as the regional disparities between China's relatively well-off eastern provinces and the poor provinces in the west. By *uncoordinated,* he was expressing concerns about deeply rooted local fragmentation, disparities between excess manufacturing capacity and underdeveloped services, and the increasingly sharp divergence between excess investment and inadequate private consumption.

But *unsustainable* was by far the most worrisome aspect of Wen's critique. Here, he was alluding to environmental degradation and pollution, but also to mounting disparities in income distribution. The subtext of his message on sustainability was that the Chinese development miracle could run out of time if the authorities didn't address the growing multiplicity of problems. After thirty years of reforms and opening up, unsustainability was the biggest danger to the development miracle. It was modern China's ultimate threat—the risk of being ensnared in the middle-income trap.

The power of this critique is that the Four Uns also provide a framework for coming up with answers. They set both an analytical and a practical agenda for the urgent and daunting task of rebalancing the Chinese economy. But they also underscore the imperatives of environmental safeguards, pollution control, and alternative (noncarbon) sources of energy.

And perhaps most critical, they speak to China's ongoing concerns about social stability—especially the need to address the mounting income inequalities that pose a serious threat to the socialist aspirations of the Harmonious Society.

Over the years since Wen Jiabao put the Four Uns on the table, the Chinese leadership has consistently used his critique to frame the policy debate. Occasionally they have tweaked the message—most recently, blaming instability more on the crisis-prone global economy than on China's internal problems.[30] But the Four Uns have played a key role in shaping the Chinese economic strategy debate—especially in developing the goals of the pro-consumption Twelfth Five-Year Plan.[31]

We should always take care not to read too much into the Chinese leadership's slogans and rhetorical flourishes. And there is a risk of giving Wen Jiabao too much credit for defining the next stage of Chinese economic development. But the Four Uns encapsulate much of what Wen brought to the economic policy debate during the ten years of his premiership. They served as a principles-based critique, anchored in the twin foundations of stability and sustainability. They provided just the wake-up call China needed.

Wen Jiabao deserves enormous credit for sparking this debate. He also gets great credit for converting this debate into the new strategic initiatives featured in the Twelfth Five-Year Plan. He merits little credit, however, for implementing solutions to the questions he posed. Notwithstanding the imperatives of rebalancing, China has dragged its feet in putting its new plan into action. That is especially the case, as will be discussed in Chapter 11, in addressing the need to fund its social welfare institutions such as social security and healthcare.

Nor should Wen Jiabao get credit for facing up to one of the biggest disconnects in the Chinese development miracle—the failure of a rapidly growing economy to generate enough jobs. Like Zhu Rongji who preceded him, Premier Wen didn't understand the consequences of an increasingly blended Chinese economy that was focusing more and more on efficiency and cost cutting to boost shareholder returns. Those costs were workers, and that meant that China had to grow at ever-faster rates to absorb its vast surplus of labor and reduce poverty. Wen's failure to appreciate that left

China struggling to stay on the treadmill—ironically, a struggle that was finessed by a hypergrowth that ultimately gave rise to the stresses and strains of the Four Uns. The critique of Wen Jiabao may well be his legacy, but he failed to grasp the source of China's deep-rooted structural problems.

Putting policies in place to force structural change is never easy, especially in a country like China, where resistance comes from deeply entrenched power blocs embedded in local governments and state-owned enterprises. Inertia has proved more difficult to overcome than the urgency of Wen Jiabao's appeal of the Four Uns might seem to suggest. Yet as the legacy of Zhu Rongji's reforms demonstrates, Premier Wen could have pushed harder at implementation. It will be up to his successor, newly installed Premier Li Keqiang, to transform the debate into action.

The Promise

November 8, 2002, was the ninetieth birthday of Milton Friedman, the high priest of the Chicago School of economics. At the Max Palevsky Cinema on the campus of the University of Chicago, Friedman's colleagues, students, and admirers gathered to celebrate the man, his work, its impact, and the community spirit he had spawned.

In keeping with academic tradition, the main event was a conference devoted to three strains of Friedman's Nobel Prize–winning research: monetary policy, social policy, and his "permanent income theory" of consumer behavior. But a final session focused on the uplifting subject of "Depression and Recovery." The main speaker was Ben Bernanke, appearing in a dual capacity as academic expert and as a newly appointed Fed governor.[32]

Bernanke provided a stylized summary of the monetary aspects of the Great Depression, as seen through the lens of the classic work by Friedman and his colleague Anna Schwartz, who was also in attendance.[33] Bernanke emphasized what he believed was a tight alignment between his views and those of Friedman and Schwartz. He stressed that their forensic analysis of "natural experiments" of the late 1920s and 1930s, especially the inexplicable movements in the money supply that could not be linked to fluctuations in the real economy, validated the important role played by the financial accelerator in the Great Depression's downward spiral.

This may not have been the most balanced treatment of this critical period. While Bernanke conceded that such "nonmonetary" factors as banking panics and business failures contributed to the Depression, he argued that their first-order impacts were relatively small, and were magnified by the financial accelerator.[34] Bernanke made no mention of Smoot-Hawley tariffs, trade wars, or the speculative stock market bubble of the late 1920s.[35] Pinning the blame almost entirely on wrong-footed monetary policy, he closed his speech with an emotional confession. On behalf of the Fed, Bernanke acknowledged to Friedman, "We did it. We're very sorry. But thanks to you, we won't do it again."[36]

That promise came from the very core of Ben Bernanke, the academic turned modern central banker. Two weeks later, in a now famous speech on deflationary risks, he took his passionate promise to Friedman one important step farther. At the time, debate was raging over whether the post-bubble U.S. economy—still coping with the aftershocks from the bursting of the equity bubble in 2000—could slip into a Japanese-style deflation. While Bernanke hoped such an outcome could be avoided, he thought it was important to present a game plan in case he was wrong—a game plan that was true to his promise to Milton Friedman.[37]

The game plan eventually served another purpose. Bernanke's speech also laid out precisely what was to come in the aftermath of the Great Crisis of 2008–9. When he delivered it, in late 2002, the Fed's main policy lever, the federal funds rate—the rate the Fed charges banks for overnight lending—was at a fifty-year low of 1 percent. The policy conundrum, as Bernanke put it, was the Fed's options in the event it had to exhaust its traditional ammunition and take the funds rate down to the "zero bound." Fear not, Bernanke argued: This is where the creative central banker can step up and use a variety of unconventional tools to stimulate the economy and avoid deflation. The answer, he maintained, could be found on the asset side of the Fed's balance sheet. Bernanke argued that if the central bank ran out of room and couldn't reduce the *price* of overnight credit below zero, it could and should operate equally aggressively on the *quantity* dimension of credit to increase the amount of money in circulation.

Bernanke went even farther and laid out a menu of unconventional choices that a zero-bound-constrained central bank might also consider as part of a quantitative easing agenda: targeting longer-term interest rates through asset purchases, spurring private sector lending via the discount window, or purchasing foreign and domestic government debt. He even went so far as to contemplate a sharp devaluation of the dollar.

The options proposed in this "what if" speech turned out to be far from idle musings. As the federal funds rate was, in fact, pushed down to zero in late 2008, Bernanke's Fed dutifully pulled out the playbook he had presented in 2002.[38] In the depths of the Great Crisis, the Fed intervened directly in frozen credit markets. Those efforts were followed by multiple rounds of "quantitative easing" and even an "operation twist" aimed at reducing the yields of longer-term securities. The asset side of the Fed's balance sheet ballooned as a consequence, going from less than $1 trillion in 2007 to more than $3 trillion by mid-2012—headed to $4 trillion by the end of 2013. Meanwhile, the value of the dollar continued its descent, declining by 25 percent from its peak in early 2002 through mid-2013.[39]

True to his promise to Milton Friedman, Bernanke did, indeed, deploy a host of unconventional weapons in an effort to prevent the dreaded financial accelerator from magnifying the recession. He claimed to have learned the lessons not only of the Great Depression but also of the more recent lost decades in Japan. But had he?

One of the toughest lessons of the 1930s concerns the perils of the so-called liquidity trap, when a crisis-battered economy is mired in a balance sheet recession and unresponsive to either monetary or fiscal stimulus. This was the nightmare described by John Maynard Keynes in the 1930s and by many economists in depicting Japan in the 1990s.[40] In a balance sheet recession, the overindebted, encumbered with collateral values that have become worth less than what they owe, focus on one thing only— basically curtailing spending and paying down excess debt. Until the deleveraging is complete, the impacts of policy stimulus in jump-starting the economy are, as Keynes feared, like "pushing on a string."[41]

There is good reason to believe that this explanation matches up well with conditions currently bearing down on the U.S. economy. Left with subpar savings, a legacy of outsize debt burdens, and underwater mortgages, overextended American consumers are now cutting back as never before. Since early 2008, inflation-adjusted personal consumption has grown, on average, by just 1.1 percent per year—fully two and a half percentage points below the precrisis norm of 3.6 percent that prevailed from 1996 to 2007.

Despite massive stimulus by Washington's monetary and fiscal authorities, balance sheet repair—or "debt rejection," as Nomura economist Richard Koo calls it—is all that seems to matter for overextended American households.[42] Some progress has been made, but it is limited at best. Household sector debt was down to 111 percent of disposable personal income in early 2013—a little more than 20 percentage points below its peak of 134 percent in 2007 but still 70 points above the 40 percent norm of the last three decades of the twentieth century. The personal savings rate stood at just 4.2 percent in the first half of 2013—up from the rock bottom of 2.3 percent in mid-2005 but far short of the 9.3 percent norm of the 1970–2000 period. Like Japan's corporate "zombies" who languished throughout the 1990s, America's zombie consumers are taking an extremely long time to climb out of a devastating balance sheet recession.

As scripted by Bernanke, this wasn't supposed to happen. The monetary fix for deflation was supposed to spark a vigorous recovery. But this supposition overlooked the alternative scenario of a balance sheet recession. The Fed, under both Greenspan and Bernanke, was steeped in denial over the risks and consequences of asset and credit bubbles. Notwithstanding the solemn promise he made to Milton Friedman, Bernanke's prescription may be the wrong medicine. By advocating open-ended unconventional easing alongside the unprecedented conventional stimulus of zero interest rates, Bernanke created the distinct possibility of an even bigger problem. The excess liquidity that is not being absorbed into the real economy or balance sheet repair is probably gravitating to another asset class. That could well be the breeding ground for the next bubble.

The plot thickens when fiscal policy is brought into this equation. The big bazooka required for crisis containment not only requires extraordinary and unconventional monetary accommodation, it also entails aggressive fiscal stimulus. America's postcrisis federal deficit and debt trajectories bear out the extent of this added dimension of policy stimulus in recent years—budget deficits that averaged 9 percent of GDP from 2009 to 2013 and a federal gross debt-to-GDP ratio that went from 86 percent to 105 percent over the same five-year interval. At the same time, federal net interest expenses held steady at 1.4 percent of GDP over this period, a remarkable result that was due in large part to the Fed's zero interest rate policy and its massive purchases of U.S. Treasury securities, which limited any backup in government borrowing costs.[43]

In effect, Bernanke's unconventional monetary policy gambit was key in allowing the federal government to run record budget deficits with impunity. This put the central bank in the unusual position of underwriting fiscal profligacy—basically blurring the distinction between monetary and fiscal policy. It also raises the distinct possibility of an intense political backlash once the Fed decides to return interest rates to more normal levels. Nothing less than the political independence of America's Federal Reserve is at risk. Far from living up to the promise of breaking with a treacherous history, Bernanke could be setting the stage for a classic policy trap from which there will be no easy escape.[44]

Codependent Leaders

The most painful lessons of history are never easily learned—especially if there are different interpretations of the forces that have shaped that history. For China, a long history of instability has instilled a deep commitment to stability. For the United States, a much shorter history of vitality and economic power has instilled a strong reaction against anything that gets in the way of free and vibrant markets.

As the products of these different histories and equally different systems of governance and resource allocation, Wen Jiabao and Ben Bernanke offered sharply contrasting approaches to the art and science of economic management. Notwithstanding the obvious dissimilarities between the two systems, the growing codependency of the U.S. and Chinese economies brings these two approaches under the same umbrella—whether their citizens and leaders like it or not. And this is where things get really interesting: To some extent, the gravity of codependency requires each nation and its leaders to assimilate the other's values.

Merging these two histories, two systems, and two approaches is very tricky—and if the effort fails it could pose the greatest threat of all to the U.S.-China economic relationship. The contrast between Wen Jiabao's emphasis on stability and Ben Bernanke's willingness to condone asset- and credit-dependent growth must be resolved if the codependency of the United States and China is to remain stable and ultimately sustainable.

Both Wen and Bernanke share the frustration of the great difficulty in achieving their mandated objectives. The framework suggested by the Four Uns provides a candid assessment of what has gone wrong in China and what must be done to fix it. Bernanke, by contrast, has been far more circumspect in offering similar critical insights for the U.S. economy. In many respects that comes with the territory in a market-based system, which relies on the magic of the "invisible hand" to do much of the economy's heavy lifting in allocating scarce resources.

The main source of tension is the stability imperative, or lack thereof, in both economies. For the United States, as noted above, stability is an afterthought, not a conscious objective of public policy.[45] That puts the externally dependent Chinese economy in a bind—it needs to formulate reactive policy strategies to cope with destabilizing shocks made in America. In part because of this vulnerability—and the increased frequency of major shocks during the crisis-torn years of 2008–12—China is now pursuing a major structural rebalancing aimed at weaning its economy from excessive reliance on exceedingly volatile external demand.

The contrast between Wen Jiabao and Ben Bernanke also speaks to the adaptability of the two systems. As noted earlier, Wen was a transition premier, challenging China to move from one model to another. Bernanke, following the example of Greenspan, was trying to come up with a new recipe for economic growth in order to satisfy the Fed's dual mandate of full employment and price stability. Psychologists will warn that codependency becomes problematic when one participant in the relationship starts to grow away from the other. If Chinese rebalancing gets under way before the United States changes its model, the psychologists may be spot-on.

Ben Bernanke grew up in the quintessential American small town of Dillon, South Carolina. In a town with a population of fewer than seven thousand and economic opportunities limited, the future Fed chairman's background fostered a deep appreciation for the challenges faced by U.S. workers and their families.[46] But with labor market distress soaring on his watch, he probably will not be remembered for his empathy with America's middle class. Wen Jiabao leaves a very different legacy. Growing up in the urban sprawl of Tianjin just east of Beijing, he brought to his leadership a humanity that resonated deeply with the Chinese people. The "People's Premier" offered empathy to China just when it was needed most—when the country was on the cusp of a major shift in its economic development model. The United States has yet to have a "people's central banker."

5

Two Takes on Strategy

WASHINGTON AND THE NDRC

S uccessful economies require far more than astute policy makers. They also need strategies—explicit or implicit—as well as the commitment and means to implement them. That requires institutions that exercise some degree of oversight in developing and monitoring the strategy function in their respective economies. On this count, the United States and China stand in particularly sharp contrast.

Since 1953, China has maintained a Soviet-style five-year planning process. For forty years, the State Planning Commission was charged with drawing up detailed targets and implementation directives for the allocation of resources in the state-owned Chinese economy. As ownership started to pass from the state into private hands, the planning function evolved. The National Development and Reform Commission (NDRC) has emerged as the modern counterpart to China's old central planning apparatus. Despite thirty years of reforms, the NDRC is still tasked with the critical function of the operational management of the Chinese economy.

The United States doesn't have an NDRC. The planning, or strategy, function of America's quintessentially market-based system remains largely in invisible hands, just as Adam Smith envisioned it nearly 250 years ago. But

Washington is hardly a disinterested observer of the U.S. economy's inner workings. In this chapter I focus on two groups in the executive branch that between them most closely resemble China's NDRC—the National Economic Council and the Office of Management and Budget. The comparison is in some ways a stretch, but it helps us see and contrast the key role of state power in guiding the decision-making process in both economies.

The NDRC has oversight over virtually all aspects of China's economic decision making. That starts with the conceptualization and design of five-year plans and extends to a wide range of implementation tactics—from monetary and fiscal policies, to the targeting of new industries, to resource and climate change policies, to the regulation of key prices, to financial and capital market reforms. The NDRC doesn't set an independent agenda but instead operates within the strategic framework established by China's senior Party leadership.

Washington's oversight is far more amorphous. America's federal budget, with expenditures comprising nearly a quarter of GDP, is the closest thing to an economic plan. The political cycle plays a vital role here—mainly by driving accountability between financial markets and voters on the one hand, and leaders and institutions charged with economic management on the other. Washington and the electorate it represents operate on a two-year election cycle, with little patience for longer-term strategy or planning. In the United States, commitment to any strategy accordingly blows hot and cold—it tends to be strong in crises and weak in periods of prosperity. Beijing, with a one-party system, can afford to take longer-term strategy far more seriously—it is basically embedded in its economic system.

In recent years, America's federal budget has become more a political battleground than a statement of strategy. Political polarization, operating through the checks and balances of the U.S. Constitution, has clogged the arteries of government-directed strategy initiatives.[1] This puts China and the United States at the opposite ends of the strategy spectrum—opening up a challenging disconnect to a sustainable codependency.

Notwithstanding their sharply contrasting institutional frameworks, the two countries' economic strategists have many basic goals in common. At the top of the list are jobs and social stability—and the sustainable growth required to achieve those objectives. Codependency ups the ante on all counts, forcing the United States and China each to focus on the strategy of the other. It remains to be seen whether Washington or the NDRC is better equipped to deal with the multiplicity of strategic challenges in their respective economies.

The NDRC

Since its inception in 1949, the People's Republic of China has relied on central planning—state-directed resource allocation—as a linchpin of its economic structure. Initially, the new government created and then empowered the State Planning Commission (SPC) to originate and implement these critical tasks. Established in 1952, the SPC framed its early efforts around the Chinese version of Soviet-style five-year plans. China's new leadership was especially taken with the Soviet Union's emerging economic and military prowess in the 1930s and 1940s and with the role central planning played in what at the time was socialism's greatest triumph. Mao's close relationship with Joseph Stalin in the 1950s only deepened China's infatuation with the so-called command economy and state ownership as pillars of socialist prosperity.[2]

But the Chinese strain of central planning was very different from the quasi-mathematical precision of the Soviet Union's fixation on "material balance planning"—an approach that relied on a detailed assessment of supply and demand conditions to guide the allocation of resources by sector, industry, and product.[3] China's version was heavily influenced by the ideological whims of Mao Zedong. While the First Five-Year Plan (1953–57) was largely successful in terms of achieving production targets,[4] the plans that immediately followed were not. The second, third, and fourth plans were unmitigated disasters, with a low point coming in the Second Five-Year Plan of 1958–62, which coincided with the disastrous Great Leap Forward, discussed in Chapter 1. The disruptions were so severe that, when the second plan ended, formal planning efforts were suspended for four years until 1966, when the "agricultural push" of the Third Five-Year Plan was launched.

The Fourth Five-Year Plan (1971–75) coincided with Mao's waning years and the final stages of the Cultural Revolution. By that point, the concept of central planning had become almost an oxymoron. The economy was in shambles and a dysfunctional SPC had all but lost control of the Chinese economy. Tensions between Chinese and Soviet leaders, which erupted in an outright split in 1960, were matched by divergences in the efficacy of their planning and in economic performance. The Soviet Union had achieved superpower status, while an isolated and unstable China had gone the opposite way.

In the years following the Cultural Revolution and Mao's death in 1976, Deng Xiaoping seized the opportunity painfully revealed by the chaos and near collapse of the Chinese economy. His call for "reforms and opening up" gave traction to the pivotal Fifth Five-Year Plan (1976–80), which set the shaky Chinese economy on a more constructive trajectory. A new strain of Chinese central planning had gained acceptance.

As the SPC recovered from the chaos of the 1960s and 1970s, it solidified its management of the vastly improved Chinese economy.[5] During the 1980s, under Premier Zhao Ziyang (who eventually rose to Party general secretary in 1987), the Chinese leadership made a key decision to move away from the rigidities of the Soviet-style planned economy. What emerged was more of a "dual-track" system, which stressed the coexistence of a state-directed and market-based economy.[6] This was China's first foray into the blended approach now known as the socialist market economy. While this evolution was cautious and gradual under Zhao, it underscores one of the most important differentiating characteristics of modern China's strategy function—adaptability.[7]

It was up to Zhu Rongji and Wen Jiabao to push ahead more aggressively to transform China's planning framework. This was in keeping with their increasingly sophisticated approaches to economic management, described in the two preceding chapters. In 1998, in the depths of the Asian Financial Crisis and at the onset of Zhu Rongji's premiership, the SPC was recast into the State Development Planning Commission. That set in motion several more years of restructuring of the central planning function. In 2003, the first year of Wen Jiabao's premiership, that reorganization coalesced into the present structure of the National Development and Reform Commission. The NDRC, in that important respect, is Premier Wen's brainchild.

The first thing to note about the NDRC is the absence of the letter P in its nomenclature. "Planning," a word that implies potentially arbitrary and rigid state-directed resource allocation, is no longer the defining characteristic of Chinese economic management. In its place are two more dynamic attributes of a blended system—development and reform. This may sound like a cosmetic or largely rhetorical change, but it was consciously intended to provide the leadership with different optics. Important steps were quickly taken in that direction—especially through the reduction in the number of numerical targets that frame the goals of more recent five-year plans. As opposed to specific industry-by-industry targets of the early plans, since the Ninth Five-Year Plan in the mid-1990s, the published list of goals has been sharply reduced in succeeding plans and now largely consists of targets for overall GDP growth and for major sectors such as consumption, investment, housing, and net exports.[8]

Notwithstanding the evolution toward more flexible oversight, there can be no mistaking the concentration of power in the hands of the NDRC. Currently staffed by only about one thousand professionals, it is one of the smallest ministries in the Chinese government. But it tends to attract the best and brightest of China's talent pool.[9] Ironically, it is not markedly different, either in functionality or in the quality of its talent pool, from Japan's now disbanded MITI (Ministry of International Trade and Industry)—the fabled elite organization that managed the Japanese "developmental state" during the high-growth era of the 1970s and 1980s.[10]

Organizationally, the head of the NDRC sits on the State Council alongside the heads of the other functional ministries, all of whom report to the premier in his capacity as head of the Chinese government. But in terms of power, the NDRC is in a league of its own. It has been dubbed "China's 'Mini-State Council'" whose "official portfolio covers almost every aspect of the national economy."[11] Its structure basically replicates that of the State Council itself; for every ministry or agency within the State Council, a small counterpart function exists inside the NDRC. But unlike China's vast bureaucracy of twenty-seven ministries employing more than five million workers, the NDRC keeps its entire professional staff under one roof—ironically, the same roof on Yuetan Street in Beijing that housed the original State Planning Agency.

This physical coincidence underscores the NDRC's deeper purpose—to coordinate the disparate parts of the far-flung Chinese government. That coordination is centered around its primary task, the design of five-year plans. Over time, the NDRC has built an elaborate and sophisticated process around this function, which now includes monitoring existing plans, overseeing background research, reviewing ministerial proposals, developing criteria for new plans, consulting with outside experts, and the actual drafting of the plan documents.[12]

The NDRC is not a one-dimensional organization. It is charged not only with the design of China's five-year plans but also with their implementation. And since implementation is defined in the broadest possible sense, the NDRC weighs in on virtually all aspects of macroeconomic stabilization—including fiscal, monetary, and currency policies. While it does not have the last word on currency and monetary decisions, its views carry considerable weight with the ultimate senior Party decision makers on the Standing Committee of the Politburo. Its role in fiscal policy is more decisive; the NDRC has the final say on investment project approvals and on the state-directed disbursement of bank credit that provides the bulk of the funding for these projects.

China's central planning does not just focus on quantity targets. Like central planners in other state-directed economies, it also focuses on price setting. This can lead to serious complications. Without market-based pricing that is driven by the real-time pressures of supply and demand, administratively determined quantity allocation often distorts pricing signals. The Soviets felt that they could solve for the right prices using math—namely, by backing out an implicit, or "shadow," price from their sector-by-sector input-output models. But frequent shortages in many of their markets threw the validity of this solution into serious question.[13] While Chinese planners don't rely on the mathematical precision of an input-output framework, the NDRC faces a similar conundrum in attempting to set both quantities and prices in such key sectors as food, energy, utilities, and selected raw materials.

The NDRC's determination of prices in these areas reflects a fuzzy interplay between economic and social policy—effectively, a weighing of the Soviet-style materials balance gap (supply and demand) against the impacts that price fluctuations for basic necessities may have on social stability. However, in light of periodic shortages of key foodstuffs and other sensitive commodities, the NDRC has had, at best, mixed success in getting administered prices "right"—underscoring one of the weakest links in its economic and market oversight capabilities.[14]

Like the State Council in which it resides, the NDRC is ultimately accountable to the leadership of the Chinese Communist Party. Thus, unlike the economic management agencies of multibranch, multiparty democracies that are constrained by horizontal checks and balances, the NDRC's accountability is largely vertical. It must seek approval for its proposals at all levels of the CCP hierarchy, from local and provincial officials up to the Standing Committee of the Politburo. Since the Party tends to speak with one voice, any debates or discussions of alternative plans obviously are not conducted on a partisan basis, as they are in democracies like the United States.[15]

This is not to say that there is total agreement over policy within China's power structure. In 2004, for example, there was an intense debate over how to restrain the economy from overheating. The NDRC favored using administrative actions dealing with sector-specific pressures to address the problem, while the central bank (The People's Bank of China) favored more orthodox monetary tightening. Unsurprisingly, the NDRC prevailed, a clear testament to its supremacy in the policy arena.[16]

The NDRC is the closest thing China has to a "super ministry." It is a cut above all the constituent ministries in the State Council. Its role is unparalleled among comparable planning functions in the world's major economies. It has responsibility for strategy, tactics, and implementation— at the macro as well as the micro level. And yet, in an extraordinary and highly controversial balancing act, it operates with both a visible and an invisible hand within the blended system of China's socialist market economy. Its strength ultimately lies in coordination and forward-looking analytics; its weakness is that it tries to do it all. The NDRC's ultimate success remains a subject of intense debate both inside and outside China.

Washington: Coordination and Accounting

Strategy—the linchpin of China's planning framework—is often scorned in Washington. While there has been a long and active debate over the role of government in American society, a debate that has become increasingly polarized in recent years, there has been broad agreement on a hands-off approach to the allocation of scarce resources into sectors, markets, and industries.

There have been important exceptions—most notably in times of crisis. The wage and price controls of the early 1970s were an ill-fated effort to deal with mounting inflationary pressures. There was a costly bailout of the savings and loan industry in the late 1980s and early 1990s. And, of course, during the Great Recession of 2008–9, the government took active ownership stakes in major banks, the auto industry, and the country's largest insurance company. But unlike China, where government ownership is an ongoing feature of a blended system, in the United States these arrangements were viewed as temporary stopgap measures.

Notwithstanding its aversion to micro intervention, Washington has long embraced the fine tuning of macroeconomic stabilization through monetary and fiscal policies. Reflecting the checks and balances within the U.S. system, macro management is broken down into two distinct functions—the monetary policy of a theoretically independent central bank, and fiscal policy as formulated jointly by the White House and the Congress.

The fiscal function—the drafting and passage of the federal budget—provides a broad umbrella for U.S. policy makers that comes closest to the strategy function of China's NDRC. It entails a diverse range of public sector activities, from defense and foreign aid to education and housing to healthcare and retirement. Coordination, to the extent that it occurs, is relegated to the annual federal government budgeting process. In theory, that process is designed so that the president proposes and the Congress approves. In practice, the politics of ever-rising polarization in the United States have all but neutered this process in recent years.[17]

In China, economic strategy is explicit, framed though five-year plans designed and implemented by the NDRC. In the United States, economic strategy, to the extent it exists, is implicit, at best, an outgrowth of the government's long and arduous fiscal deliberations. In what follows, two key actors in the fiscal dimension of U.S. economic strategy are highlighted.

The NEC. The National Economic Council, Washington's newest macro advisory body, was established under executive order by President Bill Clinton in early 1993.[18] Clinton had been elected in 1992 under the informal mantra "It's the economy, stupid," and the NEC's creation reflected his belief that the While House needed sharper focus on all matters pertaining to economic security. At the time, that meant job creation and deficit reduction, but the NEC review mechanisms that were put in place were designed to cast a much broader net over a wide array of potential policy issues—ranging from healthcare to financial markets.

"Council" has always had an important connotation in Washington—emblematic of an institutional convener of diverse constituencies. The NEC, as originally envisioned, was meant to be a coordinating council of those charged with formulating the president's economic agenda, as well as those elsewhere in the executive branch whose turf was most affected by it. The formal membership structure initially established for the NEC included the president, the vice president, and sixteen other senior officials of the executive branch, including eight cabinet secretaries, the chairman of the Council of Economic Advisers, the director of the Office of Management and Budget, and the U.S. trade representative.[19] The NEC was to be headed by a new assistant to the president for economic policy—a position first filled by Robert Rubin—and two deputy directors (domestic and international), and staffed by a small professional support team.

As specified by the executive order, the NEC was designed to focus on the coordination, consistency, and implementation of the president's domestic and international economic policy agenda. While on paper that resembles the responsibility of China's NDRC, there are enormous differences in how the two organizations go about fulfilling their missions. The NEC head count currently includes only twenty-five professionals, whereas the NDRC has closer to one thousand. Moreover, unlike the NDRC, which is structured around an internal replication of each of the twenty-seven ministries of the Chinese cabinet, the NEC serves as more of a clearinghouse for external input that draws on deep staffing across the various offices of the executive branch of the government.

As a new organization, the NEC had the opportunity to reinvent the formulation and coordination of U.S. economic policy. Robert Rubin, with a wealth of management and risk-taking experience accumulated during his twenty-six-year career on Wall Street, was well suited for that task.[20] He drew heavily on the experience of a highly successful model, the National Security Council, which was created in 1947 in the immediate aftermath of World War II in order to coordinate input and advise the president on foreign policy, intelligence gathering, and national defense. President Clinton was determined to confer NSC-like status on the economic policy process.

Rubin was quick to recognize that the NEC could be effective only if it served as an honest broker in policy deliberations. It would succeed or fail on the basis of how well it could present all sides of the debate over economic policy options—including contentious political counterpoints that would inevitably come from those on the other side of the aisle.[21] While China's NDRC performed a similar exercise in the design and development of five-year plans, the vertical, apolitical, intra-Party debate was far easier for Chinese bureaucrats to navigate.

Over the twenty-odd years since its inception and under the eight NEC directors who followed Rubin and two presidents after Clinton, the NEC has matured into an integral part of Washington's economic policy process. Its strengths are very much in keeping with its original intent: It provides coordination and coherence to the debate on tough economic issues. Its greatest weakness mirrors that of the system it inhabits—a politicization of policy. That has constrained the NEC from taking its prowess on policy coordination to the next level and creating a coherent national economic strategy. Not only is that a sharp difference between the NEC and the NDRC, it gets to the heart of one of the most important differences between the management of the U.S. and Chinese economies.

Office of Management and Budget. Process is one thing; fact-based policy implementation is another. In the art and practice of U.S. economic policy, the NEC is best suited to manage the process, whereas implementation is best addressed though the federal government's annual budgeting exercise. That's where the OMB enters America's version of an economic strategy equation.

While formally established by the Nixon administration in 1970, the roots of the Office of Management and Budget can be traced back nearly fifty years earlier. It was first set up by the Harding administration as a bureau within the U.S. Treasury Department. Its mission is straightforward—to assemble the annual budget of the federal government and help the president submit it for congressional approval.

The key word here is "assemble." The budget office doesn't make fiscal policy. Instead, it manages the broad and exceedingly complex budgeting structure that is an outgrowth of the fiscal policy debate. The resulting deficits or rare surpluses in the budget can then be applied as a tool of macroeconomic management. The federal budget provides the White House and Congress with a framework that enables them to understand how the government sets national priorities.[22] Needless to say, the second part of the OMB's mission—the congressional approval process—has proved to be most challenging.[23]

The complexity of the OMB's role is hard to overstate. Over the forty-two years since its formal inception, the federal government's total expenditures have risen from less than $200 billion, or 19 percent of the U.S. economy in 1970, to $3.5 trillion, or 23 percent of the GDP in 2012. The budget document itself has expanded from 533 pages in 1970 to 2,089 pages for fiscal year 2013.

On a functional basis, the OMB is broken down into five "resource divisions" that provide analytical support for the creation of the president's annual budget: natural resources (energy, sciences, and water); education, income maintenance, and labor; health; general government (transportation, housing, and commerce); and national security. The OMB is also responsible for the metrics of federal government performance—tracking expenditures for more than eighteen hundred federal subsidy spending programs,[24] monitoring countless programs in nearly sixty departments and offices, developing standardized procurement practices, and establishing pay and performance standards for some 2.8 million federal government workers. In short, while it does not create policy, the OMB touches virtually every other aspect of fiscal activity. It is basically Washington's accountant—feeding a well-developed budget-monitoring system into a policy process driven by the Congress and the White House.

The closest the OMB comes to shaping fiscal strategy is through the ten-year forecasts that are now required as part of the president's annual budget submission. Since the debate over U.S. fiscal policy has long been framed in terms of a five- to ten-year "fix," the ritual of long-term budget forecasts has become a key input in Washington deliberations. Unfortunately, the OMB's track record in such longer-term forecasts is terrible. In 1980, for example, it claimed that the federal budget would be in balance by

1990; instead, it ended up being in deficit by 2.4 percent of GDP. In 1990, the forecast was for a surplus of 2 percent of GDP in 2000—a far cry from the 2 percent deficit actually recorded. In 2000, the budget was expected to be in 4.5 percent surplus by 2010—a massive error relative to the actual deficit of 10 percent.[25] Obviously, business cycles and other unexpected developments, such as wars, crises, and natural disasters, complicate long-term budget forecasts. But the misses are far greater than can be explained by these circumstances.

At the same time, it's not entirely fair to blame the OMB for this record. Its estimates are driven by equally terrible economic forecasts made by the president's Council of Economic Advisers, the White House's internal economic consulting team that, as discussed in Chapter 3, provided Alan Greenspan with his entrée into senior Washington policy circles. Relying on mechanistic budget multipliers that tie tax revenues to nominal GDP and link many spending programs to inflation and labor market conditions, the economic scenarios underpinning the longer-term budgeting exercise are invariably presented to be on an improving trajectory. This dates back to the infamous "Rosy Scenario" of the Reagan administration in the 1980s—a projected vanishing act for the budget deficit that was tied to an overoptimistic assessment of U.S. economic performance. Neither happened. But that has never discouraged the ever-seductive Rosy from trying to influence the debate over U.S. deficits and debt in the years that followed.[26]

The NEC depends on OMB metrics in framing the policy debate. Largely for that reason, the relationship between the NEC and the OMB has become increasingly important to the White House economic policy process over the past twenty years. This reflects the NEC's role as a convener of input and analytics into the policy debate, and its reliance on the OMB to guide and staff much of the research required to support these efforts. Still, the collaboration between the two organizations can be episodic, driven in recent years by frequent budget crises, threats of government shutdowns, and debt ceiling deadlines. The raging debate over the future course of U.S. fiscal policy could end up being the ultimate test for NEC-OMB partnership, to say nothing of testing the long-term staying power of the U.S. economy.

Planning or Strategy?

The comparison between the NEC-OMB nexus and the NDRC underscores the vast differences in the way that the United States and China approach the formulation and implementation of economic strategy. But the differences are not just philosophical or ideological. They also reflect very different resource commitments in each country to the scope of the effort. For example, OMB staffing levels, at around five hundred, are half the NDRC's head count. This comparison may not be entirely fair since the NDRC does far more than just manage and allocate funds for the twenty-seven ministries of China's State Council. Moreover, under the guise of checks and balances, America's multiparty, three-branch, bicameral system of governance builds considerable redundancy into economic policy making. On budgetary matters alone, OMB efforts are augmented by those of the nonpartisan Congressional Budget Office, the Senate Budget Committee, and the House Budget Committee—with each of the latter two committees having a full complement of majority and minority staffers allocated along party lines.

While there are obviously sharp contrasts between the two systems, the most important operational distinctions between the economic strategy functions in the United States and China are political. China's one-party system empowers the NDRC with a focus and a single-minded commitment to a plan that lies at the heart of its development agenda. As noted earlier, vertical accountability within the hierarchy of the Party makes the implementation of China's strategy a good deal easier than that required of horizontal accountability in a multiparty United States. That enables the NDRC not only to bring the plan to life in great detail but also to pay great attention to implementation, as well as to the tools and other policy mechanisms that give China's planners the capacity to deliver.

As we have seen, there is no comparable strategy function in America's bureaucracy.[27] This is by conscious design and by steadfast belief in the wisdom of the Invisible Hand. Yes, explicit strategic initiatives often arise out of duress, more of an afterthought during times of national crisis. But in normal times, strategy is more passive and is relegated to the magic of the markets. This hands-off approach doesn't always go over well with the

American public. A failure to appreciate the "vision thing," as President George H. W. Bush scornfully called big ideas or themes (that is, strategy), came back to haunt him in his unsuccessful reelection campaign against Bill Clinton in 1992. In China, there is no such aversion to strategy as a core element of economic management.

This touches on a final aspect of the two approaches to macromanagement—the important distinction between a plan and a strategy. A plan is an organizational framework. A strategy is what gives the plan priorities and direction.[28] Bureaucrats can excel at planning. But a successful public policy strategist needs to draw on that rare combination of backward-looking experience and forward-looking imagination, while staying aligned with the delicate interplay between social, economic, and political priorities. Planning is science. Strategy is more art. Who does it better in today's complex world—the Invisible Hand or elite technocrats?

Strategy in Action

To answer that question, it pays to look at current examples of strategy in action in both countries. The American and Chinese economies are both now at critical junctures, with one very important problem in common: Their successful growth recipes of the past are not sustainable. China has taken its producer model to excess, and America has done the same with its consumer model. Complementary problems, especially of two codependent economies, often entail similar frameworks to arrive at solutions. That is very much the case today. Both the United States and China are in urgent need of strategic realignments.

How both economies respond to their rebalancing imperatives reveals much about their respective approaches to macroeconomic strategy. While I will discuss the details of their latest rebalancing initiatives in Chapters 11 and 12, at this point it is important to understand how the decision-making process has worked in China and the United States. In each case, the process has brought both the leadership and the institutional dimensions of macromanagement into play. It also provides clear examples of the interplay between political and economic considerations in the two countries.

In China, the strategy function has operated in a fairly straightforward fashion. It started with Wen Jiabao's famous critique of the Four Uns in 2007. This seemingly innocuous statement quickly became a framework of analysis that sparked intense internal debate on the wisdom of China's long successful developmental model. The Four Uns gave the NDRC its marching orders: It would need to assess ongoing and prospective trends in the Chinese economy through the lens of stability, balance, coordination, and sustainability. To the extent the economy didn't measure up, a strategic shift would be in order. It was, at least in theory, really that simple.

In the formulation of U.S. economic policy, nothing is quite that simple. False prosperity kept the nation's economic leadership in deep denial throughout a period of extraordinary excess. Wedded to their political and ideological agendas, Washington's economic policy makers wanted to believe that the unsustainable was sustainable. Unlike Wen Jiabao, who raised sustainability concerns while the Chinese economy was delivering spectacular results, U.S. authorities—especially Alan Greenspan and Ben Bernanke—never questioned sustainability. They believed instead in the fiction of sustainable imbalances.

In Washington, there was no analogue of an American-style Four Uns. The NEC, originally envisioned as an honest broker, might at least have raised such concerns as a devil's advocate—true to its multiadvocacy function as originally envisioned. Instead, it was silent. In a booming economy fixated on short-term political paybacks, there was no inclination to rock the boat. However frothy they became, markets were to be trusted, not feared, and were believed to be perfectly capable of signaling when a new approach was appropriate. Unfortunately, the signal they ultimately sent in late 2008 was far more disturbing than Washington was prepared for.

America's preference for free-market problem solving presumes that markets are self-correcting—that they contain feedback loops that don't require the surveillance of an NDRC-type institution. China's stability fixation, by contrast, doesn't count on self-correction. Unwilling to risk major boom-bust cycles, the Chinese leadership leaves much less to chance. In the late 2000s, it tasked its planners to develop metrics that tracked the risks of the Four Uns. It also gave them license to propose a plan of action if those risks became untenable.

China's approach to strategy, though seemingly mechanistic, includes an important intangible dimension as well. It's one thing to understand the analytics of Four-Un-type constraints and to develop metrics to assess the associated risks. It's another thing to discern when those metrics flash actionable warning signs. That is the judgment, or human, piece of the strategy equation.

In the case of China, the judgment call was triggered by two major external demand shocks in three years—the Great Recession of 2008–9 and Europe's sovereign debt crisis of 2011–12. These were two powerful wake-up calls for an export-led economy, and they sent a clear message to Beijing: With postcrisis recovery likely to be weak, at best, in China's two largest export markets—Europe and the United States—the once-rapid pace of export-led growth was at serious risk. For China, that meant the time was finally at hand for a major rebalancing away from exports and the external demand that supported them. That, in conjunction with mounting concerns over a broad constellation of long simmering internal imbalances, ended up being the key consideration behind China's endorsement of the pro-consumption strategy of the Twelfth Five-Year Plan.

Ironically, and as discussed in Chapters 3 and 4, the ideological capture of the U.S. central bank under Chairmen Greenspan and Bernanke all but prevented Washington from taking a China-like preemptive strike on its own unsustainable macro structure. Instead, Greenspan's free-market objectivism, coupled with Bernanke's aversion to bubble popping, encouraged the United States to push even harder for growth. That push was aimed at squeezing more growth out of America's old model rather than contemplating the possibility of a new growth recipe from a different model. In attempting to achieve that objective, the Fed went considerably farther in holding interest rates low and providing more monetary accommodation during the 2003–7 period than would have been tolerated in the NDRC-controlled Chinese economy.

Needless to say, the United States has paid a major price for this gambit: a crisis and recession on a scale never witnessed in the modern era. Debate still rages over the role that monetary and regulatory policies played in this catastrophe.[29] Unfortunately, the debate has occurred largely after the fact. That would not have happened in China: The NDRC would have jumped feet first into the precrisis policy discussion. Washington's NEC, by contrast, played no such role whatsoever. To a certain extent, this was by design. Unlike the NDRC, which is actively involved in Chinese monetary policy decisions, the NEC has no explicit say on the policy actions of the presumably independent Federal Reserve.

While the NEC can be let off the hook on grounds of separation of powers, that may not have been the best answer for the U.S. economy. It would have been well within the purview of the NEC, as stewards of macroeconomic policy, to come up with a Four-Uns-like analytical framework that explored alternative scenarios and thereby provided a counterweight to the Fed's ideological capture and related denial of sustainability risks. But it didn't do that. That meant there were no checks and balances built in to Washington's economic strategy function—a blatant abrogation of the NEC's charter as an honest broker.[30]

This lethal combination—the ideological capture of the central bank and political capture of the NEC—has done the United States great harm. Not only did it greatly impair the macro policy debate at a critical point in history, it also prevented the design and execution of a successful strategic response to rapidly unfolding macroeconomic risks such as those of the Great Crisis of 2008–9. The comparison with China is especially ironic. While China espouses socialism, ideology has had little influence on Chinese economic strategy in recent years. In the end, nothing interfered with China's single-minded focus on stability.

Good strategies are not set in stone. For economies, they must be flexible enough to adapt to changing circumstances, as dictated by either internal or external pressures. That gets to a crucial difference between the U.S. and Chinese economies. The ultimate producer now senses a combination of mounting internal pressures and a much weaker prognosis for the external, or global, economy. That has prompted China to take concrete action through the Twelfth Five-Year Plan to change its strategy by rebalancing its economy.

By contrast, Washington hasn't given up on the ultimate consumer. Feeling political pressure and falling well short of its full employment mandate, the Federal Reserve has gone back to a familiar script focused on stimulating wealth effects as the means to the regeneration of vigorous growth in personal consumption. In effect, the central bank is attempting to re-create the same type of unbalanced growth that got the United States into trouble in the first place. Ben Bernanke, like his predecessor Alan Greenspan, has been explicit in stressing the transmission effects between asset markets and aggregate demand in the real economy as the main channel by which this can occur. Bernanke has taken this connection one step farther in justifying the use of unconventional policies of quantitative easing as the principal means to restart these transmission effects in a postcrisis U.S. economy.[31]

U.S. fiscal policy, while hardly enlightened in an era of unprecedented budget deficits, is at least paying lip service to the need to consider a different economic strategy. Recognizing the headwinds holding back the 71 percent of the economy accounted for by the American consumer, the Obama administration has attempted to shift the debate to new sources of growth. Two sectors have been singled out for attention: infrastructure[32] and exports.[33] Yet the strategic agenda in both cases is not well developed. It remains to be seen if Washington can deliver on these "soft strategy" initiatives, a point to which we shall return in Chapter 11.

Meanwhile, the U.S. body politic has chosen, instead, to focus on deficit reduction as a medium-term goal for a strategy of fiscal sustainability. But lacking a consensus in an increasingly polarized Congress, it has opted for a rules-based approach to implementation of this strategic objective that relies more on formulaic across-the-board cutbacks, or sequestration, of most discretionary federal spending programs.[34] Ironically, a politicized strategy process that opts for rules over discretion in framing the national policy agenda is not all that functionally different from the mechanistic planning process long embedded in the Chinese strategy function.[35]

Structural rebalancing is never easy for any economy. It takes time—something that democracies, with their short election cycles, never seem to have much of. It also implies a focus on restructuring strategies that often lead to closures or consolidations of companies and layoffs of workers in waning sectors—another political hot button in freely elected democracies. Relative to one-party China, the United States is at a distinct disadvantage: It cannot ignore short-term political risks in a tough economic climate, and there is no effective political constituency for a longer-term strategic rebalancing. By contrast, the Four Uns, and the new strategy they entail, put China in a very different place.

The difference between the two approaches to economic strategy bears critically on the codependency between the United States and China. As stressed earlier, as China realigns its growth model to draw greater support from internal private consumption, America will struggle to replace China's seemingly open-ended supply of low-cost goods that U.S. consumers have counted on. The United States will also struggle as it starts to lose its support from surplus Chinese capital and the effective subsidy these funds have provided to interest rates and asset markets. As this aspect of codependency evolves, another important element of the U.S. strategy vacuum will get unmasked: the lack of a long-term saving strategy. How will savings-short America cope if it has less foreign saving to draw on?

The disconnects in the two approaches to strategy are not without important implications for economies and financial markets. They provide strong hints as to some of the most powerful forces that might come into play in the years ahead—namely, interest rate and currency pressures, as well as the risks of trade frictions and protectionism. Can codependency between the United States and China endure without mutually compatible strategies?

PART III

TENSIONS

HOW DO YOU KNOW WHEN there is too much of a good thing? Or, more indelicately, how do you know when a seemingly good thing isn't good? Few were asking these questions in the years before the Great Crisis of 2008–9, when tensions were mounting in the United States, China, and the rest of an unbalanced world.

But the precrisis warning signs were not limited to asset and credit markets—or even to the real economies that had grown increasingly dependent on such markets. The very fabric of globalization—the glue and shock absorbers of interconnectedness that were supposed to temper mounting imbalances between economies—was also stressed. For China and the United States, codependency magnified the strains on a new globalization. A lethal combination of cyclical bubbles and structural distortions in their economies produced escalating tensions between the two nations that have yet to be resolved.

At the core of these tensions is a zero-sum question: whether China's gains necessarily come at the cost of others, such as the United States. Globalization advocates have long argued that cross-border exchange leads to positive-sum windfalls for those engaged in global commerce. Opponents worry that one party's gains can become another's losses—more specifically, that China's export-led growth has come at the expense of American workers.

Most economists, steeped in the classic Ricardian theory of comparative advantage, fall into the positive-sum camp. Unfortunately, that theory was developed for a long-vanished era—one dominated by the cross-border exchange of tradable manufactured products. It was not designed to cope with the hyperspeed of IT-enabled connectivity that now facilitates trade in formerly nontradable services—from data processing and software development to consulting and medical diagnostics. In this modern era of globalization, the role of currencies, outsourcing and offshoring strategies, tariff and nontariff trade barriers, and the implications of savings-investment imbalances must all be seen in a very different light. Trade theory needs to be updated accordingly.

The new globalization promotes a faster and broader integration of the world than David Ricardo ever envisioned. Country-specific economic competition has been rendered obsolete by the emergence of multicountry, vertically integrated global supply chains. These new production platforms not only push the envelope on cost efficiency, they also challenge the metrics of official trade statistics, which fail to capture the distribution of production across different segments of supply chains. Statistics on "bilateral" trade imbalances do not accurately reflect these new economic relationships between nations—especially between the United States and China. What gets measured as "made in China" is more the output of an increasingly complex assembly line involving multiple nations and an increasingly globalized workforce.

Despite trade's growing multilateral character, political tensions and strategies are still framed primarily in bilateral terms. Washington, for instance, continues to view much of its international economic dilemma as a "China problem." This misses the all-important linkage between subpar U.S. saving and the inflows of surplus foreign saving that are required to satisfy America's growth addiction. The United States' massive current account deficit is a direct outgrowth of these inflows—as is the multilateral trade deficit that such a balance of payments deficit spawns. This leads to one of the biggest disconnects of the so-called U.S.-China imbalance—that there is no bilateral solution for a multilateral problem that is grounded in America's own unprecedented savings deficiency.

Learning to live with the twin tensions of globalization and macro imbalances is a challenge for any nation. But in an increasingly integrated global economy, there is great danger in fixating on a bilateral piece of a broader multilateral system. That is especially the case when doing so threatens to destabilize the economic relationship between the world's two largest economies, the United States and China.

A similar mistake also tends to overstate long-standing fears that bias Western impressions of the Chinese economy. A broad cross section of academics, policy makers, and investors harbors deep doubts about the sustainability of the Chinese development miracle. Between property bubbles and potential banking crises; risks of excess investment, environmental degradation, and currency manipulation; corruption, cyberterrorism, and theft of intellectual property, it's only a matter of time, goes the argument, before China runs off the tracks.

While all of these concerns have a certain degree of validity, they are largely prone to great exaggeration. As a rapidly growing developing economy, China confronts many of the same pitfalls once faced by today's advanced industrialized nations. Its missteps have significant implications for the broader global economy. A lot hinges on how China addresses these increasingly contentious concerns. But much also hinges on how the world copes with China.

6

A New Globalization

The conceptual case for globalization is hard to argue with. The "win-win" mantra of expanding trade sounds great for poor and rich countries alike. Underpinned by the early-nineteenth-century theories of David Ricardo, cross-border commerce has long been viewed as a major engine of economic growth and development.

But in practice, globalization is much tougher. It pits nations against one another in the rough-and-tumble arena of global competition, putting pressure on companies and their workers. The theory assures us that it will all work out in the end. Sometimes that consolation rings hollow.

An earlier globalization of the late nineteenth and early twentieth centuries sheds much light on why many have found the current strain so difficult to accept. In many respects it was a kinder and gentler globalization— taking time to evolve and affecting relatively limited sectors of the economies that engaged in trade. The current globalization, partly enabled by powerful new technologies, is both faster and broader and cuts a much larger swath in the world economy. It is a far more disruptive globalization.

The tension between the theory and practice of globalization is manageable in good times but can be destabilizing in tougher times. For China and the United States, the dominant economic drivers of globalization's new era, these tensions go hand in hand with codependency. But there is a new and important twist at work: American workers are under pressure as never before, while the bilateral trade imbalance between the United States and China has never been larger. To the extent that the unusually powerful forces of a new globalization coincide with China's rise, an equally powerful political backlash in the United States threatens to destabilize the two nations' codependency.

The costs and benefits of the U.S.-China economic relationship need to be weighed carefully in addressing these tensions. The first-round impacts are clear: Americans have been squeezed as workers but have benefited as consumers. The opposite is true for the Chinese: They have benefited as workers but are squeezed as consumers. The mirror images of codependency couldn't be sharper.

Second-round impacts, however, could be very different. Neither globalization nor codependency is static. As China and the United States face up to their rebalancing agendas, their roles in a globalized world will change. China should morph from a producer to a consumer, America ideally will wean itself from excess consumption, and the character of their interplay will shift. So will their effects on globalization.

It would be very difficult to undo globalization. That's not to say it hasn't happened in the past. But the circumstances that have led to an aborted globalization are ominous: protectionism, trade wars, depression, and military conflict. As the two leading economies in the world, the United States and China must lead by example in learning to live with globalization.

A Tale of Two Globalizations

No two economies have felt the impacts of modern globalization more than China and the United States. That's especially the case insofar as the trade dimension of globalization is concerned. As noted in Chapter 2, China has recorded an eightfold increase in its share of world trade since its economic takeoff in the early 1980s. And as the largest importer in the world, the United States consumes more low-price goods from abroad than does any other nation.

Notwithstanding the superlatives, these developments are not unique in the annals of economic history. The globalization of the late nineteenth and early twentieth centuries also brought a profound reshaping of the economic landscape. A comparison of the two globalizations—then and now—offers rich context for understanding the unusually powerful forces at work today.

The origins of Globalization 1.0 can be traced to the onset of the Industrial Revolution in the latter half of the eighteenth century. The shift from manual to mechanized production began in Great Britain and then, over the next century, spread to continental Europe, North America, and Japan—but not to China. It had the extraordinary impact of transforming largely agrarian societies into emerging manufacturing economies.

Never before had improvements in economic activity promoted such broad improvements for the overall mass of the world's population. For most of recorded history, global output barely kept pace with the expansion of population. It fluctuated with the weather—better years yielded better harvests—but produced no meaningful gains in long-term per capita incomes. According to the forensic empirics of Angus Maddison, this began to change in the early nineteenth century. By his reckoning, global output per capita grew by an average of 1.2 percent a year between 1820 and 1998, boosting GDP per person by a factor of 8.5 over that period. This renaissance resulted in nineteen-fold average increases of per capita income in the combined economies of western Europe, North America, and Japan.[1]

Globalization was not an especially important feature of the first century of the Industrial Revolution. Significant cross-border trade came with what economic historians call the Second Industrial Revolution, which commenced around 1850.[2] Over the next seventy-five years, breakthroughs in power generation—from steam to electricity and then to internal combustion—not only revolutionized assembly lines but also provided an enormous impetus to modern modes of transportation. The infrastructure of roads, bridges, highways, and ports soon followed—albeit with lengthy planning and construction lags. Cross-border commerce became more efficient and considerably cheaper. When it all fell into place in the early twentieth century, the global economy came together as never before.

An explosion in global trade and international capital flows followed. According to Maddison's estimates, the value of world merchandise exports went from $50 billion in 1870 (in 1990 dollars), or 4.6 percent of global GDP, to $212 billion by 1913, or 7.9 percent of global GDP. Europe led the way, while China and the United States lagged. Merchandise trade in China inched up from 0.7 percent of its GDP in 1870 to 1.7 percent by 1913, whereas the ratio in the United States went from 2.5 percent to 3.5 percent over this same period. North Atlantic trade surged in the late nineteenth century, especially between Britain and the United States, but the gains were asymmetrical—Britain was the exporter and the United States the importer.[3]

There is still an active debate over what brought this first wave of globalization to an end. Some argue that it was World War I; others maintain it was the trade wars and their contribution to the Great Depression of the 1930s.[4] In either case, the verdict is pretty much the same. After close to half a century of explosive gains in global trade, the world went the other way. Global exports fell by 61 percent from 1929 to 1932 and did not begin to recover for decades. In 1950, merchandise exports were just 5.5 percent of world GDP—down sharply from the 9 percent peak in 1929 and nearly back to the 4.6 percent share that Maddison estimated for 1870.[5] Globalization 1.0 was history.

With depression and World War II, a long hiatus in globalization was hardly surprising. The world had turned inward and had lost both its appetite and its wherewithal for cross-border linkages. That changed dramatically beginning in the 1950s. The postwar resurgence of world trade happened in two distinct phases. A gradual rebound occurred through the early 1970s, as overall merchandise exports went from 5.5 percent of world GDP in 1950 back to 10.5 percent in 1973, slightly above their 9 percent peak in the late 1920s. Then, over the next thirty-five years, global trade really took off. According to IMF statistics, total exports rose from 18.5 percent of world GDP in 1990 to 26.9 percent by 2004—on their way to a record 32.4 percent in 2008.[6] The confluence of trade liberalization, new technological breakthroughs, sharply reduced transportation costs, and broad gains in global economic activity ushered in a Second Golden Age of Globalization that is still in place today.

This current wave of globalization differs from the first one on three counts: scope, means, and speed. The *scope* of Globalization 1.0 was narrow. It was largely confined to cross-border exchange of tangible goods—raw materials and other components and inputs into manufacturing processes—that were extracted or produced by blue-collar workers. This trade was an important outgrowth of European empire building, dominated by resource-related exchange between imperial powers and their colonies.[7] Cross-border commerce was concentrated within individual empires: The British dominated North Atlantic trade, France did the same with Africa and Asia, and Spain had closer ties with South America. Relatively little trade took place between one imperial system and another.[8]

The second wave of globalization added a new ingredient: Rapidly expanding exchange of tangible goods was augmented by trade of formerly nontradable services—largely knowledge-based output generated by white-collar workers. While the broadening of price reductions that arose from this development was beneficial for the world's consumers, it exposed a whole new segment of workers to tough cyclical pressures for the first time ever. Since the start of the Industrial Revolution, blue-collar factory workers had borne the brunt of the downside of the business cycle. They had grown accustomed to the hardship of temporary bouts of economic distress and to the dislocations caused by global competition. White-collar knowledge workers, meanwhile, had led a more sheltered life. Domestic business cycles were far less severe for services, and global pressures were not a factor for relatively insular services that were basically nontradable. That all changed with Globalization 2.0. White-collar workers also felt the harsh winds of the business cycle and global competitive pressures.

The current *means* of cross-border connectivity also stand in sharp contrast with those that facilitated Globalization 1.0. Not until the latter stages of the first wave did motor vehicles come into existence. Ships and then railroads provided the major means of exchange. Port facilities and rail transportation networks took time to construct and link up to local distribution hubs. Researchers have found that the sharp reduction in transportation costs, rather than trade liberalization, appears to have accounted for most of the surge in world trade in the late nineteenth and early twentieth centuries.[9]

Globalization 2.0 relies on a very different global transportation and de-livery system: For tangible goods, that entails advanced container ships, more elaborate rail systems, an increasingly advanced fleet of trucks and other forms of motor vehicles, and aircraft. The arrival of the Internet in the 1990s greatly enhanced the logistics of global supply chains, which underpinned new modes of production and cross-border exchange in trad-able manufacturing.

But for Globalization 2.0, the most dramatic breakthrough came in the Internet's dissemination of intangible products: services. With the click of the mouse, digitized information—the essence of knowledge-based output—could be made available instantaneously anywhere in the world. Suddenly, a wide range of white-collar workers—from software programmers and en-gineers to medical technicians and consultants—were connected from low-cost offshore platforms such as Bangalore and Shanghai to desktops in the developed world. This led to a massive compression in the prices of many knowledge-based services that benefited consumers around the world. But it also squeezed information, or white-collar, workers in once-sheltered oc-cupations and as a result had a major impact on job security in what had long been the most secure part of the labor market.

Finally, there are sharp contrasts in the *speed* by which the two waves of globalization evolved. According to many historical accounts, it took close to 150 years, from the onset of the Industrial Revolution in the late eighteenth century, before Globalization 1.0 hit its stride. This time, it has been much quicker. The extraordinary pace of technological change and the rapid absorption of new technologies have caused the current wave of globalization to proceed at breakneck speed. This is consistent with accel-erating trends in technology absorption that have long been evident. For example, it took 38 years for the radio to reach fifty million households in the early part of the century; for television, similar penetration rates were hit in 13 years, for cable TV in 10 years, and for the Internet in only 5 years.[10] Not surprisingly, Globalization 2.0 attained its critical mass in less than 20 years—considerably shorter than the 150 years it took for Globalization 1.0.

The time compression of technology absorption throws a wrench into nations' ability to cope with globalization. The first wave of globalization gave the major economies of the world ample time to adjust to a new world order. That was not the case in the second wave. It has evolved at hyper-speed—in keeping with the churning of an increasingly fast-paced world. In many respect this has been very unsettling to both individuals and nations.

The leisurely pace of Globalization 1.0's evolution also gave nation-states the luxury of time to build relationships among themselves. Successful relationship building, even between imperial powers and their colonies, framed the earlier globalization as more of a shared opportunity. Even after the disruption of World War I, the world's political leaders reaffirmed their support for trade liberalization and renewed globalization.[11] It would take a severe depression to derail this early strain of globalization.

By contrast, there has been nothing slow about the second wave of glo-balization. The speed of forced assimilation between nation-states has unmasked tensions between rich countries and poor ones. The failure of the world to successfully conclude the latest round of multilateral trade negotiations—the so-called Doha Round—is an important case in point.[12] The battle over farm subsidy reductions between large developing nations, such as India and Brazil, and major economies in the developed world has been especially intense. But the collapse of the Doha Round is not the only problem. Tensions have also arisen over potential repercussions of uncon-ventional monetary easing by major developed economies. The liquidity in-jections of quantitative easing—as noted in Chapter 4, a stimulus focused on an expansion of the quantity of credit—have sparked concerns from major developing nations, from Brazil to South Korea, over the possibil-ity of "currency wars." These fears stem from a potential realignment of foreign exchange rates that could reduce currencies in the developed world and boost those in the developing economies of Asia and South America and impair their export-led growth.[13]

Codependency has not been enough to alleviate these stresses and strains of Globalization 2.0. As much as the world intellectually appreci-ates the mutual gains that can eventually come from trade, the reality of sudden immersion into Globalization 2.0 has been much tougher to cope with. The United States and China share a common misgiving over the new globalization for many of the same reasons.

Tough Circumstances

Not only is the current wave of globalization more testing than the first one in terms of scope, means, and speed, it has recently encountered much tougher circumstances in the aftermath of the Great Crisis and Recession. That complicates the situation, especially for codependent nations like the United States and China.

From the U.S. side, unrelenting pressures on consumers and on companies and their workers, to say nothing of heightened uncertainty over fiscal, monetary, and regulatory policies, only exacerbate the unease of a subpar recovery and increase concerns over the prospects of meaningful improvement. These pressures contribute to a general anxiety that has become one of the defining features of the political conversation in the United States.

The repercussions of this angst have recently taken a destructive turn. Rather than accept responsibility for its role in creating false prosperity—namely, promoting policies that have fostered subpar saving, a profusion of asset and credit bubbles, dereliction of regulatory oversight, the deskilling of the American workforce—the U.S. body politic has chosen instead to pin the blame on others.

China has emerged as America's favorite foreign scapegoat. As a major beneficiary of globalization, it has become a source of special resentment for countries like the United States, which are having a hard time coping with the new globalization. It is not just a large trade deficit with China that has become a lightning rod in this scapegoating. Two sets of additional pressures are at work: the newfound prowess of Chinese companies and the increased vulnerability of America's white-collar workers.

Competitive leapfrogging. Businesses are on the leading edge of those facing heightened competitive pressures. The hyperspeed of Globalization 2.0 has proved challenging for all companies. China has been particularly adept at taking advantage of competitive opportunities in key industries. Its success has not always gone over well with the rest of the world and has caused particular resentment in the United States that has heightened tensions between the two nations.

Examples from two leading-edge industries—information technology hardware and telecommunications equipment—underscore the speed with which China has emerged on the global stage. In both cases, Chinese industry went from uncompetitive as recently as 1990 to a position of global dominance by 2004.[14] The gains since 2000 are particularly impressive. At that time, the global export shares of Chinese companies ranked thirteenth in the world in information technology and fifth in telecom equipment. Just four years later, China was number one in worldwide export shares in both industries.

The flip side of China's extraordinary ascendancy has been others' loss of market share. The United States and Japan have felt the heat in each of these key industries. For both IT and telecom products, Japan went from first position in 1990 to fifth in 2004. Meanwhile, global export shares of U.S. companies also plunged—in IT from 19 percent in 1990 to 11 percent by 2004 (although still holding on to second place over this period) and in telecom from 14 percent in 1990 to just 7 percent (going from second to third place) by 2004.

China's competitive leapfrogging occurred at a particularly opportune moment, when the global trade cycle was on a record upswing. That means these two industries were able to boost market share at precisely the moment when the volume of global trade was expanding as never before. Not only did Chinese industries quickly emerge on the global stage, but they got a bigger slice of a much larger pie. Research by Yale professor Peter Schott comes to a similar conclusion on the speed of China's newfound export prowess—finding that Chinese exports were able to achieve a significant overlap on a product-by-product basis with those of other developed economies in a surprisingly short period of time, from 1972 to 2001.[15] But he also notes that the quality of Chinese exports became increasingly inferior to those of more advanced economies over this same period, casting China's so-called competitive threat in a different light.

There is, of course, great dispute over how China has achieved these stunning results on export prowess in a relatively short time frame. U.S. charges of currency manipulation, unfair subsidies enjoyed by state-owned enterprises, illegal technology and intellectual property transfer, and uncompetitive pricing practices (dumping) are all part of the long list of grievances that drive the contentious charges leveled by many in corporate America and Washington alike. While there is some validity to some of these charges, especially the unfair trading practices that have been adjudicated by the World Trade Organization, others, such as currency manipulation and even intellectual property theft, are more debatable. These prickly aspects of codependency and their role in promoting competitive leapfrogging are taken up in greater detail in Chapter 8.

White-collar shock. The globalization of services is a big deal for the American workforce as it injects a very different set of pressures into the labor market. Unlike the production of goods, which rises and falls with the business cycle, fluctuations in demand for the services-based necessities of life such as utilities, telecommunications, and shelter tend to be more muted. Moreover, for most of modern history, services were performed in person, in close geographic proximity to the markets they serve—relatively immune to international competition. While that remains true for providers of most personal services, such as teachers, barbers, and gardeners, larger-scale global networks have emerged in many transactions-intensive services industries, such as transportation, retail trade, and finance, as well as many professional services as accounting, consulting, legal counsel, and temporary office staffing. This is a huge change. Competition in these areas used to be constricted by national boundaries. The services had to be tailored to local laws, regulatory regimes, national accounting practices, and other customs. Today many of the geographic constrictions that stemmed from these nation-specific constraints on services can now be resolved on consolidated Internet-based platforms.

The bulk of the work in services involves information- and knowledge-based tasks—from data management to the analytics of consulting, from transactions processing to the development of marketing strategies, from supply-chain logistics to financial advisory work. By U.S. Labor Department nomenclature, these endeavors are performed by workers in two major occupational categories: managers and professionals on the one hand and sales, administrative support, and other office workers on the other. According to the Bureau of Labor Statistics, about 80 percent of all workers employed in services can be classified as white-collar. Similarly, about 80 percent of all white-collar workers in the United States are employed in the services sector.

Moreover, the line between manufacturing and services has become blurred over time. Manufacturing companies also have important back-office and services functions that employ a wide range of white-collar workers in auditing, accounting, process control, sales, marketing, and internal consulting. The Bureau of Labor Statistics estimates that white-collar workers now account for about 40 percent of total manufacturing employment in the United States.

Adding them all up, irrespective of the sectoral classification of the parent company, nearly eighty-seven million U.S. workers can be now classified as white-collar. That boils down to 61 percent of total nonfarm employment—ten times the 5.9 percent share of so-called blue-collar production workers.[16] For most of the modern history of the U.S. labor market, production workers have been on the leading edge of facing competitive and cyclical pressures. White-collar workers, whether in services or to a lesser extent in manufacturing, have been relatively sheltered.

That has all changed with the IT-enabled globalization of services, which has transformed many nontradables into tradables.[17] The reason is not just the Internet and the related connectivity of many low-wage offshore knowledge workers to desktops around the world. It is also sharply improved education, training, and language skills in the foreign pool of such workers—improvements in the quality of offshore white-collar talent platforms that make cross-border connectivity well worth the effort.

India, with its legendary business-process outsourcing industry, was the first offshore alternative to pose a serious threat to American white-collar job security. In the early 1990s, companies like Infosys, Wipro, and Tata Consulting Services began their migration up the value chain from data processing and call centers to higher value-added analytics, consulting, and systems solutions. U.S. companies were quick to embrace the India solution, moving significant portions of their back-office, transactions processing, and other support functions to India to take advantage of its well-educated, English-speaking, low-wage talent pool. While the numbers weren't large—at least at first—the perception of a serious threat was very real. And as the big gorilla in development circles and a major beneficiary of globalization, China suffered guilt by association.

Alan Blinder of Princeton University has tried to estimate U.S. workers' exposure to "offshoring"—the IT-enabled substitution of foreign white-collar workers for domestic ones. Based on a detailed analysis of some 291 occupations, Blinder puts potential "offshorability" at between 22 percent and 29 percent of the total American workforce.[18] If we take the average of this range, his estimates suggest about one-quarter of the U.S. workforce could be threatened over time by this new strain of job displacement.

Such a broad incidence of first-time victims underscores the potential for a widening outbreak of "white-collar shock." To the extent that Blinder is correct, vast numbers of U.S. knowledge workers unaccustomed to tough competitive pressures could over time be exposed to a new strain of job insecurity. Adding to other sources of job insecurity that have arisen in a tough postcrisis climate, the political backlash against globalization can only become sharper in the face of the new concerns of white-collar shock.[19] Rational or not, it is precisely such sentiments that stoke fears of the antiglobalization crowd and direct the angst toward globalization's "new champions," such as China.[20]

Rethinking Ricardo

Contrary to widespread belief, there is no theory of globalization. It is instead a conceptual framework that is based on some of the oldest and most basic theories of economics. The early-nineteenth-century work of the famed British economist David Ricardo, which gave rise to the theories of comparative advantage and international specialization, have become the intellectual pillars of globalization.[21] Those who question globalization are often accused of violating the sacred code of economics. Yet the real question is not the theory itself but the relevance of its applications in today's world. The serious critics of globalization worry that its theoretical foundations are balanced on the head of a very ancient pin. Rapidly spreading industrialization and a modern services economy speak to a very different world from Ricardo's heavily agricultural era. So does the explosion of global trade, which now has some thirty times the share of world GDP that it did during his lifetime. So does the emergence of multicountry global supply chains, which, as will be discussed in Chapter 7, render the simple Ricardian models of exchange between producer and consumer economies largely obsolete.

The pro-globalization crowd tries to squeeze these new realities into an old theory.[22] On the surface, the Ricardian solution is quite comforting. It argues that the inevitable strains of trade disputes between nations will work out just fine in the end. A modern translation of the theory still rests on the classic foundations of relative productivity growth and competition, arguing that nations will specialize in the production of goods where their labor forces are the most efficient. In the early nineteenth century, Ricardo argued that it was England's productivity advantage in cloth versus Portugal's in wine that made trade beneficial to both nations. Today, it could be toys in China and "fracked" natural gas in the United States.

The link to globalization comes in the implications for international specialization when the traditional model is opened up to include nontradable services. In the past, as labor in a high-cost developed nation came under pressure from trade with a low-wage developing economy, displaced workers sought refuge in nontradable services. That refuge was more or less a safety net for those who had lost their jobs due to trade. However, for this strategy to be effective, transitional remedies of education, retraining, and reskilling of exposed workers would also be required—in effect, preparing the victims of international competition for new livelihoods.

In many respects, this was all part of a grand unifying theory of capitalism—Ricardo's building blocks fit quite neatly with the ebb and flow of companies and industries as posited in the "creative destruction" of Joseph Schumpeter.[23] It was acceptable if competitive pressures put traditional manufacturers out of business. Entrepreneurs and their retrained workers could then move up the value chain into new, more technologically advanced manufacturing industries. Or they could migrate to the more sheltered nontradable services sector. In either case, the theory of comparative advantage suggested a wide range of options for a nation whose tradable industries were fading, while allowing consumers in the meantime to benefit from ever-cheaper goods and the associated expansion of purchasing power. The elegance of the Ricardian solution in a rough-and-tumble Schumpeterian world spawned the win-win mantra of modern globalization.

But as should be evident from the description above of Globalization 2.0, the long-standing assurance that services are nontradable hasn't withstood the test of time. As they become increasingly tradable, the degree of shelter afforded to the workers who toil in services becomes less secure. In an IT-connected world, those insecurities can emerge quickly. The reverberations of white-collar shock spread equally quickly. Even if information workers don't sense immediate risks to their own jobs, they have firsthand knowledge of other white-collar workers who have not been so lucky. That rapidly spreading fear has had a profound impact on a once sheltered and vast segment of the U.S. labor market. It erodes their confidence as consumers and it angers them as voters. It is an important component of the backlash against globalization.

In keeping with these concerns, some prominent economists have raised serious questions about the modern-day relevance of Ricardian theories. Two stand out as particularly noteworthy. The first came out of a 2000 collaboration between William Baumol, the eminent economist, and Ralph Gomory, the equally eminent mathematician.[24] At its core, their argument is very simple—it's all about scale. Unlike the Ricardian era, when the law of diminishing returns constrained the expansion of the scale of business establishments in a largely rural and agricultural world, today's circumstances are all about the increasing returns of large-scale industrial enterprises.

That simple premise seriously complicates the elegance of the Ricardian solution. In the early nineteenth century, when resource endowments and other factors of production were largely fixed, the theory of comparative advantage pointed to one optimal, or mutually beneficial, solution for nations engaged in cross-border trade—in the words of Gomory and Baumol, it was "the unique state of stable equilibrium . . . automatically selected by the Invisible Hand."[25] In today's large-scale world, there is no such unique equilibrium. In industries such as motor vehicles, computer and telecommunications hardware, and pharmaceuticals, huge start-up costs (including research and development), in conjunction with mass assembly lines, point to increasing returns from an expansion of scale by what Gomory and Baumol refer to as "retainable" industries—those with a lasting presence. That, in turn, points to a scalable range of many possible trading configurations between nations—leading to a multiplicity of outcomes of varying degrees of mutual desirability between nations.[26] The "multiple equilibria" result introduces the possibility of inherent conflicts between a large number of solutions that could conceivably result, and related conflicts between the nations that endorse such a range of scalable outcomes.

Gomory and Baumol stress that these conflicts are very real features of today's activist government policy agendas, which are aimed at enhancing competitive positions of industries by focusing on the sources of scalable expansion, such as investment in new capacity, research and development, and education. Since the theory of comparative advantage is silent on the distribution of gains from trade—namely, on the share of output that goes to each trading nation—Gomory and Baumol warn that the tension between multiple outcomes could lead to trade frictions and protectionism, especially between developed and developing nations. This is a point that seems especially relevant to the mounting frictions between the United States and China.

The toughest criticism came from Nobel laureate Paul Samuelson, who more than any modern economist was responsible for the translation of Ricardian foundations into contemporary economics. In a provocative paper near the end of his life, Samuelson made the theoretical point that a technological innovation that boosts Chinese worker productivity could also give China some of the comparative advantage that previously had belonged to the United States."[27] Samuelson demonstrated that, contrary to the basic theory of comparative advantage, competition from a low-wage technologically equipped imitator, such as China, could put pressures on U.S. exports. That means that under certain circumstances, China's "catch-up"—the essence of economic development—could lead to lower worker wages and a permanent loss of American per capita income. And just like that, win-win globalization becomes "lose-win."

While Samuelson tended to downplay these "intuitively obvious" results, as he described them, his paper caused an enormous stir, not just in academia but also in policy and political circles. One of Ricardo's greatest champions was laying out a contrary case that was tied to a fairly realistic depiction of U.S.-Chinese codependency. In a rejoinder to the vigorous reaction—both supportive and critical—Samuelson offered no apologies. He reaffirmed his core position as an unflinching apostle of free trade and comparative advantage, but warned "that advanced nations can expect to encounter in a biased way some possible preponderance of win-lose inventions from abroad."[28] In other words, complacency is not the answer to today's fast-moving globalization. If I may put words in Samuelson's mouth, he was cautioning that the United States shouldn't bask forever in the warm glow of Ricardo.[29] Instead, he implied, it was time to take China seriously.

These critiques, and others that have surfaced over the years, have not negated Ricardian trade theory as a pillar of economic theory and practice.[30] They do, however, suggest that strict application of the theory has become more and more of a stretch in the era of Globalization 2.0.[31] Under ideal circumstances—or "proper circumstances" as qualified by Baumol[32]—free trade can still deliver optimal results for the broader global economy. But it is not clear whether all participants, codependent or not, are engaging in global commerce on a "fair enough" basis to allow the theory to work as stipulated. This is yet another area where the imbalances of codependency can come into play—the considerations that delineate the boundaries between what is fair enough and what is not. The globalization debate hangs on the resolution of that critical issue. So does the codependency between the United States and China.

Reality Check

We live in an imperfect world. Globalization's harsh realities, as well as its opportunities, are an outgrowth of the rough edges of today's nearly $80 trillion global economy.[33] Imperfect as it is, globalization also frames the codependency between the Chinese and American economies. It provides great context for the world's most important bilateral relationship.

On one level, it's a context of sharp contrasts. China is a large developing economy with a well-articulated growth strategy. It operates as a blended system—a socialist market economy. The United States is the world's largest economy, with an amorphous strategy. While it embraces and celebrates the core principles of capitalism, it constantly struggles with many of capitalism's most fundamental features: competition, unregulated markets, free trade, equal opportunity.

Many have argued that globalization shrinks the world by bringing economies like America's and China's closer together.[34] Notwithstanding the cross-border linkages of globalization, the image of a smaller world is mis-leading. If anything, globalization has created the opposite. Connectivity and integration have enlarged the opportunities for globalized economies. To the extent that globalization prompts further shifts in trade liberaliza-tion and a reduction of trade barriers—thereby fulfilling the key assump-tions of the Ricardian Dream—an expanding world economy should enjoy great and lasting reward.

The elegance of theory notwithstanding, reality is a different matter alto-gether. China and the United States both understand the theory and would like nothing more than to reap the promised benefits. But neither trusts the other to play by the same rules. They live, instead, in Ralph Gomory and William Baumol's alternative reality of inherent conflicts. The conflicts arise because neither nation has cracked the code of economic prosper-ity. Instead they have come to rely on government policies—framed by market-based socialism in China and the increasingly activist trade policies in the United States—to turbocharge the ever-challenging fundamentals of development and growth.

The outcome, in both cases, has fallen well short of perfection. As we concluded in Chapter 1, it has led the U.S. and Chinese economies both into a precarious false prosperity—spurred by an unsustainable domestic consumption binge in America and an export-led growth bonanza in China that was underpinned by excess U.S. consumption. In today's postcrisis era, the payback from that false prosperity has left both economies with serious sustainability challenges that have, in turn, undermined their com-mitments to globalization.

For example, the U.S. Congress included a "Buy American" provision in its 2009 stimulus bill that was intended to cope with the Great Reces-sion. At the same time, as part of its own stimulus package, China directed government procurement policies toward favored treatment of indigenous, or homegrown, innovation.[35] These protectionist actions are not exactly in keeping with the spirit of globalization. But, as noted in Chapter 2 and de-veloped in more detail below, an even bigger challenge looms: a consumer-led reduction in China's surplus saving that could threaten America's major source of external funding. All in all, and consistent with the critique of Gomory and Baumol, there is good reason to worry about an escalation of conflicts between these two nations that could make it very difficult for them to remain committed to globalization and to the codependency that binds them together.

Neither, of course, will admit that openly. Both nations continue to talk the talk of globalization. But walking the walk has become another matter—especially where free trade is concerned. As Berkeley professor Laura Tyson aptly put it twenty-five years ago, "managed trade" is the only alternative for the United States in today's imperfectly globalized world—in effect, "using trade policies to promote and protect industries and technologies that we believe to be important to our well-being."[36] These were not the musings of an ivory tower academic. Tyson went on to succeed Robert Rubin as the second director of the National Economic Council—the closest thing Washington has to a national economic strategy office.

Meanwhile, as will be described in Chapter 12, China's NDRC-based strategists have recently made an overt effort to support seven strategic emerging industries over the next ten years. By using their planning framework to provide direct assistance to this group of leading-edge high-technology industries—from alternative (noncarbon) energy and advanced materials to biotech and electric cars—China, in many respects, is borrowing from the Tyson script. And, of course, this fits all too well with Samuelson's example of technology outsourcing to Chinese "imitators" that he posited could pose a serious threat to U.S. living standards.

Such examples of industrial policy—the conscious intervention by governments in support of companies and sectors—violate the key assumptions of Ricardian comparative advantage that are the crux of pro-globalization case. The theory works its charm only in the absence of such market interventions. Of course, it is not just China and the United States that have relied on industrial policies. Japan and Europe have long favored state subsidies, state ownership, and other measures to support key industries, as have most developing countries. Apparently, economic development is far too important to be left to the markets.

So what is Globalization 2.0? It is clearly about linkages—broader and faster than the world has ever seen. But it is also about white-collar shock, insecurity, and political backlash. This leaves U.S.-China codependency in a very tricky place. In theory, a robust globalization has the potential to be the superglue of market-based integration. It could anchor the two nations in the mutually beneficial "Chimerica" synthesis that historian Niall Ferguson has suggested.[37] That would cement their codependency.

But it turns out that today's strain of globalization falls far short of that ideal. Market frictions and policy intervention are the rule, not the exception. Political buy-in is missing. And an oversimplistic rationale for globalization sits on the crumbling foundations of ancient theories that are out of step with a modern world. In short, Globalization 2.0 cannot solve the great global growth dilemma. Nor can it alleviate the tensions that have arisen between America and China. That leaves their codependency very much in human hands—specifically, in the hands of policy makers and politicians and in the strategies they embrace to solve their growth dilemmas.

How that works out remains to be seen. The nations' political cycles are not aligned to promote cooperation. With historically high structural unemployment, neither political party in the United States seems willing to cast its lot with trade liberalization and globalization. Nor does the new leadership in China seem about to embrace a quick and aggressive shift toward free-market reforms of its powerful state-owned enterprises.[38] While reluctant to say so publicly, both U.S. and Chinese policy makers increasingly view globalization as part of the problem, and not the solution, for their codependent economies. Can this codependency be sustained in such a climate?

7

Bilateralism in a Multilateral World

At the top of the list of contradictions plaguing an unbalanced global economy is the stubborn insistence on bilateral remedies for multilateral problems. Persistent trade tensions between the United States and China are a case in point. They provide only a narrow and distorted window into far broader problems for both of these codependent economies.

There is little dispute on the facts. The official data show that a large trade imbalance exists between the United States and China. But saying this masks a deeper and more significant point: the true breadth and scope of the U.S. trade deficit and its sources. On one level the focus on China is understandable. In 2012, the United States trade deficit with China hit $315 billion, a record, and accounted for 43 percent of America's total merchandise trade gap of $728 billion. Japan, which accounted for the second-largest piece of the overall trade deficit, was only 10 percent of the total. The sheer size of the bilateral imbalance with China has led many politicians and economists to conclude that there needs to be a "Chinese solution" to America's economic woes.

But while the U.S.-China trade deficit is indeed large, this bilateral imbalance did not arise in a vacuum. It is one piece of a multilateral trade deficit that includes more than half of America's trading partners. In 2012, the United States ran deficits with 102 countries—up from 98 in 2011 and 88 in 2010.

In economics jargon, this is known as a multilateral trade imbalance—a deficit with many countries. And it reflects a deeper problem in the U.S. economy: an unprecedented shortfall of national saving. Lacking in savings and wanting to grow, the United States must import surplus savings from abroad—and it must run massive current account and multilateral trade deficits to attract that foreign capital. This is where China fits into the equation: It is a key piece of the mechanism by which America copes with the growth challenges that might otherwise arise from a lack of saving.

The heart of the matter is that the United States' multilateral trade imbalance is not made in China. It is made at home, by a nation seemingly incapable of saving. Yet if the Chinese piece of America's trade deficit is neutralized—either by trade sanctions or a currency "fix"—without addressing the underlying source of the multilateral imbalance, then the bilateral solution will backfire. America would continue to import surplus savings from abroad, but from somewhere else. The U.S.-China deficit would then be shifted to America's other trading partners. To the extent that those trading partners are higher-cost producers than the Chinese, a reasonable presumption, the result will be the same as a tax hike on American consumers—hardly the remedy politicians are seeking.

Therein lies the problem. If the United States doesn't address its savings shortfall—an unfortunate though distinctly possible outcome given outsize federal budget deficits for as far as the eye can see—it is doomed to run chronic multilateral trade deficits. Against that backdrop, trying to eliminate the Chinese piece of a massive U.S. trade deficit would accomplish little other than shifting one piece of the trade gap to others.

Bilateral myopia also misses another key point: cross-border linkages of global supply chains and the resulting distortions to trade flows between nations. Flows of intermediate components and parts—partially completed goods that are further processed in several countries before being put in the hands of consumers—now make up close to 40 percent of annualized global trade.[1] But because of the accounting deficiencies of international trade statistics, countries like China, which serve as the assembly and distribution hub for many such platforms, get credited with a disproportionate share of exports from multicountry supply chains. That tends to exaggerate bilateral trade deficits—and aggravate political tensions—with major recipients of those exports like the United States. Not only does the growth of multicountry supply chains suggest that China's role in America's trade imbalance is overstated, it offers further evidence that Washington's inclination to get tough with China is a misdirected strategy.

This points to a serious misunderstanding of codependency: There are no bilateral fixes to multilateral problems. The U.S.-China trade debate misses this point entirely. If the United States doesn't improve its own saving rate, it will continue to be plagued by trade imbalances and the attendant pressures on jobs and hard-pressed U.S. families. Pushing for a stronger renminbi will make no difference. America's most fundamental macroeconomic imbalance with many countries cannot be resolved through a revaluation of one currency. The U.S. growth debate has been hijacked by the Chinese currency issue for far too long.

America's Chronic Saving Problem

The United States doesn't save. The problem is not just individuals but the entire economy. America's broadest measure of domestic saving—the sum of depreciation-adjusted, or net, savings of businesses, households, and the government sector—fell into negative territory in 2008 and plunged to minus 2 percent of national income in 2009 before easing to minus 0.8 percent in 2010 and then inching up to just 0.4 percent in 2011–12.[2] That is the largest savings shortfall for a leading nation in modern history.

A brief technical digression is warranted here. The "net" saving rate is what matters most for economic growth. When we strip out the portion of reported (or "gross") saving that is earmarked for the wear and tear, or depreciation, of a country's capital stock, the net saving rate measures what's left over to fund the expansion of productive capacity. The United States, with a negative net national saving rate, doesn't have any. America suffers from a complete lack of the domestic savings needed to enlarge the scale of its economy.

This has enormous consequences for economic growth. Savings are the seed corn of future prosperity. A positive saving rate helps finance the new investments in productive capital that are vital to support economic expansion. Without savings, no economy can increase its citizens' prosperity over time. When it has a savings shortfall, an economy basically has two choices—uncover a new source of savings or give up on future growth. Unwilling to compromise on its growth aspirations, the United States has chosen the first option. It has turned to surplus savings from abroad to plug the hole.

This where China and the world's other surplus savers, like Japan and Germany, enter the macro equation. International trade and saving are inextricably linked. If a nation's consumers, businesses, and government collectively try to spend more than they produce, that country is effectively living beyond its means and must draw down its domestic saving to make up the shortfall. That is fine as long as there is a savings buffer to draw on. But there may be times when any surplus of domestic savings has been depleted and the economy turns to savings from abroad to fund its excess spending. At that point, its "current account balance," or the difference between national saving and investment and the broadest measure of any economy's financial position with the rest of the world that is sometimes referred to as the balance of payments, goes into deficit.

This is precisely the current state of affairs for the United States. For most of the period since the end of World War II, the U.S. current account was in surplus—that is, America saved more than it invested.[3] But with its sharply declining net national saving rate having fallen into negative territory since 2008, the United States has run a deficit on its current account for all but one year since 1982. America's international imbalance is extreme by any standards. Its current account deficit of $440 billion in 2012 was nearly $350 billion more than the second-largest such deficit elsewhere in the world.[4]

This massive imbalance is key to the other piece of the story—the trade deficit. A nation running balance of payments deficits does not get foreign capital just for the asking. It must also run a trade deficit on goods and services. That is exactly what has happened in America, and with good reason: As the United States buys more goods from abroad than it sells to foreign customers, it exports a surplus of dollars overseas. That dollar surplus—the so-called capital account surplus, which balances the current account deficit—is then exchanged for local currencies by America's trading partners. As a result, the United States receives capital inflows from abroad, which provides the external funding it needs to plug its shortfall of domestic saving. Without the trade deficit, there would be no transfer of funds to finance America's excess spending.[5] For the United States, these two international deficits—trade and the current account—are inseparable. Over the past ten years, the cumulative shortfalls in dollar terms have been comparable: U.S. current account deficits between 2003 and 2012 add up to $5.8 trillion, or 82 percent of the total merchandise trade deficit of $7.1 trillion recorded over the same period.

This international accounting framework does not determine how the trade deficits are parceled out or which countries provide the foreign capital. The deficit financing the United States receives from abroad could originate from any of the world's nearly two hundred countries, or all of them.[6] Experience tells us, however, that capital flows and trade imbalances are intrinsically multilateral. An economy as large as America's with an outsize savings shortfall must run trade deficits with many countries in order to secure the incremental funding it needs to maintain economic growth.

The causes of America's chronic savings shortfall are an important part of the story, especially insofar as codependency with China is concerned. While economists have long debated the reasons behind shifts in saving, in recent years, three main factors appear to have been at work—the bubble economy, the role of the dollar as a reserve currency, and a lack of incentives for saving.[7]

The Bubble Economy. First, as we saw in Chapter 1, America's false prosperity is traceable to asset and credit bubbles. As asset appreciation takes hold, the character of a nation's economy can change—especially if economic actors (households and businesses) are given the means to extract purchasing power from rapidly expanding asset bubbles. That's where America's credit bubble came into play. It provided an ever-increasing population of homeowners with an easy way to convert their soaring home values into ATM-like machines. These wealth effects allowed the United States to shed its identity as an income-based economy and become an asset-dependent economy. This transition began in the latter half of the 1990s and continued largely unabated through 2007. At its height, both spending and saving were heavily reliant on asset and credit markets.

The problem with asset-dependent economies is that they often go to excess—just like the bubbles they are built on. That happened in Japan in the late 1980s, and in the United States beginning in the late 1990s. In both cases, when the bubbles burst in the private sector, the public sector had to pick up the pieces, running massive budget deficits to temper lethal crises and to compensate for the subsequent shortfalls in private demand.

The United States' situation, however, was especially dire. Household saving was already sharply depressed before the crisis, and the federal government had already established a trend of persistently large budget deficits.[8] When the crisis hit, the subsequent plunge of economic activity created a massive shortfall of government revenues that, when accompanied by aggressive countercyclical fiscal policy, amplified existing fiscal deficits. This government "dis-saving" compounded the country's preexisting saving problem. It effectively spread the large savings gap from the private to the public sector—thereby completing the chain of excess for the bubble-dependent and savings-short U.S. economy.

The Dollar. The second factor is what former French President Valéry Giscard d'Estaing called the "exorbitant privilege" afforded to the United States as the issuer of the world's preeminent reserve currency.[9] According to this argument, the strong demand for dollar-based reserves has allowed the United States to borrow from abroad with impunity. Excess foreign borrowing by any large-deficit economy would normally permit the lender to exact tough concessions on the terms by which the loan was provided. For the savings-short U.S. economy, with its unprecedented demand for foreign capital, tougher terms would have implied a weaker dollar, higher longer-term interest rates, or both. But that has never happened—at least not yet. Interest rates on U.S. Treasury securities—the amount the country must pay to borrow money—were lower in 2012 than they have ever been. Undisciplined by the markets, the world's hegemon has not hesitated to borrow the surplus savings of other nations on extremely favorable terms. America got away without saving, in part because it benefited enormously from the "kindness of strangers."[10]

Savings Incentives. Third, as the quintessential consumer society, the United States has made little effort to address its longer-term saving problem. While few dispute that enhanced saving is necessary for sustained economic growth, there was always an excuse to defer the heavy lifting for another day. Since the Great Crisis, the aversion to facing the imperative of long-term saving has only deepened. Some warned that saving would be a drag on the economy. Haunting memories of the "paradox of thrift" were dredged up from the 1930s.[11] While saving was good for one, went the argument, it was bad for all. It would hobble aggregate demand precisely when the U.S. economy needed more demand.

Largely as a result of such arguments, the case for saving has fallen on hard times. And that's too bad. American families—especially the seventy-seven million baby boomers who have now started retiring—desperately need to feel more secure about their financial futures. Increased saving, or the expectations that enhanced incentives might make saving more attractive in the future, could play an important role in fostering that security. While a balance needs to be struck between the short-term tradeoffs of spending versus saving and the medium- to longer-term objectives of financial security, that is not an excuse for failing to engage in an active debate over America's saving dilemma. This topic will be taken up in greater detail in Chapter 11.

Saving is the central unifying element in the codependency between the United States and China. All you have to know at this point is one thing: Savings-short nations run multilateral trade deficits. Without sustained improvement in domestic saving, America will never pull itself out of its current account and trade deficits. And that means China, with its large trade and saving surpluses, will probably remain in Washington's political crosshairs for as long as this key issue is unresolved.

China's Surplus Saving Problem

China has the opposite problem. The mirror image of savings-short America, China saves too much. Its overall saving rate—gross, not net, in this case—was at 49.5 percent of its GDP in 2012.[12] Not only is that about 10 percentage points above its norm in the final two decades of the twentieth century, but it is only 3 percentage points below China's record high of 53.4 percent recorded in 2008, which was the highest domestic saving rate registered for any major economy in the post–World War II era. China's sharply elevated gross saving rate was more than four times the 12 percent gross saving rate in the United States in 2009–12.

Just as America's low saving rate is a reflection of its identity as a consumer society, China's high rate is equally critical to its identity as a producer economy. The implications of this pro-saving bias are precisely the opposite of those in the United States. Unlike America, which has to draw on foreign saving to sustain economic growth, China relies heavily on domestic saving to fund its massive fixed investment program, which in turn underpins the commitments to urbanization, infrastructure, and construction of state-of-the-art manufacturing facilities that support the Chinese export machine.

Notwithstanding the huge portion of its GDP that goes to capital investment—about 46 percent in 2013—China still has enough savings left over to run a large current account surplus. Since 1991, its current account has been in surplus for all but one year (1993). The surplus has averaged 3.3 percent of GDP since 1990 and soared to a record 10.1 percent in 2007 before falling back to around 2.6 percent in 2012. Despite the recent decline, however, China's current account surplus was $239 billion in 2013, the largest in the world.[13]

Like America, whose current account deficit requires large trade deficits, China's current account surplus has comparable implications for its trade balance—namely, trade surpluses that have averaged 4 percent of GDP since 1990. The disposition of China's surplus saving is an important and highly sensitive aspect of its economic and financial relationships with the rest of the world. As noted in Chapter 2, China's large and expanding current account surpluses have led to a massive buildup of foreign exchange reserves—going from $11 billion in 1990 to $3.5 trillion by mid-2013.

All this ties up China's macroeconomic story in a very neat package. The savings surplus and the current account and trade surpluses its excess saving has spawned are critical features of the Chinese economy, which remains excessively dependent on exports as a major source of economic growth and development. As noted in Chapter 2, the resulting sharp buildup of foreign exchange reserves has forced Chinese currency managers into massive investments in dollar-denominated assets. That serves the dual purpose of maintaining a competitive renminbi and also helping savings-short America fund its own growth agenda. Anything that supports America's consumer demand, of course, also fits quite well with China's growth strategy: It provides the foreign demand support that Chinese exporters rely upon. While all this sounds like the mutually beneficial trappings of an ideal codependency, there are many in Washington who are far from convinced.

As with America's deficit saving, the hows and whys of China's penchant for surplus saving are an important part of the story. Four main factors are at work: China's mercantilist growth model, the lack of a social safety net, the financial repression of Chinese households, and the lack of a credible dividend policy for state-owned enterprises.

Mercantilism. As stressed in Chapter 1, China's mercantilist, export-led growth model has been a linchpin of its stunning success over the past three-plus decades. Relying on trade as an engine of growth requires both high savings, to fund the expansion of export-producing industries, and currency suppression (a managed float, in recent years) to ensure that exports are well priced in world markets. China has followed that script to a tee. Yet the Four Uns, described in Chapter 4, suggest that the country is on the brink of shifting to a different, more balanced growth strategy. Until that shift is farther along, the savings imperatives of the mercantilist approach are likely to remain a powerful force shaping the Chinese economy.

The safety net. There can be no mistaking the fear-driven motives behind high levels of household-sector saving in China. Under the old model of state ownership, cradle-to-grave support from the so-called iron rice bowl gave the Chinese people a sense of security. While there was no promise of upward mobility, families at least knew that the state would provide the basic necessities of life, most notably retirement income, healthcare, and even shelter. There was no urgency to save.

That was then. As state-owned enterprise reforms intensified in the mid-1990s, the iron rice bowl was dismantled and a deepening insecurity gripped the Chinese populace. With households lacking investment options—let alone the discretionary income that is required to implement a personal investment strategy—a strong preference for precautionary saving emerged.[14] A rapidly aging population, traceable to the one-child family planning policy, reinforced this trend. Given the current paucity of funding for social security and healthcare, these precautionary saving motives seem likely to remain powerful. The good news is that Chinese leaders have identified safety net funding as a major priority in the Twelfth Five-Year Plan. But it has yet to happen.

Financial repression. Individual Chinese savers face severe constraints on what their savings can earn. Tightly regulated interest rates on bank deposits have resulted in negative returns in inflation-adjusted terms since 2003. Facing limitations on both interest income and investment alternatives, individuals must compensate by saving more. Some researchers have estimated that this form of financial repression has reduced the personal income share of the Chinese GDP by as much as 5 to 10 percentage points, requiring a comparable amount of precautionary saving as an offset.[15]

Corporate saving. Finally, the surge in Chinese household saving over the past decade has been accompanied by an even larger increase in corporate saving, especially by state-owned enterprises. Since 2000, about 60 percent of the total surge in China's national saving can be traced to sharp increases in corporate saving.[16] This is partly a consequence of the financial repression imposed on Chinese households, which allows banks to enjoy subsidized access to funding. Banks can then offer cut-rate lending to large Chinese companies, which, in turn, subsidizes growth in retained earnings and thereby supports China's investment-led growth.

There is a relatively straightforward policy fix that could address the excesses of enterprise saving in China. It would focus both on a liberalization of deposit rates and a rethinking of corporate dividend policies. Mandatory dividend payments were first required of China's state-owned enterprises in 2007 in an effort to capture a portion of excess corporate saving. While this was a step in the right direction, it is generally agreed that it was not enough. Increased dividends, together with higher yields on bank deposits, would go a long way toward tempering the imbalances in the Chinese saving structure. That would increase personal income, require greater discipline of banks, and reduce subsidized lending to state-owned enterprises. Such a policy would, in effect, shift excess returns from capital back to labor—thus reducing the need for precautionary household saving.[17] It could well be an important initiative of China's newly installed leadership under Xi Jinping and Li Keqiang.

Putting the two pieces of the U.S.-China saving story together gets right to the heart of the powerful codependency between these two economies. America, the deficit saver, needs imported capital in order to grow. China, the surplus saver, needs to make certain that its export demand is well supported by the deficit economy. Two unbalanced economies, each needing support from the other. The ultimate symbiosis of codependency—who could ask for more?

102 Deficits

In 2012, the United States ran trade deficits with 102 countries. Some were bigger than others—and some were tiny, like the deficit with Côte d'Ivoire. But the number is still 102, a large and diverse mix of bilateral deficits.

Like Japan's during the 1980s, China's share of America's multilateral trade deficit has far outdistanced that of any other country. Over the decade ending in 2012, China accounted for 33.5 percent of the cumulative U.S. multilateral trade gap. And the Chinese portion has been rising—averaging 42.6 percent between 2009 and 2012.

The comparison with Japan is important. Japan offered the first modern example of a significant bilateral concentration in the U.S. multilateral deficit. Over the decade of the 1980s, the bilateral U.S.-Japan deficit accounted, on average, for 40 percent of the total U.S. merchandise trade deficit—nearly 10 percentage points more than the share traceable to China over the decade ending in 2012. The imbalance with Japan ended up being a major source of tension in the world economy. It led to Japan-bashing, the Plaza Accord on yen revaluation, monstrous Japanese asset bubbles, and Japan's postbubble carnage of two lost decades and counting.

But even though its share of the total deficit is smaller, the threat posed by China is a much bigger deal in the United States today than the challenge coming from Japan during the 1980s. The primary reason for this difference is the state of the U.S. economy. The United States is in much worse shape today than it was in the 1980s.

Back then, the United States was a saver, with a net national saving rate averaging 5.7 percent of GDP from 1980 to 1989. By contrast, that rate has averaged just 1.8 percent since 2000 and just 0.7 percent since 2005. Largely as a result, the overall merchandise trade gap—just 2 percent of GDP in the 1980s—has widened to 5 percent since 2000. That means the trade imbalance between the United States and Japan, while a bigger piece of the overall U.S. trade deficit in the 1980s than today's imbalance with China, had a much smaller impact on overall GDP. That's all Washington cares about, especially with acute pressures continuing to bear down on middle-class American workers.

But the number is still 102. And that means that a China-centric fix won't work. America's multilateral trade deficit is an outgrowth of the biggest saving shortfall in history. If that saving problem is not addressed, closing down trade with one of the 102 countries means that piece will simply get redistributed to the other 101.

From the Chinese perspective, the persistent bilateral trade imbalance with the United States is equally perplexing. China has made great progress in reducing its current account and trade surplus over the past five years, with latter being cut nearly in half from 2008 to 2012. Yet with the narrowing of its multilateral imbalance, the outsize bilateral imbalance with the United States sticks out all the more. That poses a very tough question: How does a nation significantly reduce its multilateral trade imbalance and yet still experience a sharp deterioration in the bilateral balance with its largest trading partner?

Supply Chain Economics

The answer can be found in one of the newest and most powerful features of Globalization 2.0—the rapid expansion of global supply chains. The Ricardian construct, under which goods are produced in one country and exported to another country to be consumed, is long gone. Global production is now fragmented across a broad swath of nations, with components and parts flowing from country to country before being assembled into their final form and exported to their ultimate destination.

Such integrated global supply chains benefit producers as well as consumers, both of whom take advantage of lower production costs and more efficient delivery systems. At the same time, the trend seriously complicates the official metrics of international trade. For example, if a finished good is shipped from China to the United States, where it is consumed, China gets credit for 100 percent of the value of the export, even if the only value added by a Chinese company was to assemble components manufactured elsewhere. It makes little sense to bemoan gross trade flows from China if the bulk of the production and employment behind such trade took place in other countries. The growing network of global supply chains forces us to ask to what extent our trade data with China might be seriously distorted.

Over the past twenty years, China has been a major beneficiary of the vertical integration of Asian and global production chains. It has become the major assembly and distribution hub of a massive flow of East-West trade, taking intermediate goods from a vast network of supplier nations and assembling them into their final forms for consumption in the United States and other developed economies. Yet traditional trade statistics are out of step with the new flows of supply chain production. Of particular relevance to our analysis are distortions to bilateral trade data between the United States and China that have inflamed the public on a sensitive issue. By missing the critical distinction between components and parts that come from elsewhere in the supply chain and those that reflect the indigenous value added of Chinese production, these biases seriously distort one of the key economic impacts of U.S.-Chinese codependency.

Apple's product family offers a particularly striking example of these distortions. In a study published in 2008, three researchers from the University of California examined the specifics of the iPod supply chain for 2005.[18] Based on a detailed parts list provided by Apple as well as pricing and profit margin information from designated suppliers, they broke down one model of the iPod into six major components and tracked them through the production process: the research and development and design blueprint developed by Apple in Cupertino, California; Japanese display and hard drives manufactured by Toshiba in China; processors made in the United States; memory made mainly in South Korea and Japan; and a lithium-ion battery made in Japan. The iPod's components were assembled in China at Inventec Appliances (a Taiwanese company) and then shipped as finished products to the United States and elsewhere. The study concluded that China contributed around 3 percent of the iPod's value added. But U.S. trade statistics credited China with all of the approximately $1 billion gross flow of these products as they were valued at the point of entry into the United States.

Li and Fung, the world's largest clothing "manufacturer," provides another example of supply chain management at the other end of the product spectrum. Founded in Hong Kong in 1906, the company stresses its evolution from a "sourcing agent to a global supply chain manager." It owns no factories but sits astride a network of more than fifteen thousand suppliers operating in more than forty economies worldwide—with a heavy tilt toward Asia, especially China.[19]

Relying on IT-enabled connectivity and the new efficiencies of global logistics, Li and Fung has revolutionized the piece-by-piece approach to the manufacturing and assembly of clothing that stocks the shelves of major retailers around the world, ranging from Walmart to Liz Claiborne. If you buy a Li and Fung dress at The Limited that is labeled "Made in China," the Chinese value added turns out to be only about 5 percent of the sales price. Ironically, even though 100 percent of the import's value is officially credited to China, as much as 85 percent of the value may be attributable to American inputs, such as design, marketing, logistics, transport, and retailing.[20]

While there are plenty of other examples that illustrate the problems with using bilateral trade statistics to capture the complex realities of supply chain production in a multilateral world, it remains a tough sell in Washington. China's trade statistics show that about 40 percent of its total exports have been previously processed in other countries. Moreover, China alone is estimated to have accounted for fully 67 percent of all processed exports in the world over the 2000–2008 time period.[21] This only hints at China's role in Asian supply chains.

Academic researchers have been hard at work trying to fill this gap in our knowledge. While gross flows between countries are relatively easy to capture, it is much harder to figure out the "net" flows, the value added on a country-by-country basis up and down the supply chain. Input-output tools—specifically, detailed estimates of the interindustry flows within and across economies—bring the characteristics of vertical supply chains into sharper focus. That requires combining a large number of country-specific input-output tables into an integrated global matrix. Such efforts are now under way at the United Nations, the Organisation for Economic Cooperation and Development (OECD), Japan's Institute of Development Economics, and the World Trade Organization (WTO).

In January 2013, the first findings from such an effort were released from a joint WTO-OECD initiative on "Trade in Value Added (TiVA)."[22] Several important conclusions have emerged from the new TiVA database and other research: First, vertical supply chains are a big deal in the modern global economy. Trade of intermediate goods now accounts for about 40 percent of gross nonfuel trade flows.[23] Over the past three decades, the share of exports that can be attributed to a vertical supply chain from other countries has been substantial and growing.[24] This phenomenon applies even to the United States, the world's largest consumer. In 1972, vertical supply chains and imports from other countries accounted for only 6 percent of U.S. exports, but by 1997 that share had doubled to 12 percent, and by TiVA data remains close to that share today.[25]

Second, the value added attributable to China through bilateral statistics is seriously overstated, particularly for high-end technology goods. The best estimates suggest that about 36 percent of the total value of China's global exports is attributable to components and parts of foreign origin. Moreover, foreign suppliers account for at least 80 percent of the value added in high-end Chinese technology exports of computers, other office equipment, and telecommunications equipment. As we saw in Chapter 6, these are the same industries in which China has enjoyed great success at competitive leapfrogging; these numbers mean that foreign suppliers have captured the bulk of these gains.[26]

Third, much of the foreign value added that is incorrectly attributed to China by traditional trade statistics is in fact traceable to other Asian countries. China is a major hub for assembly and distribution in East-West trade within the increasingly integrated Asian regional trade network. In 2002, 60 percent of China's imports of intermediate goods came from nearby countries, with Japan, South Korea, Taiwan, Singapore, and Hong Kong accounting for about half that total.[27] Specifically, Japan accounts for 22 percent of the foreign value added that is currently misattributed to China, and another 28 percent comes from South Korea, Taiwan, Singapore, and Hong Kong.[28]

These results help us frame the bilateral U.S.-China trade deficit in a broader multilateral context. They suggest that U.S. imports of goods from China are overstated by about 44 percent—meaning that while official data have China accounting for 11.1 percent of total American imports, in reality the number on a Chinese value-added basis is closer to 7.7 percent.[29] If we apply these findings to U.S. exports, we find that the United States produces much greater value domestically than does China, with domestic industries contributing 87.1 percent of the value added. Correcting for these supply chain distortions would significantly reduce the stated trade deficit between the United States and China. In 2011 it would have been cut by 37 percent, from $295 billion to $187 billion.[30] While that's still a big number, it brings China closer to the rest of the pack when we assess the mix of America's outsize multilateral trade deficit.

That should be the basic point of the supply chain story insofar as the United States is concerned. Rather than fixate on China as a bilateral threat, we can more accurately see it as the hub of a massive, integrated, pan-regional export machine—in effect, a proxy for a large collection of tightly connected Asian economies that provide low-cost goods to a savings-short U.S. economy. America's import needs are now increasingly sourced through such multicountry supply chains. While China may be the final stop in this chain of production, assembly, and distribution, it is far from the only cog in the global trade machine that the United States has come to rely on. The bilateral trade data seriously mislead us about the multilateral origins of this critical feature of codependency.

The Currency Trap

Currencies measure relative prices between nations. They rise and fall on the basis of comparative shifts in economic and financial fundamentals. Governments can attempt to limit or manage the fluctuations, but eventually they gravitate toward equilibrium. Bilateral exchange rates, such as between the United States and China, tie the fluctuations to country pairs. These bilateral rates are very different from broader trade-weighted, or effective, exchange rates that relate a nation's currency to a large collection of its trading partners. The fixation on country-specific currencies is another manifestation of the misplaced emphasis on bilateral analysis of multilateral problems in a globalized world.

This distinction has obvious importance for both the United States and China. America, with its shortfall of savings and its current account and multilateral trade deficits, worries about the role the dollar plays in causing these problems. But it should pay more attention to broad trade-weighted currency metrics—the relationship of the dollar to average currency levels for a broad cross-section of economies elsewhere in the world. Instead, Washington has long focused on bilateral exchange rates—with the yen in the 1980s and now with the renminbi. As it did with Japan, this mistake today creates serious risks—not only for China and the United States but also for the broader global economy.

The currency issue stands out as a lightning rod in the U.S.-China economic debate. Although America's political parties rarely agree on anything these days, as detailed in Chapter 10, there has been strong bipartisan support since 2005 for actions that would force China to revalue the renminbi sharply upward against the U.S. dollar. Yet what a mistake that would be. Trying to address a multilateral problem with a bilateral fix is like squeezing a partially filled water balloon. The water simply sloshes to the other end of the balloon. Relying on a bilateral currency adjustment to address America's multilateral trade problem misses the most basic point of all: Without addressing the source of the multilateral imbalance—the chronic saving problem—attacking the Chinese piece of the U.S. trade deficit would simply send it somewhere else.

That "somewhere else" could pose a serious problem for American families. As noted earlier, China's role as a low-cost supplier to U.S. consumers is a three-legged stool: It produces a wide range of products that are exported to America; it sits at the center of a global supply chain that assembles and feeds products into U.S. distribution channels; and it houses offshore production platforms for subsidiaries of U.S. multinational corporations, creating cost savings that get passed on to American consumers.

A sharp renminbi revaluation of the sort demanded by Washington could knock out all three legs. And then what? Unless Washington miraculously addresses the national saving issue at the same time that it forces a Chinese currency revaluation, the U.S. economy would still face the same external funding dilemma—a large current account deficit and a massive multilateral trade imbalance.

But there would be an added twist from this misdirected effort at a political remedy: Hard-pressed American families would be squeezed even more. Depending on the magnitude of the currency adjustment, or the compensatory tariff, America could lose all the benefits of China's role as its leading external supplier. The already thin profit margins of Chinese exporters would collapse, and many of these companies would go out of business, curtailing supply and driving up prices of U.S. imports. The economics of supply chain management and offshore subsidiaries would be severely undermined. And America would then be forced to do without its vital China-centric support system that has provided the ample sources of low-cost goods and financial capital that a saving-short U.S. economy so desperately needs.

Moreover, if America were to turn to other trading partners to fill the void left by a loss of Chinese imports, U.S. consumers and producers would face greater costs for two reasons: For starters, reconstructing supply chains and interlocking webs of offshore subsidiaries won't occur overnight. It has taken more than twenty years for China, a broad network of associated suppliers, and U.S. multinationals to assemble this complex global sourcing platform. If Humpty Dumpty is pushed off the wall, it will take considerable time to put all the pieces back together again.

On paper, the United States has a second option. There are 101 other countries with which it runs trade deficits. It could certainly turn to them to plug the hole that would be left if China were forced to abdicate its position as America's leading foreign supplier. Who might they be? Consider the others on the top ten list of importers into the United States: Canada (number 2), Mexico (3), Japan (4), Germany (5), the United Kingdom (6), South Korea (7), France (8), Taiwan (9), and Ireland (10). While they could conceivably step up and fill China's place, they might not provide the answer Washington wants.

It turns out that foreign suppliers two through nine are all much higher-cost producers than China. That underscores why a "Chinese solution" to America's trade deficit would penalize U.S. consumers. Based on official data from the U.S. government, average manufacturing compensation in these nine nations, weighted by their shares of imports into the U.S., works out to about $26 per hour in 2010—whereas the comparable rate in China was $2.30.[31] That means if the Chinese piece of U.S. import demand were redistributed to America's nine next largest foreign suppliers—a perfectly reasonable approximation of the initial response to a sharp appreciation of the renminbi or the imposition of high tariffs on Chinese trade—the cost difference, and the associated rise in U.S. import prices it would undoubtedly trigger, would act as a large tax hike on American consumers. They would in effect have less income to either spend or save. The depressing effects of the resulting shortfall in demand would raise the federal deficit, and the already depressed U.S. saving rate might fall even farther. In short, attempts at a bilateral currency "fix" to America's multilateral saving and current-account funding problems would only make its existing problems worse.

Unfortunately, there's far more to the risks of such a policy blunder. If, in fact, Washington finally imposed trade sanctions on China, Beijing would probably retaliate. Such a scenario is described in Chapter 10, but the bottom line is worth stressing here: Depending on the degree of political hostility that sanctions occasioned between the two nations, China might well play its trump card—selling off its massive position in U.S. Treasuries. That would put an end to America's "exorbitant privilege"—the ability to secure foreign funding on extremely favorable terms. In light of the sharp increases in U.S. government debt in recent years, such a backup in borrowing costs would be especially problematic. It could light the fuse on a long dormant U.S. debt bomb, perhaps even bringing an end to America's fantasy of a sustainable false prosperity.[32]

This nightmare scenario would also hit the codependent Chinese economy hard. It would be another devastating blow to the external-demand support for China's export machine, but it also would undermine the value of its enormous $3.5 trillion portfolio of foreign exchange reserves, which is heavily overweighted with dollar-based assets. So why would China dare retaliate in the event of U.S. trade sanctions if it had to bear those risks? As argued in Chapter 10, when faced with an act of economic war, there is good reason to expect China to counter in kind, with political and nationalistic considerations outweighing immediate economic or financial consequences.

Like the choice between true and false prosperity described in Chapter 1, the trade war scenario is another manifestation of the toughest balancing act of codependency: the weighing of economic pressures against domestic politics. The difference between bilateral and multilateral perspectives is key here for both the United States and China. For far too long Washington has been blaming China for problems made in America: an unprecedented savings shortfall, a loss of competitiveness, and the lack of a long-term strategic vision. Every year since 2005, Washington has demanded roughly a 25–30 percent appreciation of the renminbi against the dollar as a bilateral remedy to these tough problems.[33] This demand not only misses the fact that the Chinese currency has actually appreciated by 35 percent against the dollar since mid-2005, it ignores the most important message of America's macro imbalances: There can be no bilateral fix for multilateral problems of a savings-short economy.

For its part, China needs to be far more cognizant of the responsibilities that come with its role as one of the greatest beneficiaries of Globalization 2.0. Were it not for the explosion of global trade since 2000 and the voracious, albeit bubble-induced, appetite in the United States for goods made in China, the export-led Chinese development miracle simply would not have happened. As is true of its codependent partner, China's thirst for growth has led to unsustainable domestic and international imbalances. As China moves up the growth and development ladder, it is all the more critical that the Chinese face up to these imbalances and take tough feedback from the rest of the world far more seriously.

8

The China Gripe

n May 2012, a few weeks after the annual Strategic and Economic Dialogue (S&ED) between the United States and China, a subcommittee of the Senate Banking Committee held yet another hearing on the U.S.-China relationship.[1] It was hoping to get advice from a panel of experts on the usefulness of the S&ED as a high-level forum of engagement on key policy issues in the economic and foreign affairs arenas. What emerged instead was a bit of classic Washington theater.

I was one of those providing testimony that day, as was an old friend, C. Fred Bergsten, founder of the Peterson Institute for International Economics and one of Washington's most highly sought advisers on international economic policy. He and I used to agree on most issues, but the case of China had driven a wedge between us.

Long a hawk on the Chinese currency issue, Bergsten has consistently called for a sharp one-time revaluation of the renminbi against the dollar. Over the years his testimony has provided much of the ammunition behind the various anti-Chinese currency bills introduced in Congress.

As Bergsten was responding to a question from Senator Michael Bennet of Colorado on a U.S.-China trade dispute over solar panels, the following exchange occurred.

> *Mr. Bergsten:* China cheats. . . . Free trade is good for our economy, but when one country cheats, you want to counter it . . .
> *Mr. Roach:* Just for the record, I strongly object to the word "cheat" to characterize China's behavior as a developing economy.
> *Mr. Bergsten:* I want to reiterate it.

Bergsten went on to elaborate what he meant by cheating. He cited a familiar laundry list of complaints about China, including currency manipulation and subsidized credit for Chinese exporters. Nothing he said surprised anyone in the hearing room, and that's the point. Fred Bergsten personifies an attitude that is pervasive in Washington: the belief that since China does not play by our rules in the economic arena, it should face strong retaliatory actions by the U.S. government. The many who agree with him are not just on Capitol Hill but also include leading academics, as well as many business leaders and senior representatives from labor unions and industry trade associations.

While I objected for the record, I knew that few of the senators present that day were open to the other side of the debate. Republicans and Democrats alike have pretty much made up their minds about China. The U.S. Congress levels a constant barrage of complaints about China's alleged cheating, which it wants to believe has taken a serious toll on the U.S. economy and American workers.

The China Gripe is emblematic of a pervasive mindset that has an important bearing on the two economies' codependency. It shapes public opinion and legislative actions, and also colors Washington's domestic and international economic agenda. The Gripe is also cloaked in suspicion over the legitimacy of China's growth strategy and fears of the inevitable collapse. In assessing the prospects for U.S.-China codependency, it is thus important to have a clear understanding of the validity of these complaints and concerns.

Currency Manipulation

China manages its currency exchange rate. Unlike Japan, which bought into the Plaza Accord of 1985 and effectively outsourced the management of its currency to other industrial economies—ultimately with disastrous consequences—China has elected to keep a tight rein on the renminbi.

Still, management and manipulation are two different things. Nations have long managed their currencies for a variety of reasons. A fixed exchange rate—"pegging" one nation's currency to another—has been viewed by some, like Hong Kong and the United Arab Emirates, as an anchor of macroeconomic stability. Others, especially developing economies like India, Peru, and Pakistan, prefer what is called a "managed float," placing limits on the natural gravity of currency movements in an effort to temper the adverse impacts that foreign exchange market volatility might have on embryonic and vulnerable financial systems and economies.

Manipulation, on the other hand, has a pejorative connotation—implying a deliberate effort to use currency policy to inflict economic damage on others. It is not a concept grounded in economic theory but one that emerges from political considerations at the international and the individual country level.[2] Talk of Chinese currency manipulation has long resonated in the halls of the U.S. Congress. It was a central feature of the original anti-China tariff bills introduced by Senators Charles Schumer and Lindsey Graham in 2005, and of an alternative version offered by Senators Max Baucus and Chuck Grassley in 2006.

The insertion of the manipulation construct into the China currency debate can be traced to the International Monetary Fund. The revised articles of agreement of the IMF—in effect, its constitutional charter—explicitly forbid a country to manipulate its currency to gain unfair competitive advantage.[3] In keeping with this principle, the U.S. Treasury has been required under law since 1988 to issue a semiannual report to the Congress assessing whether any of America's trading partners is guilty of currency manipulation as implied by IMF conventions.[4]

The earliest Treasury reports named several manipulators. The first report, in October 1988, charged South Korea and Taiwan as manipulators, and warnings were issued to Singapore and Hong Kong—which were later elevated to declarations of full manipulator status. China was warned in 1990 and graduated to full manipulator status during 1992–94. And that's pretty much been it, apart from periodic warnings to the abovementioned nations. Since the inception of Treasury's semiannual foreign exchange report, Asian countries stand alone in Washington's search for currency manipulators.

This debate bears critically on the spirit as well as the specifics of U.S.-China codependency. If one party is consciously trying to inflict economic damage on the other, the impact on the other could be serious enough to draw the entire relationship into question. The trick comes in the assessment of motive, especially in being able to make the distinction between the economic and political sources of the alleged manipulation.

Fortunately, Treasury has been mandated by Congress to rely on both multilateral and bilateral trade criteria in rendering a currency manipulation verdict. On that basis, and despite intense bipartisan political pressure to declare China a currency manipulator, it is not hard to see why U.S. authorities have refrained from rendering such a judgment in recent years. Notwithstanding its large and growing *bilateral* imbalance with the United States—albeit, as noted earlier, one that is grounded in America's saving shortfall and is exaggerated by supply chains and Chinese subsidiaries of Western multinationals—China has made great progress in reducing its *multilateral* trade and current account imbalances since 2007. The U.S. Treasury has correctly taken this development into consideration in making an important distinction between China's active management of the renminbi and an outright intent to inflict damage on the U.S. economy.[5]

China's status as a developing economy is an often overlooked consideration in this debate. Even as the second-largest economy in the world, on its way to number one sometime in the next ten to twenty years, China remains far behind in per capita GDP and in the extent of its persistent poverty. It still has an underdeveloped financial system and limited policy tools to cope with the increasing volatility of world financial markets. Flows of financial capital remain restricted both going in and leaving China—meaning that it has only partially opened its capital account. And the renminbi is not a fully convertible currency in foreign exchange markets, meaning that it cannot be freely exchanged in unlimited amounts for other currencies around the world.

These classic characteristics of a developing economy, together with its fixation on stability, have made China unwilling to expose its still fragile system to treacherous global markets. Its reliance on the dollar rather than on its own currency to finance its huge trade surplus has put it, by Stanford economist Ronald McKinnon's reckoning, in the "historically unusual position of being an immature creditor."[6]

Moreover, while China may not be moving its currency as fast as an impatient and troubled world wants, at least there have been significant shifts in the right direction. As noted earlier, the renminbi has appreciated by 35 percent against the dollar since mid-2005, while China's current account surplus has shrunk dramatically, from 10.1 percent of GDP in 2007 to 2.6 percent in 2012.

Largely as a result, the evolution of China's foreign exchange regime has been in keeping with the transitions in its real economy and financial system. From 1993 to 2005, the renminbi was fixed, or pegged, to the dollar. Since then, the country has adopted a managed float. As China's capital markets continue to develop, we should expect further progress on opening the capital account, moving to a convertible currency, and then ultimately adopting a freely floating foreign exchange regime with currency values set in the marketplace. The recent growth of an international, or offshore, renminbi trading market is an important step in that direction, as were mid-2013 hints of accelerated capital account reforms.[7] If China holds to this course, in McKinnon's parlance it will eventually become a more mature creditor, relying less on active currency management and more on market-determined outcomes.

Until then, China's controlled management of its currency seems both wise and prudent in order to insulate an embryonic financial system and a still "unstable and unbalanced" economy from the volatile world it inhabits. Seeking to cushion itself from external instability is very different from accusations of a purposely damaging manipulation.[8] It is also a more palatable conclusion for sustainable codependency with the United States. If these are the footprints of manipulation, China is guilty of a misdemeanor, not a felony.

Unfair Trading Practices

Charges of unfair subsidies, together with the predatory pricing and dumping in international markets they can spawn, have long been key elements

of the China Gripe. State-directed support of the socialist market economy, many believe, tilts the playing field. China's extraordinary competitive leapfrogging would not have happened, goes the argument, were it not
for a wide range of subsidies—ranging from cut-rate finance and prefer-
ential pricing to discriminatory taxes and government-sponsored incuba-
tion of new technologies. Fred Bergsten's imagery of China as a cheater is
grounded in these concerns.

There is no doubt that the parameters, to say nothing of the rules of engagement, of industrial development are very different in a blended system
like China's from those of a free-market economy like that of the United
States. But the question that bears on disputes over the trading practices of
these two codependent nations is a relative one—specifically, measuring
their behavior against the laws and standards of internationally accepted
conventions. Fortunately, there is an objective set of metrics that allows us
to answer the questions of fairness that have been raised over Chinese trading practices.

They come from the "dispute database" of the World Trade Organization, formally established in 1995 as the successor to GATT—the General
Agreement on Tariffs and Trade, which was set up in 1947 as the governance structure for global trade. China's admission to the WTO in 2001,
after long and arduous negotiations ultimately concluded by Premier Zhu
Rongji, was a pivotal event in many ways. It forced China to align its tariff
structure, agricultural subsidies, and export pricing mechanism with global
standards. It even forced harmonization of intellectual property enforcement mechanisms between China and existing WTO members.

But most of all, entry into the WTO put China on notice that it would be
accountable to the rules-based trading system of the West. And it provided
the rest of the organization's members with a process they could rely on to
adjudicate disputes with China over actions that they believed were having
unfair impacts on their economies. In short, it put teeth into the China
Gripe—if the United States has a problem with China's trading practices,
it now knows where to go and how to attempt to resolve the problem. The
record of WTO disputes provides us with hard data with which to measure the validity of this aspect of the gripe. Through the filing of formal
charges and countercharges, a body of evidence has been created over the

past twelve years that provides a candid assessment of how well China has done on this front.

Contrary to the popular storyline, the WTO disputes data do not paint a picture of rampant abuses by China and its companies. Since WTO's formal inception in 1995, a grand total of 455 disputes had been filed with the organization through 2012. China was charged in 30 instances, coming in third behind the United States (119 cases) and the European Union (73). China edged out India (21 cases) and has been on the receiving end of considerably more complaints than Japan (15), South Korea (14), or Mexico (14).[9]

Of the 30 disputes filed against China during its membership in the WTO, half (15) were initiated by the United States. By contrast, China initiated only 8 of the 119 complaints that had been filed against the United States since the inception of the WTO.[10]

Moreover, there were six instances of multiple party claims filed against China (by two or three countries) in its first eleven years in the WTO, usually with the United States and Europe joining forces. That reduces China's dispute count to 19 separate trade issues. WTO panels rendered 6 verdicts against China on these 19 issues.[11] On the other 13 cases—the earliest of which date back to 2008, with most filed since 2010—consultations and final adjudication are still open, not surprising for a long and arduous process, which in most cases takes at least two to three years to run its course.[12] A careful examination of this record points to three key conclusions:

First, the auto parts case of 2006–9, which focused on China's use of tariffs to favor domestic over imported auto parts, forced China to recognize the need for *fair treatment up and down the supply chain*.[13] While it is the hub of Asia's global supply chains, China is not simply an assembler of parts made elsewhere—it still adds much value through domestic production of parts and components. A discriminatory tariff structure that allowed it to insert Chinese-made parts unfairly into its supply chains was struck down. The WTO verdict in this instance affirmed that China had not been playing by the rules of fair and equitable global supply chain economics.

Second, the integrated circuits case of 2004–5—the first WTO dispute initiated against China by the United Sates—bears directly on China's attempts to use its tax code as a back-door means of protecting its newest industries.[14] The United States took issue with China's efforts to rely on value-added tax (VAT) refunds as a means to protect and subsidize an emerging high-tech industry—invariably a key focus in nations like China with activist industrial policies. The WTO dispute panel ruled in favor of the United States, and China agreed to drop the practice. In doing so, China was forced to recognize that *there is a limit in using tax incentives to incubate new industries.*

Third, the 2007–10 intellectual property rights case goes to the heart of one of the loudest complaints of the China Gripe: China's alleged lack of respect for international copyright and trademark laws, and its tolerance of counterfeiting and piracy.[15] As part of its 2001 WTO accession agreement China had agreed to adhere to the Trade-Related Aspects of Intellectual Property Rights conventions (TRIPS). Mounting U.S. concerns over Chinese compliance with these standards resulted in another landmark WTO dispute, with significant rulings against China in the trademarks and copyrights areas. I will discuss this point in greater detail below, but the WTO verdict in this instance sent a powerful message to China that it needs to take seriously the responsibility to *respect the intellectual capital that is embedded in the innovations of others.*

It is also important to note the lessons learned from two lesser WTO disputes brought by the United States against China. In a 2007 case involving tax refunds or exemptions granted to Chinese exporters, the United States and Mexico tried to argue against China's use of tax incentives to promote state-owned enterprise purchases of domestically produced goods over those which could be imported from abroad.[16] Four months into this particular dispute, China agreed to settle and bring its import and export substitution incentives in compliance with WTO standards. Similarly, a 2008 case aimed at Xinhua News Agency's alleged stranglehold on the distribution of news in the Chinese financial services industry was settled before the dispute panel rendered a verdict.[17] Foreign financial information providers such as Bloomberg and Dow Jones were freed from onerous Chinese regulations that had attempted to put their commercial activities under the Xinhua umbrella. Given the limited development of Chinese financial markets at the time, the broader consequences of this agreement were minimal.

Meticulous research by Gary Clyde Hufbauer and Jared Woollacott of the Peterson Institute for International Economics largely corroborates these findings.[18] They highlight eight WTO disputes brought by the United States against China over the 2001–10 period, noting findings in favor of the United States in all eight. While this count exceeds the six judgments against China noted above, the discrepancy is largely technical, coming in two disputes where the verdict was either mixed (a 2007 complaint over Chinese restrictions on the distribution of audiovisual and print media) or still open (a 2009 complaint over Chinese restrictions of raw materials exports).

Hufbauer and Woollacott also detail the U.S. trade actions against China that have been taken outside the WTO framework—specifically, antidumping measures, countervailing duties, and intellectual property–related actions.[19] Putting it all together, there can be no mistaking the numerous complaints over unfair trading practices that have leveled by the United States against China since 2001. But Hufbauer and Woollacott make their most important contribution by placing an order of magnitude on the total volume of trade flows associated with these disputes. In 2009 they found that just 12 percent of the two-way trade between the United States and China was so affected, a nontrivial amount, to be sure, but hardly validation of the charge of widespread cheating leveled against China by the authors' boss, none other than Fred Bergsten, at the time director of the Peterson Institute of International Economics.

The wheels of progress often turn slowly. Such is the case with the trade dispute mechanism. So far, it has forced China to face up to serious transgressions in three key areas—supply chain economics, industrial policy, and intellectual property rights. This is progress. Given its success rate, the real question is why the West hasn't used the WTO more often.[20]

Intellectual Property Rights

While the WTO dispute arbitration process has led to some meaningful progress in addressing some of the more contentious aspects of China's behavior in the global economy, postsettlement compliance and enforcement remain real issues. Nowhere is that more obvious than in the critical area of intellectual property rights (IPR). Despite the WTO settlement on copyright and trademark infringement in 2010, there are still reports of a steady stream of Chinese piracy and other forms of intellectual property theft.[21] For a long time, the rule in China seemed to be that anything goes, from knockoff clothing and golf clubs to pirated DVDs and software. Add in frequent claims of industrial espionage and cyberattacks (discussed below), and it's a wonder that any foreign company would do business in China.

But the numbers suggest otherwise. Over the decade ending in 2012, $1.5 trillion of foreign direct investment poured into China from companies around the world, an inflow second only to that going into the United States.[22] If intellectual property theft in China is as serious a threat as the anecdotes suggest, why were foreign companies so eager to place so much of their capital and core technologies at such obvious risk?

The answer is that foreign companies have more or less learned to live with this problem. When they set up operations in any offshore market, they understand that their business models and practices—including proprietary design and production technologies—will eventually be assimilated in the foreign economies where they operate. Foreign direct investment does not come with an ironclad cocoon of permanent insulation.

In China, the veil of intellectual property protection may be more porous than elsewhere, but apparently that has not deterred countless multinational corporations from taking advantage of China's lower costs or seeking access to its potentially large domestic markets. The data on foreign intellectual property complaints also offer some support for this point. A recent study of Chinese patent infringement cases in 2010 concludes that just 4.3 percent of them involved at least one foreign party—hardly an overwhelming outcry from an exploited world.[23]

All this is not to say that intellectual property violations aren't a serious problem in China. Nearly forty-three thousand civil IPR cases were filed in the local people's courts in 2010—40 percent more than were filed in 2009.[24] Of course, there are two ways to interpret these trends: One, there is a raging epidemic of intellectual property theft in China. Or two, China's judicial system is now rising to the challenge in bringing such a large number of these cases to court.

The truth is probably somewhere in between. China does have a major and worrisome problem with IPR. In that important sense, the China Gripe

is accurate. But the legal actions on Chinese intellectual property infringement have been largely between domestic litigants. Foreign party–initiated
actions have been relatively few. While this may suggest that that foreign
companies are willing to put up with a lot in order to establish toeholds
in domestic Chinese markets—consistent with surging foreign direct investment into China—it may also suggest that the violations are less of a
problem than commonly perceived in the West. Without minimizing the
IPR threat, it is fair to observe that it has yet to derail U.S.-China codependency. Of course, that doesn't mean such a derailment can't happen in the
future—a possibility that looms especially large in light of the recent escalation of cyberhacking, which will be discussed shortly.

Irrespective of the sources of the IPR complaints—domestic or foreign—
the judicial system data indicate that Chinese authorities have stepped up
their efforts to tackle the issue. That is an encouraging development. Compliance with the 2010 WTO verdict on intellectual property infringement
appears to have played an important role in this new emphasis. Stepped-
up Chinese compliance efforts demonstrate that the WTO's rules-based
pressures, which have resulted in confiscation of pirated products, legal actions against copycat producers, and stricter enforcement of international
copyright and patent laws, can actually lead to a modification of Chinese
behavior.[25]

But another motive is probably at work. As China recognizes that its
growth potential will increasingly depend on its future successes as a
knowledge-based economy, it knows that it will not be able to get away
with a double standard on intellectual property protection. Just as the world
needs assurances from China that it will respect these rights, the Next
China will need the same from others.[26]

China is already focusing on just such a future. Its patents are surging
as it lays the foundation for a transition to a knowledge-based economy.
In 2010, it granted 135,000 new patents—up 25 percent from 2009 and
now third in the world behind Japan and the United States. Between 1995
and 2008, China accounted for 35.6 percent of the global growth in patent filings; the United States accounted for 22 percent over the same time
period.[27] Like other aspects in its sprint to development, China has come a
long way in its emerging patent leadership in a very short time.

It is only a matter of time before China will develop a full complement of national brands whose owners will insist that their trademarks and patents receive protection. This is an important aspect of any consumer society. As China makes the transition from the producer to the consumer model, brand awareness—and brand protection—will probably get much greater emphasis. That means China will face a serious challenge in protecting its own intellectual property. It must ensure that its scientists, innovators, and entrepreneurs enjoy the same legal safeguards as others in the world. But it can't expect this quid pro quo if it doesn't live up to its own obligations to respect foreign intellectual property.

A final, and controversial, aspect of the intellectual property piece of the China Gripe also needs airing. In a still poor developing economy with a large and very fragmented population, Chinese enforcement of antipiracy laws is very challenging. Knockoff production lines can spring up quickly in remote locations, and go in and out of business rapidly.[28] The lack of a well-developed rule of law and local monitoring and compliance procedures make it exceedingly difficult to limit such activities.

That raises thorny comparative issues. Today's advanced industrial economies, when they were at a stage of economic development equivalent to China's, were little better at protecting intellectual property.[29] The history of American and European patent and copyright compliance is replete with flagrant abuses of technology transfers.[30] Early in the Industrial Revolution, transgressions ranged from industrial espionage to illegal recruitment and even kidnapping of foreign workers with knowledge of proprietary production techniques. Later abuses included limited enforcement of foreign intellectual property rights, trademark counterfeiting, and "trivial" and "interlocking" patents that resulted in false claims of proprietary products and ideas.[31] Largely out of recognition of these precedents, developing economies have been granted some transitional leeway on matters of TRIPS compliance to WTO rules.[32] Whether this dispensation is fair in light of the historical record of today's developed nations remains a contentious question.

The speed of Chinese development only compounds this problem. China has had to come into conformity with global IPR standards in a relatively short period of time. Unlike that of the developed world, which has been steeped in a culture of intellectual property protection since the fifteenth century, the legal framework in China is all very new.[33] The first Chinese patent law came into force only in 1985, and it hardly brought an immediate sea change of understanding and acceptance. In the early years after the law's enactment, few inside China even understood what it meant. None of this is an excuse for China to receive special dispensation on intellectual property enforcement. But it does help us understand the context of the task it faces in coping with this key aspect of the China Gripe.

Cyberhacking

Cybercrimes are sweeping the world—a clear testament to the dark side of Globalization 2.0. Particularly worrisome is a sharp escalation of computer and network hacking, a forcible intrusion into secure information-based technology systems of governments, companies, and defense establishments. According to data monitored by Akami Technologies, Inc., a leading computer security company, "attack traffic" involving its customers around the world surged by more than 200 percent in 2012. A Verizon survey reveals that the top three "threat actors" were China (accounting for 30 percent of such incursions), followed by Romania (28 percent) and the United States (18 percent).[34]

China's cyberhacking activities have been the subject of intense focus in the Western media, especially the incursions allegedly sponsored by the Chinese military that appear to be aimed at a broad cross section of U.S. companies and defense installations.[35] Initial accusations of such attacks were largely focused on specific incidents and circumstantial evidence pertaining to the scope of China's cyberwarfare capabilities, as well as to the military ties of Chinese technology companies and educational institutions.[36] But the precise trail of such activity—especially Chinese intrusions into U.S. systems—was not clearly delineated.[37]

That has changed on the heels of a detailed investigation released in 2013 by Mandiant, a private cybersecurity company, that revealed a systematic pattern of Chinese-sponsored cyberattacks on the United States over a multiyear time frame—attacks that have been traced to a Shanghai-based cyberespionage unit embedded in the People's Liberation Army (PLA).[38]

These charges are consistent with a recent report of the U.S. Department of Defense, which concludes that "the Chinese utilize a large, well-organized network to facilitate collection of sensitive information and export-controlled technology from U.S. defense sources."[39]

Chinese officials have disputed the evidence and have claimed that their country has also been subjected to a surge of U.S.-sponsored cyberattacks against their public institutions, as well as their military and defense facilities.[40] Recent revelations of extensive cyberespionage activities by the U.S. National Security Agency (NSA)—especially the so-called PRISM and TAO (Tailor Access Operations) programs—add credence to these claims and suggest that America's cyberhacking efforts may well be comparable to those of the Chinese.[41]

This issue poses a serious threat to the stability of U.S.-Chinese co-dependency. Unlike the currency and unfair–trade practices issues, the cyberhacking threat does not lend itself to a long process of adjudication. As a potential national security risk, it must be addressed immediately. It has already prompted high-level military talks between the two countries, as well as the establishment of a working group of senior officials from both governments. It has also sparked the introduction of a cyberterrorism bill in the United States Senate that is basically directed at China.[42]

This development could drive a major wedge between the two nations. Deployment of increasingly sophisticated cyberhacking capabilities as a medium of intellectual property theft raises a host of issues, including the acquisition by China's PLA of new military offensive capability aimed at neutralizing the clear advantage currently held by America's powerful arsenal of information technology–enabled weaponry. In addition, it poses a new threat to U.S. job security by targeting the intellectual property that defines the innovations-based core competencies of corporate America.

Cyberhacking also bears directly on one of the most dramatic characteristics of China's development—competitive leapfrogging. The examples discussed in Chapter 6 focused on the information technology and telecommunications and equipment industries and were set in the pre-cyber era of the 1990s. But the 2013 Mandiant report alleges that Chinese hacking is also being aimed at four industries in the United States that are counterparts of China's new strategic emerging industries featured so prominently in the Twelfth Five-Year Plan.[43] If such SEI initiatives are, indeed, facilitated by cyberhacking, leapfrogging risks becoming an illegal shortcut that deserves prompt adjudication in the WTO.

Notwithstanding these concerns from the U.S. side, as reiterated by Vice President Joe Biden at the July 2013 U.S.-China Strategic and Economic Dialogue, Washington has lost the high ground on this very sensitive issue. Disclosure of extensive NSA cyberespionage activities involving America's allies in Europe, Japan, South America, and the Middle East makes U.S. claims especially audacious. U.S. Secretary of State John Kerry's retort that such activities are "not unusual for lots of nations" is symptomatic of the classic denial and hypocrisy of codependency.[44] It is hard for the United States to demand accountability from the Chinese when there is culpability on both sides of this equation.

Despite the growing threats of cyberhacking, it is important not to lose sight of the tradeoffs between the openness required of an innovations-based culture and protection of computer-based repositories of knowledge. If the United States were now to err on the side of moving to a more closed architecture in response to Chinese hacking, it might put the very process of knowledge creation at risk—undermining one of America's greatest competitive strengths.[45] Before rushing to judgment, Washington needs to think carefully about this strategic imperative.

China, for its part, has good reason to address the cybersecurity issue, especially if it wants to move up the value chain and embrace the knowledge- and innovations-based activities that are identified in the Twelfth Five-Year Plan. As noted earlier, when the Chinese develop intellectual property of their own, including but not limited to SEI initiatives, they, too, will demand protection for their newfound innovations under the provisions of international patent and copyright laws.

The epidemic of cyberhacking is no doubt here to stay. As senior Google executives Eric Schmidt and Jared Cohen put it, "This is a cat-and-mouse game that will play out as long as the Internet exists."[46] The growing prevalence of long, complex, and vulnerable global supply chains, in which China plays a central role, only adds to the temptations of hackers. All this points to a worrisome bottom line on cyberhacking: The United States and China are both aggressors in this area, deepening a growing sense of distrust that can only destabilize the codependency between the two nations. The gripe, in this case, is both legitimate and serious—and one that both countries have in common.

Collapse

In 2001, an American lawyer of Chinese descent named Gordon Chang published a book entitled *The Coming Collapse of China*.[47] On the cusp of China's WTO accession, Chang warned that the PRC had between five and ten years before the Communist Party fell from power amid social and economic chaos. During the next ten years, China averaged 10 percent annual growth in its GDP, with no signs that the Party was losing its grip on power.

It is unfair to single out Gordon Chang. I've certainly had my share of bad calls. But Chang personifies a cottage industry of China doubters who have long predicted the demise of the Chinese economy. The reasons vary: Property bubbles, a banking crisis, corruption, social unrest, human rights violations, and environmental catastrophes are all woven into the fabric of gripping China-collapse scenarios. China's persistent refusal to succumb to these crises hasn't silenced the disaster crowd.

No discussion of the China Gripe would be complete without a look at these claims. They certainly bear on the prospects of codependency between the United States and China. If a disaster is around the corner for China, its relationship with the United States would obviously be radically altered. Here we explore three leading doomsday scenarios.

The property bubble. One pundit famously said that China is "Dubai times a thousand."[48] In other words, if you thought the bursting of the property bubble in Dubai was bad, wait until it happens in China.

Chinese officials would be the first to concede that there have been speculative excesses in the nation's residential property markets in recent years. That's why they have clamped down. The latest restrictions on property market excesses began in earnest in April 2010, when the government implemented new regulations aimed at curtailing multiple property purchases by speculators. Down payment requirements that had been set at 20 percent were raised to 30 percent for a first home, 50 percent for a second home, and 100 percent for purchases of a third or subsequent unit.

Since then, even in the face of slowing overall GDP growth in 2011–12, the government has kept its focus and has continued to limit the availability of credit to high-end property developers in China's dozen or so first-tier cities.

The campaign has worked. By mid-2012, home prices were declining at a modest rate in fifty of the seventy cities that China monitors on a monthly basis. Yet this "soft landing" in the residential property market hardly portends the dreaded crash landing in the broader economy that many seem to fear from a bursting of the Chinese property bubble and a precipitous plunge in home prices.

Property market concerns fit into a deeper aspect of the China Gripe, fears of a massive investment overhang in the real economy. It is true that total fixed investment is approaching an unprecedented 50 percent of Chinese GDP—well in excess of investment shares that historically have been recorded by other major economies. But this is not nearly as serious a problem as many in the West maintain.

First of all, real estate accounts for only about 15–20 percent of total fixed investment in China—or no more than 10 percent of the overall GDP. Moreover, in terms of floor space completed, residential properties make up about half of China's total real estate investment. That means residential property investment accounts for no more than 5 percent of Chinese GDP and considerably less than that for the speculative high-end properties concentrated in the so-called first-tier cities in coastal China. A major fall in the value of such properties would not, by itself, do extensive damage to the Chinese economy.

Still, a fear of property bubbles is certainly understandable—especially in light of what has recently happened in the United States and parts of Europe—to say nothing of the bursting of a monstrous property bubble in Japan in the early 1990s. But China differs from these economies in one important respect: Its demand for shelter is underpinned by the most powerful urbanization in modern history.

The urban share of the Chinese population reached 51.3 percent in 2011, exceeding 50 percent for the first time in history, and rose further to 52.6 percent in 2012. As recently as 1980, the urban share was below 20 percent. By adding between 15 million and 20 million people a year to its cities, China is expected to increase its urban population by more than 300 million people—essentially equal to the current U.S. population—by 2030. That's slightly different from Dubai, where a monstrous property bubble rested on an indigenous population base of just 1.3 million citizens.

With urbanization on that scale and at that speed, China has no choice but to run a high investment economy. Urbanization requires shelter, commercial and office buildings, and infrastructure—all of which must be in place before new citizens arrive. That puts the criticism of China's high-investment economy in a very different light. Investment is the means toward an end—the end, in this case, is the stock of productive capital that any economy needs to drive longer-term productivity and growth. Thirty years ago, in the aftermath of the Cultural Revolution, that stock was negligible. Despite surging investment since then, China's stock of capital remains woefully deficient, especially when measured against the steady growth of its urban workforce, where productivity potential is of greatest importance. That suggests China will need to run a high-investment economy for years to come.[49]

Many warnings about the property-bubble syndrome point to "ghost cities" in places like Ordos, Inner Mongolia—largely uninhabited by human beings—as an example of China's excesses. Yet ghost cities are not uncommon in China. In fact, they are the rule as China moves preemptively to build new cities in order to absorb its extraordinary influx of new urban residents. Shanghai, Pudong, was China's first well-known example in the 1990s. It now has a population of some 5.5 million. According to a recent study by McKinsey, by 2025, more than 220 Chinese cities will have at least one million people living in them.[50] That would be nearly double the current count, and about eight times the number that currently exist in the United States. At that rate, China will have to construct between another fifty and one hundred urban complexes in the next two decades to absorb the influx of new dwellers. All in all, high anxiety over the bursting of a massive Chinese property bubble is seriously exaggerated.

The banking crisis. China has a relatively new banking system that, despite its short history, has experienced several major problems. Commercial banking didn't commence in earnest until the mid-1980s, when four large state-owned banks were carved out of the central bank. With a lending function that was largely akin to that of a fiscal agent—directing state-appropriated "policy loans" to state-owned enterprises—bank lending officers had little experience in distinguishing between good and bad credit. As a result, China's banks were plagued by nonperforming loans—eventually requiring capital injections totaling around 4 trillion renminbi, or 25 percent of GDP, in the first half of the 2000s.[51]

After that, the Chinese banking system got its act together. Bad loans were transferred to newly constituted asset management companies and auctioned off at market-clearing prices. The newly recapitalized major banks subsequently reduced their exposure to poor quality credit. System-wide, nonperforming bank loans fell to less than 2 percent of total assets by 2010—well below the 4 percent to 5 percent that is the norm in the developed world.[52]

The improvement in the publicly stated loan quality of Chinese banks masked a deterioration in off–balance sheet credits that occurred during the Great Crisis of 2008–9, when banks were asked to fund much of China's massive 4 trillion renminbi fiscal stimulus. This was accomplished in a clandestine fashion, with lending largely channeled through bonds issued by local government investment vehicles (LGIVs). According to the Chinese Banking and Regulatory Commission, local government debt totaled USD $1.7 trillion at the end of 2010—equal to approximately 30 percent of Chinese GDP, not much different from bad loan exposure during the banking crisis a decade earlier.[53]

It turns out that about half of these loans were on the banks' books before the Great Crisis. But with the local government revenue stream under pressure from the crisis-induced slowing of the economy and the drying up of property transactions, the LGIVs' debt-servicing capacity became increasingly problematic. By the end of 2010, the Chinese Banking and Regulatory Commission admitted that about 20 percent of the LGIV lending, or 2–3 trillion renminbi, could be classified as nonperforming. Conversely, that means about 80 percent of the new lending was judged to be credit worthy, not surprising since about three-fourths of the late 2008 stimulus was directed at infrastructure. Like the exaggerated fears of the housing bubble, bank-directed support to infrastructure spending must be seen in the context of China's massive urbanization. While many of these projects suffer short-term cash-flow shortfalls that would classify them as nonperforming loans by Western standards, their longer-term economics look much stronger. Still, the bad loans that piled up in the aftermath of the Great Crisis are enough to boost China's nonperforming bank loan exposure to roughly 6 percent of Chinese GDP—not a trivial figure, but not likely to bring down the economy.

Finally, China has a liquid banking system that can withstand anything but a major crash in the real economy. The systemwide loan-to-deposit ratio is now about 65 percent—well below the 120 percent that caused problems elsewhere in Asia in the late 1990s and more recently in Europe.[54] China's financial sector is far from perfect. There has been an increase in low-quality bank lending since late 2008. But fears of a major banking crisis are vastly overblown.

Corruption. China's corruption is deep-rooted and systemic. It is a serious problem. But the question at hand is whether corruption has the potential to bring the economy down or have a material bearing on the codependency between the U.S. and Chinese economies. The answer is, no.

Corruption in China has long been viewed as an outgrowth of the traditional tension between local and central power. In Wen Jiabao's terminology, it stems from the third of the Four Uns—an uncoordinated system. Fragmented societies tend to coalesce around disparate power blocs, and China is a case in point. Because it lacks a well-developed rule of law and the political accountability of a multiparty system, its power blocs tend to live by their own rules. All too often, these rules have been compromised. Just as the localization of power bred corruption in the Ming and Qing dynasties,[55] the same has occurred in modern China, with its many inbred relationships between local Party officials and business leaders.

Media attention to Chinese corruption tends to be dominated by sensational accounts of high-profile cases. The so-called "recent events in Chongqing"—as the events surrounding the fall of Bo Xilai are still depicted in official circles—is the latest such example, as is the all too predictable anticorruption backlash led by Premier Wen Jiabao discussed in Chapter 4.[56] In 2006 it was Chen Liangyu, former Party secretary and mayor of Shanghai, who was sent to prison for bribery and embezzlement of public pension funds. In 1995 it was Beijing Party Secretary Chen Xitong. And so on.

While it makes for great reading, the litany of these high-profile cases detracts from a more basic and insidious aspect of the problem—the profusion of corruption among lower-level bureaucrats and local officials. According to statistics compiled by the People's Procuratorate (China's state court system), in 2010–11 an average of almost thirty-five thousand individuals per year settled criminal charges of corruption, bribery, misappropriation of public funds, fraud, and abuse of power.[57] While that's about 8 percent higher than the number who settled such charges over the prior three years, 2007–9, there is good reason to believe that the corruption problem could be a good deal worse than these statistics suggest: Missing in this tally are the equally alarming reports of widespread corruption in the Chinese military.[58]

China's new senior leadership has singled out corruption as a major issue on its policy agenda. Xi Jinping, the newly installed general secretary of the Chinese Communist Party, warned in no uncertain terms on assuming the reins of power in November 2012 that corruption could lead to "the collapse of the Party and the downfall of the state."[59] Wang Qishan, one of seven members of the new Standing Committee of the Politburo, China's most senior Party leaders, has been given operational responsibility for the anticorruption campaign as chairman of the Central Discipline Inspection Commission. The combination of Wang's record as a credible and forceful reformer in financial and economic matters and Xi's commitment from the top is encouraging, although the burden of proof obviously will be on them to deliver.[60]

Finally, and contrary to what many might expect, the global metrics of corruption don't flag China for special attention. It has long scored reasonably well on the Corruption Perceptions Index assembled by Transparency International.[61] Compared with other nations in the so-called BRIC group, China, ranking 80th on corruption out of 176 countries in the world in 2012, placed lower than Brazil (69th) but higher than India (94th) and well above Russia (133rd). Its overall corruption score has improved significantly since the mid-1990s. In fact, since 1996, China has enjoyed the greatest improvement in corruption perception of all the BRIC nations; Brazil was second, followed by India, while Russia has consistently been ranked as the most corrupt BRIC and near the bottom in the worldwide rankings.

To be sure, the broad metrics don't do justice to this aspect of the China

Gripe. Nor does the familiar refrain "everybody does it." For China, as for any nation, it doesn't work to excuse corruption by hiding behind the worse examples of others. It makes little difference whether there are tendencies toward corruption elsewhere around the world. The point is that the core principles of governance and economic management can be undermined by the corruption of power. For China, on the cusp of a critical strategic change in its growth model, that is the bottom line.

While corruption hasn't created serious problems for the Chinese economy in the recent past, it may do so the future. Corrupt decision making didn't derail the old producer model because it was more or less subsumed in the state-directed resource allocation of a blended system. But the coming era of consumer-led growth, where there is greater empowerment of the public voice, could be very different. In moving from a producer model to a consumer society, the Next China will undoubtedly have to take corruption far more seriously.

So What's Really the Gripe?

China is far from perfect—especially in the eyes of those in American academic, policy, and business circles who view the Chinese economy as a threat to American renewal and prosperity. Struggling middle-class American workers also increasingly look at the Chinese growth juggernaut with considerable trepidation. But there is a difference between concerns and complaints. The trick is in the important distinction between legitimate gripes and misperceptions.

Misperceptions of China stem from the confluence of two things: the problems of the U.S. economy and the sharp contrasts between the two systems. The blended Chinese model—the socialist market economy—operates by a different set of rules from the market-based system that underpins the U.S. economy. The disparities are many: standards of living, political systems, the roles of strategy and planning, demographic constraints, urbanization, stability mandates, and saving imbalances, just to name a few. Sometimes these contrasts work to the advantage of codependency—each economy offers something the other is missing—but not always. A tough economic climate in the United States is especially likely to bring out conflict.

The China Gripe arises out of this combination of difficult times and contrasts between the two systems. History is also a factor—especially the disturbing imagery of a militaristic Red China of the 1950s and 1960s. Out of this combination of context, contrasts, and history, the China Gripe has been a dark cloud looming over the nation's codependent relationship with the United States.

While there is clear legitimacy to many of the concerns embedded in the gripe, there is also considerable exaggeration. China's foreign exchange rate is managed in order to maintain stability, not manipulated to inflict damage on the United States. China has indeed used industrial policy in ways that disadvantage other nations, but WTO membership is forcing it to conform to global norms in tradable goods and in the protection of intellectual property rights. Its violations are far from trivial on both counts, but research shows that a relatively small portion of cross-border trade between the two economies has been adversely affected. Nor is the Chinese economy facing the imminent crisis that many fear. Neither property bubbles nor the banking system nor corruption threatens an imminent collapse. Of all the concerns that have given rise to the Gripe, charges of cyberterrorism are the most disconcerting—but they raise serious questions about the trustworthiness of both America's and China's engagement with the rapidly shifting technologies of Globalization 2.0. They must be taken seriously—both by China's new leadership and by senior government officials in the United States and elsewhere in the world.

As with any economy, there are, of course, many other things that can go wrong in China or that Americans can find distasteful about China. Human rights issues, environmental degradation and pollution, and widening income inequalities are just a few of the issues that have gotten considerable attention both inside and outside of China. These are all serious problems that pose immense challenges to China and its system of governance. In particular, history does not look kindly on regimes that have ignored human rights and corruption. There is good reason to engage and push China to see these problems from a different perspective. That they have not yet derailed the modern development miracle does not mean that can't happen in the future.

In the end, however, the Gripe is more an attitude than anything else. Accusations of cheating testify to a destructive erosion in this attitude. Where that comes from says as much about the character of the United States as it does about China. The distortion of China's faults is both an outgrowth of the disaffection inside of America and a candid and objective assessment of the flaws of the Chinese system.

Yet there is a real risk that perception becomes reality insofar as the China Gripe is concerned. Republicans and Democrats alike demonized China during a highly contentious U.S. presidential campaign in 2012. Such bipartisan vilification won't fade quickly. To the contrary, there is the distinct possibility that it could poison the well and do lasting damage to the American public's impressions of its codependent partner. Sustainable codependency means learning to live with each other—finding a common ground and putting the Gripe in perspective. That means being tough when necessary, but also knowing where to draw the line. Until or unless that happens, the Gripe can become reality and the relationship can only suffer.

PART IV

WARNING SHOTS

THE MARRIAGE BETWEEN China and the United States was never bliss-
ful. Now they are at risk of going their separate ways. That's due as much
to America's angst as to China's newfound strength. Sustainable codependency, especially a version based on trust and mutual respect, is a tall order
for any two economies. The dream of a lasting partnership—a new symbiosis
in a globalized world—was at best a passing fancy. But unless China and the
United States establish a more mature and constructive relationship, there is
a real risk of a major breakup—the ultimate betrayal of codependency.

The immediate challenge for both nations is to figure out how to cope
with the aftermath of a wrenching string of crises and face up to the imperatives of postcrisis rebalancing. The Great Crisis and its aftermath have
triggered significant and protracted shortfalls in economic activity in the
developed world, threatening the external demand that underpins China's
export-led growth model. The Chinese leadership understands the implications of this upheaval. It knows full well that while its current strategy

has delivered spectacularly over the past thirty years, these results were an outgrowth of a powerful surge in global demand and trade that has now fizzled out.

The Great Crisis, together with increasingly worrisome internal imbalances, is a clarion warning to China that the old model must be rethought. Changing from export- and investment-led growth to a model that derives more support from internal private consumption is its most obvious and really its only sustainable answer. Acceptance of structural change is equally vital, but much harder to come by, in the United States. In large part, that reflects America's strategy deficit. Unlike China, the United States doesn't believe in strategies framed around multiyear plans. To the contrary, it looks with great disdain on meddlesome intervention by the state and instead places trust in the inherent magic of its market-based system to come up with the right formula for employment, income generation, wealth creation, and resource allocation.

Unfortunately, it is no longer clear that America's hands-off approach to economic management is capable of delivering as it has in the past. Washington has an intellectual understanding of the imperatives to save more and spend less, but it lacks the political will to do so. Inertia remains a powerful force in U.S. political and policy circles, where the consensus is still focused on re-creating yet another round of consumer-led growth. If that mindset prevails, the Next America could very much resemble the Last America—saddled with the excesses of domestic demand, a persistent shortfall of saving, never-ending current account and budget deficits, and the risk of another wrenching crisis. Under those circumstances, sustainability would become the biggest risk for postcrisis America—as it is for China.

In the fourth part of the book I focus on many of the forces putting codependency under pressure—both fact and fiction. The tensions of a crisis-prone world are in many respects a powerful signaling mechanism as to what went wrong in both China and the United States. The United States paid a huge price for an unsustainable consumption binge, and China tied its successes far too much to America's excesses. The Great Crisis and its aftershocks are all about the unwinding of those excesses. They provide an unmistakable wake-up call to both nations that the old growth models were not built to last.

A nightmare can also be a wake-up call—usually a frightening one. And there is one big nightmare that has long been lurking in the subconscious state of the codependent relationship between the United States and China: mounting trade frictions, protectionism, and a repeat of the devastating trade war of the 1930s. This possibility is explored through a "dream analysis"—not to bring Freud and Jung into our psychodrama but to underscore how such a bad dream could actually come true in today's vulnerable and insecure world.

It is always tempting to dismiss such disasters as unthinkable. Why would either nation be so foolish as to fall into one of modern history's worst traps? Yet a similar complacency led to the excesses that culminated in the Great Crisis of 2008–9, as well as to the subsequent pyrotechnics in Europe. In that respect, it is critical not to lose sight of the destructive effects of the Smoot-Hawley tariff of 1930 and the devastating impacts they had in sparking a full-blown global trade war. There is a nontrivial chance that a comparable blunder lurks in the dark shadows of U.S.-China codependency. The lesson is painfully clear: Never say never, especially when there are plenty of warning signs that the unthinkable is, in fact, becoming dishearteningly thinkable.

9

Imbalances and the Great Crisis

I t was the ultimate consumer who hit the wall first. In the aftermath of the Lehman Brothers bankruptcy in September 2008, a festering economic crisis turned into a catastrophic meltdown. Two bursting bubbles—property and credit—fed on each other and U.S. consumer demand plunged as never before. It was a capitulation heard around the world. An interdependent, unbalanced global economy was brought to its knees.

For the vast majority of policy makers and politicians, who had come to believe that imbalances either didn't matter or were sustainable indefinitely, the Great Crisis came as an especially rude awakening. With the deficit spender in free fall, the world's surplus savers, long dependent on exports to support their growth machines, were quickly in trouble. The crisis-driven collapse in aggregate demand sparked by the downfall of the American consumer had brought down the global house of cards. Suddenly, the imbalances that most considered benign had put the interdependent global economy and its systemically impaired financial system in a vise. There was nowhere to hide.

China was hardly spared. By late 2008, it had entered the functional equivalent of recession. Its economy was at a virtual standstill, and layoffs were mounting on a massive scale. Long fixated on social stability, China responded with an aggressive stimulus program, and the economy bounced back smartly in the second half of 2009. But the stimulus was not without consequences. It compounded many of China's precrisis imbalances and sowed the seeds for new risks.

With hindsight, it is now painfully clear that years of unbalanced growth in the world economy were a recipe for disaster. A vocal minority shared a sense of foreboding that the lopsided pattern of global economic growth was unsustainable.[1] But few thought the end was imminent. Cassandra is never heard in good times. Only when the crisis arrives and the denial cracks does the obvious actually penetrate most people's thinking.

The Great Crisis of 2008–9, and the Great Recession it triggered, should have been wake-up calls for the restoration of economic sanity. Yet there is little reason to believe that the authorities understood that. They certainly didn't in Washington, where postcrisis policies of massive monetary and fiscal stimulus were aimed at rekindling the animal spirits and the reckless risk taking of bruised and battered consumers. They also didn't appear to get it in Beijing, where Chinese officials drew on postcrisis stimulus measures that only exacerbated the Four Uns of Wen Jiabao.

Yet what if the orthodox reflationary policy initiatives work, or at least deliver a recovery in economic growth that for a while resembles those of the past? Can the world economy take another bout of unbalanced growth led by still overextended American consumers and equally unbalanced Chinese producers? Do political considerations—short-term election cycles in the United States and an undercurrent of pressures on China's one-party system—encourage the authorities to opt for yet another bout of false prosperity? The Great Crisis is a strong warning that the world should do everything in its power to avoid such a reckless gambit. Can China and the United States resist that temptation?

Game Over for the American Consumer

The Great Recession is called that with good reason: It hit with a vengeance few had ever seen. For the American consumer, the biggest consumer in the world and a significant portion of the external demand that sustained the Chinese economy, it was game over. Over the six-quarter period from the first quarter of 2008 through the second quarter of 2009, U.S. personal consumption expenditures fell, in inflation-adjusted terms, at a 1.8 percent average annual rate. While a 1.8 percent annualized decline doesn't sound like much, it was the worst contraction in consumer demand in the post–World War II American economy.

U.S. consumer demand had of course fallen in earlier business cycles. But those declines were fleeting and far less severe. The only thing close in terms of order of magnitude came in 1980, on the heels of the Federal Reserve's ill-conceived imposition of credit controls in a desperate effort to contain a serious inflation problem. In the second quarter of that year, real consumption plunged at an 8.7 percent annual rate. But the Fed quickly abandoned that effort and the consumer snapped back.

Other than that, consumer downturns were generally mild and short-lived—contractions in "hard-goods" spending on items such as motor vehicles, furniture, and appliances were tempered by sustained spending on such basic necessities as food, shelter, and utilities. The U.S. economy would suffer periodic recessions, but the resilient consumer was the bulwark of the nation's cyclical defenses.

Then came the Great Recession. After an unprecedented sixty-four consecutive quarters of growth in real consumption expenditures—from the first quarter of 1992 through the final quarter of 2007—the American consumer pulled back as never before. The weakening actually predated the pyrotechnics of the Lehman failure, but it was relatively gentle at first—with inflation-adjusted consumption recording "zero growth" in the first half of 2008. Then the wheels came off: back-to-back declines averaging 3.8 percent in the last two quarters of 2008, followed by aftershocks of 1.5 percent average annualized declines in the first two quarters of 2009. The carnage over that four-quarter period—a 2.7 percent contraction in real U.S. personal consumption expenditures from mid-2008 to mid-2009—was unprecedented in modern history.

Not surprisingly, it devastated the broader economy. The unemployment rate shot up from 4.9 percent in early 2008 to 10 percent by October 2009, as businesses shed 8.8 million jobs in just two years. The recession gathered force with extraordinary speed. At the worst point, the inflation-adjusted gross national product (real GDP) fell at an 8.3 percent average annual rate in the fourth quarter of 2008 followed by a 5.4 percent drop in the first quarter of 2009—the sharpest back-to-back quarterly declines for the U.S. economy in the postwar era.

By the time the dust settled, real GDP had dropped by 4.3 percent from its peak in late 2007, before hitting bottom in mid-2009. The contraction was more than double the 1.9 percent norm of the previous eight post–World War II downturns, and it lasted about seven months longer. It shattered all records in the annals of modern U.S. business cycle history.[2]

Much has been made over the linkage between the Great Crisis and the Great Recession. Recessions in the aftermath of financial crises, go the logic and the research that underpins it, are always severe.[3] Where there is a big crisis there is almost always a big recession. But this painful experience also carries a deeper lesson.

In this case, the financial crisis poured high-octane fuel on a fire that had been smoldering for years. The American consumer had long been overdependent on two massive bubbles—property and credit. Both were going to burst, crisis or not. And in fact that bursting was well under way before the Great Crisis hit in autumn 2008. The housing bubble had started to deflate in late 2006, and the credit bubble was punctured in the summer of 2007, when the subprime mortgage market first came under pressure.

At first, the bursting of the twin bubbles seemed to give off only a gentle hissing sound. But between the failure of Bear Stearns in March 2008 and the bankruptcy of Lehman Brothers six months later, the hissing became a roar. On the heels of the Lehman shock, the overleveraged U.S. financial system froze up and set in motion a chain of events on Wall Street and in Washington that obliterated any remaining vestiges of consumer and business confidence. America's animal spirits turned inward, and already weakened consumer demand collapsed—a collapse that was all the more severe because it had rested on the false prosperity of now deflated asset and credit bubbles.

To this day, there remains a contentious "chicken or egg" debate: What came first? Was it the bursting of the bubbles, or the crisis? Was it soaring unemployment or the capitulation of the American consumer? Was it a monetary policy blunder or the lack of regulatory oversight? Cause and effect are never easy to disentangle from major economic or historical events, especially so soon after they occur. But that may be beside the point for the purpose of our analysis.

There can be little dispute that the American consumer—the bubble-dependent, savings-short, excessively indebted American consumer—was at ground zero in the Great Recession. With consumer demand in free fall, business demand—especially the so-called derived demands for employment and capital spending that are heavily dependent on consumer demand—was quick to follow.

But it doesn't end there. The same bruised and battered American consumer is likely to remain at the epicenter of the postcrisis aftermath for many years. And economic growth in these years is likely to be exceptionally weak compared to recoveries of the past. That's the conclusion that follows from the script of a balance-sheet recession, when the stress on the economy works its way through the assets and liabilities of economic actors—in this case, consumers.[4] With balance sheet repair proceeding slowly in the aftermath of the Great Recession, the U.S. recovery will be facing stiff headwinds for years to come.[5] That conclusion has enormous consequences for the rest of the world—especially China.

Collapse in Global Trade

The capitulation of the world's ultimate consumer wreaked havoc on global trade. In 2009, the volume of world trade plunged by 10.6 percent—the first year of outright contraction since a 1.8 percent drop in 1982 and by far the sharpest annual decline of the post–World War II era.[6] Except for the 61 percent implosion in the first three years of the Great Depression (1930–32), nothing has ever come close to the 2009 decline in trade.[7]

The plunge in 2009 was hardly surprising in light of the year's extraordinary decline in global economic activity. Still, many believe that a crisis-induced contraction of trade finance—driven by a generalized freezing of global credit markets starting in late 2008—greatly amplified the downturn in the physical volume of cross-border trade. If correct, that would imply that the precipitous drop in world trade in 2009 was largely an idiosyncratic event—a consequence of a rare "perfect storm" in the credit markets that was at center stage in the Great Crisis.

It turns out that this interpretation is greatly exaggerated. While the sharp tightening of credit conditions did play a role, a broad consensus of researchers has concluded that most of the decline—about 70 percent of the fall in world merchandise trade in 2009—is attributable to the rare 0.6 percent drop in global GDP that year.[8]

Several factors were at work. First, the output shock itself was exceptional. For a global economy that had averaged 3.4 percent annual growth since 1980, without a decline in even one of the twenty-nine precrisis years, the output decline of 0.6 percent in 2009 was an extraordinary aberration. Second, it is not that rare for the trade cycle to react more sharply than the output, or GDP, cycle. Conditions in the recent precrisis period were ripe for just that outcome. Growth in world trade had been blistering. In the six years before the crisis, 2003–8, global trade volumes increased by an average of 7.4 percent a year, taking the trade share of world GDP to a record 32 percent in 2008. In that frothy environment, it is hardly shocking that an output shock took its greatest toll on one of globalization's most prominent linkages.[9]

This is not to minimize the impact of "financial frictions" on the trade cycle during the depth of the crisis.[10] They certainly worsened the impact of the demand shock—especially for financially vulnerable firms in developing economies.[11] But it is a real stretch to argue that the sharp contraction in the trade cycle was traceable mainly to the near meltdown of the financial system.

No one was spared from the contraction of global trade in 2009. The developed world—the source of the crisis—was hit hardest, with trade volumes plunging by 12.2 percent. But there would be no decoupling for the export-led developing world, where the volume of trade still fell by 8.1 percent in 2009—the sharpest decline in modern history. The percentage decline in the developing world doesn't do justice to the severity of the shock. Between 2000 and 2008, developing and emerging economies' trade volumes had surged an average of 10.5 percent a year. The 8.1 percent drop in 2009 thus represented a shortfall of 18.6 percentage points from that precrisis growth trend—actually a tad worse than the 17.8-point shortfall evident in the advanced economies relative to their nine-year precrisis growth trend.

Developing Asia was hit especially hard. Exports had risen to a record 45 percent of the collective GDP of its fourteen largest economies in 2007—an astonishing increase of 10 percentage points over the preceding ten years.[12] The fastest-growing region in the world, developing Asia, was one of the major beneficiaries of globalization and the associated surge in global trade. But when the recession hit, the export share of the combined GDP of these countries plunged to 35 percent in 2009—back to levels last seen in the depths of the Asian financial crisis of the late 1990s. As the newly ascendant engine of pan-regional trade and economic growth, China was on the leading edge of this collapse.

The Chinese Producer Hits the Wall

For export-led China, the shock was especially severe. Here was an economy whose export share had surged from just 5 percent of GDP in 1979 to 37 percent in 2007—far outstripping the growth of any other sector. In the precrisis tranquility of March 2007, Premier Wen Jiabao posed what many thought to be a rhetorical commentary on the paradox of the Four Uns, questioning whether a seemingly vibrant Chinese economy could stay the course or ultimately succumb to an "unbalanced, unstable, uncoordinated and unsustainable" endgame. For a year or so, the premier's critique seemed like idle conjecture. But the shock, literally just around the corner, would provide powerful validation of the Four Uns as an operative construct for risk assessment of the Chinese economy.

As late as July 2008, China's exports were still surging by 26 percent relative to levels of a year earlier. Then the tide went out. By February 2009, just seven months later, the surge had become an outright collapse, with Chinese exports having plunged 27 percent from year-earlier levels. At the same time, sequential growth in China's quarterly GDP had slowed to a virtual standstill, and industrial output comparisons fell into the low single digits (3 percent growth in early 2009). Most telling of all, government survey data suggest that well over twenty million migrant workers had lost jobs in export-led industries, especially in Guangdong province.[13] The worst-case scenario had come to pass. The Chinese economy had entered the functional equivalent of recession.

The alarm bells went off across China—from the Zhongnanhai senior leadership compound in Beijing down to provincial and local government units, especially those in the export-sensitive coastal regions like Guangdong. All the stability tripwires had been breached, and China moved quickly to hit the stimulus button. The monetary policy stance was shifted immediately from "moderately tight" to "moderately loose," in the parlance of the People's Bank of China, and interest rates were slashed by more than 2 percentage points. Fiscal policy was quick to follow.

The heavy artillery—China's version of America's Big Bazooka—came in the form of a massive fiscal stimulus announced in November 2008. Initially committing four trillion renminbi (more than USD $575 billion), or about 12 percent of China's 2008 GDP, the Chinese leadership wasted no time in marshaling enormous support for the economy. While this headline figure overstated the actual fiscal stimulus, there can be little doubt of its impact.[14]

As the first major economy to respond to the crisis, China also became the first to recover—with year-over-year GDP growth rebounding to 11.4 percent by the fourth quarter of 2009, nearly 5 percentage points faster than the 6.6 percent cyclical trough hit in the first quarter of the year. What's particularly intriguing about the 2008 stimulus package is what it says about leadership perceptions of the resilient character of the Chinese economy, namely, the sectors that could be trusted to deliver recovery after a severe crunch. The bulk of the stimulus went to infrastructure: railroads, highways, airport construction, and the electrical power grid; there was also significant support for rural village infrastructure and low-income housing. Relatively little went to social welfare or other initiatives that might have supported private consumption. Unlike the United States, where a $787 billion fiscal stimulus had trouble finding "shovel-ready" traction, China was quick to implement its shovel-ready spending initiatives.

In March 2007, Premier Wen used the Four Uns to warn of mounting risks to the old model—setting in motion the debate over a new one. Yet the details of China's 2008 countercyclical stimulus reveal that its policy makers weren't ready to try out the new recipe. Instead, they sought more immediate traction that could be achieved only by turning to the well-oiled producer model of the past.

As China came out of its short but sharp recession, its having doubled down on the old model became all the more apparent; in effect, it dug itself an even deeper hole as seen through the lens of Premier Wen's Four Uns. This was a disturbing development. The fixed investment share of Chinese GDP rose from an already elevated 40 percent to 45 percent between 2008 and early 2010—then increased further to 46 percent by 2011—while the long-depressed private consumption share hovered around 35 percent. The real side of the Chinese economy had in effect become more unbalanced. Meanwhile, the stimulus also took a toll on the financial sector, with commercial banks risking off–balance sheet exposure to deteriorating credit quality by lending aggressively to shaky local government investment units.

All this underscores one of the most daunting challenges that China faces. The leadership fully understands the case for rebalancing toward a new consumer-led growth model. But can it pull it off—especially when unexpected shocks force stability-fixated policy makers back into their comfort zone with the time-tested model of the past?

Aftershocks

The sequel to the Great Crisis is in some ways even more disturbing than its antecedent. In 2011, for the second time in three years, the world was hit with another major crisis—this one made in Europe.

As noted earlier, these two crises were joined. The unusually sharp contraction in global economic activity in 2009 clobbered Europe with an asymmetrical shock, one that had especially lethal consequences for its "peripheral" economies, those of Portugal, Ireland, Italy, Greece, and Spain. The slowdown unmasked a number of serious strains that had been festering in these countries for years—chronic fiscal deficits and sovereign debt overhangs, a significant erosion of competitiveness, and postbubble vulnerabilities of an interlinked bank-centric financial system. And it led to the bursting of a different kind of bubble, the so-called convergence bubble that had allowed the peripheral economies to secure financing in sovereign debt markets on the same terms that were accorded to the much stronger "core" European economies such as those of Germany and France.

The now notorious case of Greece, the poster child of the euro crisis, is the most obvious and important case in point. In the early 1990s, the Greek government had to pay close to 25 percent interest in order to borrow for ten years in international capital markets, more than three times the roughly 7.5 percent financing cost that Germany and France had to pay at that point in time. But then over the course of the decade to come, Greek interest rates converged on those in Germany, as investors drew comfort from the coming unification of the European Monetary Union and the single currency that was to be launched on January 1, 1999. That comfort translated into a conviction that the integrity of Greece as a borrower was basically equivalent to that of Germany—effectively dismissing the possibility altogether that the Greek government might default on its ever-rising debt obligations.

From 2000 to 2007, the difference between Greek and Germany interest rates—the so-called spread—all but evaporated. The Greek economy benefited significantly from the interest rate convergence play during that period, which boosted home prices, equity markets, consumer and business expectations, and ultimately the country's GDP growth. As a result, the Greek economy actually outperformed Germany's, the so-called engine of Europe. From 1999 to early 2008, real GDP rose 40 percent in Greece, almost three times the 15 percent increase in Germany over the same period. It didn't seem to matter that Greece's underlying productivity growth was weak, that its budget deficit was too high, and that its sovereign debt load was mounting. Being able to borrow at German interest rates allowed Greece to sidestep the imperatives of fiscal discipline, improved competitiveness, and faster productivity growth.

But then it all came to a sickening end in late 2008. As world credit markets froze up in the aftermath of the Lehman failure, investors rethought the wisdom of their risky bets—including the euro convergence trade. Suddenly, spreads started to widen sharply not just for Greece but for the other peripheral economies of Europe, such as those of Ireland, Portugal, Spain, and even Italy, all of which had been inattentive to their mounting structural problems. But there was a deeper message behind this development: Financial markets were effectively rethinking their once sanguine assessment of default risk, recognizing that it no longer made sense to give Greece and the other peripheral economies the same benefit of the doubt as Germany in making good on their sovereign debt obligations.

Events in Greece in 2011–12 validated these newfound fears. With its ten-year government borrowing costs shooting up to 30 percent in 2011 and the government lacking the funds to roll over, or refinance, its existing debt obligations at these punitive rates, Greece was forced to seek a bailout: backstop funding from the IMF and the European Union. But there were important strings attached to the disbursement of these funds—namely, sharp increases in taxes and massive cutbacks in government spending on a wide range of social programs. This austerity campaign didn't exactly go over well in Greece. The Greek government fell in mid-2012, and massive protests spilled over into the streets in the months that followed. The political debate inside Greece conformed to the fears that were gripping financial markets—that a "Grexit" (Greece pulling out of the European Monetary Union) was a much higher probability than had previously been thought.

While the extreme events in Greece subsided in late 2012, comparable developments played out in several other European economies—not just in Portugal, Ireland, and Cyprus but also in two of Europe's biggest economies, those of Spain and Italy.[15] In all these cases the risks swung away from liquidity concerns toward the more lethal problems of debt sustainability and solvency. Their worry was no longer about borrowing more money in the markets but about having the wherewithal to service the debts they already have. One by one, many of Europe's once high-flying economies sagged back into recession in 2012–13, the second downturn in three years, as fiscal austerity took its toll on government spending and aggregate demand.

As in all crises, the endgame here is uncertain. For Europe, the challenge is formidable. The sad case of Greece allowed the darkest fears to surface. Without a fiscal and political union, the days of its monetary union could be numbered.[16] The crisis has put acute pressures on the funding costs of the peripheral economies, raising the on-again, off-again possibility that one of them may actually pull out of the monetary union and trade in the euro for its old currency. If that were to occur, the fear in many quarters is that of a domino effect of exits and the ultimate unwinding of the European Monetary Union, one of the pillars of modern international finance.

While European authorities have moved aggressively, if belatedly, to stave off such a disastrous outcome, the jury is out on whether they will succeed. The European Central Bank has taken the tactical lead in these efforts, committing all of its considerable resources to doing "whatever it takes" to save the euro, in the words of its president, Mario Draghi.[17] Ultimately, the fate of the currency union rests less on the firepower of its central bank than on the delicate balancing act between massive debt burdens and social stability. The debate remains intense over sustainable debt trajectories for Europe's overindebted peripheral economies.

Muddling through now looks like the best outcome for Europe, orchestrated by a series of incremental steps toward enhanced unification. But the damage has been done and the postcrisis aftershocks of the euro breakup scare prompted not only renewed recession in late 2012 but also the likelihood of a disappointingly weak recovery.

The Euro crisis offers four conclusions that have important implications for both China and the United States—to say nothing of the rest of the global economy:

One, many roads lead to false prosperity and they can all be treacherous. Japan tried it with property and equity bubbles, the United States with property and credit bubbles, and now Europe with its interest rate convergence bubble. When the bubbles burst, as they always do, the journey is over.

Two, financial markets can make serious mistakes in assessing risks. The bubbles that brought down Japan, the United States, and Europe were outgrowths of serious mistakes that were made by investors in valuing underlying assets, from property to equities to credit and sovereign debt instruments. Policy blunders exacerbated those mistakes, especially by central banks in Japan and the United States. In Europe, it was more of a political blunder of rushing to embrace a flawed currency union.

Three, a crisis exacts a serious and lasting toll on real economies. Consistent with the findings of Reinhart and Rogoff, Japan, the United States, and now Europe are struggling with postcrisis difficulties—and are likely to do so for years to come.[18] The penchant for a quick fix that ducks the structural imperatives of balance sheet repair—for corporations in Japan, consumers in the United States, and sovereign governments in Europe—can sow the seeds for the next crisis.

Four, the so-called austerity debate—facing up to fiscal excesses in tough times—is far from settled.[19] The United States and Europe have distinctly different views on this burning issue. Notwithstanding enormous political infighting over a "fiscal cliff" and debt ceilings, Washington has opted for the open-ended Keynesian stimulus approach. Europe is more solidly in the austerity camp. However, neither has much to brag about in terms of the efficacy of the approach it favors. Economic recovery has been unusually anemic in the United States, and Europe's latest recession is likely to be followed by comparably weak recovery.

For China, renewed recession in Europe, combined with lingering weakness in the U.S. economic recovery, has only made it tougher to keep running on the same treadmill. Collectively, these two economies account for about 40 percent of the external demand that supports the Chinese export machine. In light of its stability imperative, the demand shortfalls in Europe and Japan make it vital for China to consider new sources of growth.

Nor has the U.S. economy been spared the impacts of Europe's woes or the feedback effects those headwinds are prompting elsewhere in the world. With the American consumer likely to remain subdued for years to come, the United States has turned increasingly to export-led growth. For a while, that strategy seemed to be working. Exports accounted for about 40 percent of the (admittedly feeble) increase in real GDP in the first three years of postcrisis recovery from mid-2009 to mid-2012. Without those gains, the 2.4 percent average growth trajectory would have been closer to 1.7 percent, and the sharply elevated U.S. unemployment rate would have been even a good deal higher than it is today.

But as the world slowed again in 2012, the export-led impetus to America's weak recovery also started to wane. That, in turn, spawned additional collateral damage through trade linkages to China and elsewhere in Asia's China-centric supply chain. And then the Asia slowdown came back to haunt Europe, leading to further ripple effects on the United States, and so on. Interdependence has its virtues, but it can also create a chain of increasingly intractable vulnerabilities.

Predicting the next shock is, of course, impossible. But the key point to keep in mind is that it doesn't take a big one to derail a weak and fragile recovery. The all too frequent aftershocks following the Great Crisis—of which the Euro crisis is the most prominent—not only create the danger of relapses but also demonstrate the ever-present complications that are likely to dog American and Chinese economic management for years to come.

The Wake-Up Call

Unfortunately, there is nothing particularly new about the string of crises that began in 2008. As stressed above, the most recent ones were unusually severe, but they actually follow on the heels of a steady stream of major crises that has beset the world economy for more than thirty years. Starting with the Latin American debt crisis of the early 1980s, the list includes the 1987 stock market crash, the U.S. savings and loan crisis (1990), the bursting of Japan's bubbles (1990), Mexico's peso crisis (1995), the Asian financial crisis (1997), the demise of Long-Term Capital Management (1998), the dotcom blowup (2000), U.S. corporate accounting scandals (2001), and then, of course, the subprime mortgage collapse (2007) and Europe's sovereign debt crisis (2010). Eleven shocks in thirty years—the world has been lurching from crisis to crisis with painful regularity, with the crises becoming increasingly complex and severe over time.

While the sources differ, the responses to these crises all have a familiar ring. Well-intentioned authorities rush to the scene and promise never to let it happen again. They take actions—initially monetary and fiscal to stop the hemorrhaging—but then adopt a regulatory fix to address the problems of the latest crisis just uncovered. Stock market circuit breakers were instituted after the crash of 1987, new foreign exchange regimes after the Asian financial crisis, Sarbanes-Oxley regulations after the U.S. accounting scandals, and the Dodd-Frank financial reforms after America's recent subprime crisis.

Unfortunately, this penchant for the backward-looking postcrisis fix introduces a new complication. It presumes that the next crisis will replicate the last one. But it almost never happens that way. What typically does happen instead is that after the crisis runs its course and time passes, the authorities invariably get lulled into complacency, mistaking the natural tendency of postcrisis healing for the apparent success of their new regulatory remedies. Eventually, however, that success gets called into question by a new flaw—one that was not captured by the backward-looking measures—and the process starts all over again.[20] The past three decades have brought one crisis roughly every three years.

This is a sad commentary on the state of the global policy architecture. It depicts a politicized crisis-response mechanism driven by the unrelenting search for a quick fix.[21] A reluctance to craft forward-looking solutions lies at the heart of the political economy of false prosperity. The authorities are unwilling to tamper with growth—even if the growth ultimately is unsustainable. More often than not, policy makers actually try to re-create the same strain of economic growth that was just discredited in a crisis. As already noted, that's what the Fed is trying to do in the United States, and that is what China did in the aftermath of its downturn in 2008–9.

Yet the crises that began in 2008 are of a very different ilk than earlier ones. Their scope and severity, to say nothing of their complexity, raise deep questions about economic management for individual nations as well as for the broader global economy. This latter point is obviously of great importance in an era of globalization, where the global policy architecture—largely left in the hands of the International Monetary Fund and, more recently, the G-20 group of the world's largest twenty economies—lacks both policy tools and an enforcement mechanism that would make such tools effective.

A flawed global policy architecture means that world leaders are, by default, operating under an erroneous presumption—that the best global policy is the sum of the best national policies. This approach pits nations against one another rather than providing a collective framework of oversight and coordinated policy implementation. As the European crisis painfully illustrates, the need for collective action raises basic questions of national sovereignty—whether individual national states are willing to subsume country-specific considerations into the broader welfare of an integrated economic union. That's an obvious problem for Europe, but it's an equally serious challenge for a sustainable globalization.

The Great Crisis and its aftermath are major wake-up calls for China and the United States. In the case of China, the alarm went off with Wen Jiabao's Four Uns and the eventual recognition that an unbalanced and unstable Chinese economy is not immune to a global crisis. First posed as an intellectual construct—a framework of debate—the paradox of the Four Uns has now been validated by two massive shocks in three years from China's two largest sources of external demand, first the United States, now Europe. Many argued that the U.S. subprime crisis should be dismissed as a one-off event—a hundred-year storm that could hardly be expected to strike again soon.[22] To the extent that Chinese leaders accepted this explanation, they might have been inclined to conclude that they, too, could stay the course—that after a period of healing, the storm-ravaged U.S. economy had not only survived but would regain its footing and again support China's external demand.

The powerful echo in Europe should dispel that view. With one crisis begetting another, the notion of a once-in-a-century one-off disturbance has been discredited. Moreover, since postcrisis recoveries are well known for chronic weakness,[23] the export-led Chinese economy won't be able to count on vigor from its two largest sources of demand for many years. For externally dependent China, wake-up calls don't come any louder than that. The old model needs to go for that reason alone.

We can draw a similar conclusion for the United States. Lacking a stability constraint like China's, undisciplined U.S. authorities have not hesitated to roll the dice on growth. Starting in the mid-1990s, one bubble begot another, fueling an excess consumption binge that left the world's ultimate consumer ripe for the biggest fall in modern history. That fall is America's wake-up call—a challenge to rethink the framework required for prudent management of the U.S. economy.

But more than a wake-up call, the Great Crisis is also a shot across the bow of U.S.-Chinese codependency. Traditional sources of growth in both economies have been dealt serious blows—each with lasting implications for the other. China can no longer count on deriving growth from U.S. consumers who buy much of what it produces. At the same time, savings-short America could lose some of its support from the largest foreign buyer of Treasuries, as consumer-led China starts to draw down its surplus savings.

The economic effects of codependency are one thing. But the Crisis and its aftermath could also have a chilling impact on another aspect of the relationship—the two nations' political rapport. As the United States lingers in a subpar recovery, Washington risks getting swept up in the polemics of blame—especially in singling out China as a scapegoat. Meanwhile, as China continues to prosper, its nationalistic pride has taken on a more strident tone—making it all the more difficult for the Chinese to accept criticism from abroad. The Great Crisis could do yet another serious disservice if it worsens the economic and political frictions between the United States and China. We take up that very risk in greater detail in the following chapter.

Now or Never

There is also an important wake-up call for the stewards of the global economy. It is not a coincidence that beginning in the late 1990s and continuing through the run-up to the Great Crisis there was an ominous deterioration in most measures of global imbalances. The world was entering an era of ever-widening current account surpluses and deficits.[24] The disparities between spenders and savers kept setting new records—the nations that were big spenders were spending more, and big savers were saving more.

Yet there was nothing but complacency about the risks of these mounting imbalances. They hadn't derailed the global economy yet, went the argument of some of the world's most experienced and wisest thinkers.[25] Who could say how and when the story might change?

Looking back on that false tranquility, one can see plenty of warning signs that the "sustainable imbalances" thesis was dead wrong. The United States was a classic example. America's massive current account deficit was a direct outgrowth of its chronic lack of domestic saving. Yet that saving shortfall was itself a function of consumers' rush to embrace the dreams of asset-dependent consumption. Why save out of current income if your largest asset (the home) could automatically do the saving for you? The only problem with that strategy—and the current account deficits it spawned— is that it was held together by a daisy chain of asset and credit bubbles.

America's contribution to global imbalances—the biggest current account deficit in modern history—stemmed from the massive bubbles it learned to rely on as substitutes for saving and income-based consumer purchasing power. When those bubbles burst, the unthinkable happened—an unprecedented pullback of consumer demand. That alone is testament as to how ludicrous it was to believe that America's imbalances were sustainable.

The same can be said for most of the world's other major imbalances in the decade before the Great Crisis—especially the current account surpluses in China and Germany. The former was an outgrowth of the financial repression and insecurity of Chinese households. The latter stemmed from a policy of export-led growth that was supported by the pan-European interest rate convergence bubble discussed earlier and the artificial support that bubble temporarily provided for an important source of German external demand, the peripheral economies of Europe. The Great Crisis brought into question the sustainability of both of these outsize current account surpluses.

In short, every one of the world's major imbalances not only was unsustainable but also played an important role in sparking the steady stream of recent crises. This destabilizing sequence of events offers lessons for individual economies as well as for the world as a whole. It is no longer acceptable simply to pay lip service to the need for global rebalancing. Global governance, both at the narrow G-20 level and the broad IMF level, needs to be empowered to address this problem.[26] For that to work there can be no escaping two of the toughest issues of all: the tug-of-war between national sovereignty and supranational accountability, and the political economy of false prosperity. Sustainable globalization requires nothing less than intense examination and ultimate resolution of these issues.

Time is the enemy of the lasting fix. The farther a crisis fades into the past, the less leaders and citizens are inclined to heed its warnings. Too often, the temptation is to deploy policies aimed at a quick fix and then dig in, buy time, and hope that the new problem will blow over. Yet that's not the message that should be taken from the Great Crisis—by China, the United States, or the world at large. The history of the past three decades tells us that the insidious interplay among these imbalances doesn't fade with time. The crises they trigger and the aftershocks they spawn only get larger with each recurrence. If there has ever been a time to face up to the imperatives of global rebalancing, it is now. Denial could lead to a new round of global imbalances—and an even greater crisis with devastating consequences for China, the United States, and the rest of the global economy.

10

Smoot-Hawley Redux

When it comes to the intersection of politics and economics, never say never. That's especially true in tough times, when economic pressures invariably create a clamor for political action. Bad policy decisions in such circumstances have had profound and lasting implications for many economies.

The U.S.-China economic relationship is hardly immune to such a possibility. Since 2005, America's Congress has repeatedly threatened anti-China trade and currency initiatives. The good news is that no such legislation has yet become law. The bad news is that past performance may not be a good predictor of future decisions.

The Smoot-Hawley Tariff Act of 1930 provides a vivid worst-case scenario of what happens when trade skirmishes turn into open war. This one piece of legislation raised average tariffs by close to 20 percent on almost nine hundred items imported into the United States.[1] By triggering strong counteractions from America's major trading partners, it is widely thought to have sparked a global trade war—helping to turn a world financial downturn into the Great Depression. Many experts consider it the worst economic policy blunder in modern U.S. history.

Could it happen again? Of course not, according to the ever-complacent consensus. Mindful of the lessons of the 1930s and steeped in the theory and practice of free trade, no sane political leader in the United States or China would start a trade war by shooting with live ammunition. But these risks should not simply be assumed away. The same complacent consensus believed in the fairy tales of sustainable imbalances, benign asset and credit bubbles, and the self-interest of market participants in a free capitalist society. Never say never.

Mark Twain said that history rarely repeats itself, but it often rhymes. Washington's penchant for China bashing is one of those rhymes that is particularly disconcerting. Unlike the broad shotgun approach of Smoot-Hawley, an anti-China currency or trade bill would be targeted at just one purported adversary. But codependency makes that one target vital to American interests. Unlike in 1930, when the United States was running trade and savings surpluses, China is the main foreign funder of today's deficits and a major supplier of cheap goods that American consumers crave. That makes the United States far more vulnerable today than it was back then to any retaliatory actions that a trade war with China might trigger.

Alas, this is not about logic. It is about the politics of job security—and an irrational conviction that the only way to give hard-pressed U.S. workers a fair shake is to make China flinch. Never mind that most of America's deep-seated economic problems—its lack of saving, the deskilling of its workers, the hollowing out of once competitive industries, and its inadequate infrastructure—are of its own making. The message from Washington is that it is easier to cast blame than tackle hard issues.

Never mind also the ominous implications a Chinese retaliation might have for financial markets and the real U.S. economy. The politics of fear ignores the risk of collateral damage—precisely the mistake made by Senator Reed Smoot and Congressman Willis Hawley nearly eighty-five years ago.

Two Senators and a Currency

The current escalation of anti-China protectionist sentiment took an ominous turn on April 6, 2005. On that day, in a surprising vote on the floor of the U.S. Senate, a large bipartisan majority of sixty-seven senators re-

fused to table, or put aside, the Schumer-Graham Chinese currency reform amendment to a routine State Department funding bill. While it was
hardly the first time Congress had talked about getting tough with China, it
was the first time live bullets had been loaded into the chamber. As U.S.
Senator Charles Schumer put it a few weeks later, "It is time to speak softly
and carry a big stick."[2]

Schumer, a liberal Democrat from New York, and Lindsey Graham, a
conservative Republican from South Carolina, made an unlikely political
tag team. Schumer had never set foot in China when he cosponsored the
currency bill. "That didn't matter," he said a year later, over his first breakfast in Beijing. "I only had to go to Japan once in the late 1980s to take care
of the yen."[3] That was his glib way of saying just as it didn't require him to
spend a lot of time in Japan to play a role in pushing for a stronger yen, he
didn't need a lot of China time to have a similar impact on the renminbi.
Educated as a lawyer (although he never practiced law), Schumer made his
mark as a senator by championing the plight of the middle class. He quickly
came to the view that China posed a serious threat to that constituency.

Lindsey Graham, also trained as a lawyer, was the first Republican to
be elected in his South Carolina congressional district since 1977. Repre-
senting a nonunion state whose textile industry had been hollowed out by
foreign competition, he too found that China came with the territory. As
the China-fearing conservative, Graham was the perfect counterweight to
the liberal Schumer. Together they have been an effective force in cutting
across the ideological divide and appealing to a bipartisan groundswell of
anti-China sentiment in the U.S. Congress.

Schumer and Graham's China tactics were never a practical plan of action.
The use of countervailing tariffs to retaliate for alleged currency manipulation is probably not even compliant with WTO rules. The proposal was political theater, meant to stir up national debate and make Beijing squirm.

It did just that. Beginning in 2005, a steady stream of anti-China legislation was introduced in both houses of Congress. Schumer and Graham
themselves, along with various cosponsors, put forward and then withdrew
several such proposals. By one tabulation, more than 110 legislative initiatives targeting Chinese currency and trade issues were introduced in the
Congress between 2005 and 2012.[4] Most of them died in committee. But
they have kept alive the anti-China drumbeat in Congress.

Two bills actually made it to the floor. On September 29, 2010, by an overwhelming bipartisan margin of 348–79, the U.S. House of Representatives passed the Currency Reform for Fair Trade Act of 2010, basically an anti-China currency bill that would have imposed steep tariffs on China to compensate for its alleged currency manipulation.[5] A year later, on October 11, 2011, a similar bill, the Currency Exchange Rate Oversight Act of 2011, passed in the Senate by an equally large bipartisan margin, 63–35.[6] Neither bill was taken up at the same time by the other house, so neither ever made it to the president's desk.[7]

While the structure of these legislative initiatives has evolved over the years, a basic three-step approach has remained largely the same: First, the bills outlaw currency manipulation as it is defined by IMF conventions. Second, they authorize the president to name currency manipulators based on some exchange rate valuation criteria that would be used to determine the extent of the manipulation. Finally, they mandate the imposition of duties to compensate for the damage done by the manipulation.

While the proposed laws did not name China explicitly, there was little doubt whom the first target would have been. Since damage conveyed through the currency affects all goods shipped from China to the United States, the manipulation penalty could amount to tens of billions of dollars in duties. The 2005 Schumer-Graham bill set the undervaluation of Chinese goods at 27.5 percent, which would have resulted in tariffs totaling $67 billion on some $243 billion of imports from China at the time.

Several refinements to this approach have been introduced since Schumer and Graham first proposed it. The most important one was to shift the onus of proving currency manipulation from the Congress to the U.S. Treasury. Under advice from legal counsel, Congress realized that any verdict it might render on currency valuation could be deemed arbitrary. So it turned over this determination to others, proposing that the trigger for action be tied to the U.S. Treasury's semiannual "Report to Congress on International Economic and Exchange Rate Policies." If Treasury were to reach a manipulation verdict—something it had not done since 1994—after obligatory consultations with the accused manipulator, the duties would be automatically triggered under the new law.

The fact that no legislation has resulted does not make these proposals an empty threat. They served the important purpose of drawing attention—

in the United States as well as China—to the significance of trade-related tensions in shaping the economic agendas of both of these codependent countries. Both sides took these concerns seriously, and that reaction is at least partly responsible for two major developments since Senators Schumer and Graham first offered their remedy: a shift in the Chinese foreign exchange regime to a managed float in July 2005, and the establishment of a formal high-level economic and strategic dialogue (first semiannually, now annually) between the top leaders in both countries. These are positive steps but, in the general scheme of things, small ones in alleviating the unrelenting buildup of U.S.-Sino trade tensions. Perhaps they would have occurred in any case. But it is probably not a coincidence that they followed on the heels of the pressures brought by the two senators.

Upping the Ante

Bluster can take the U.S. Congress only so far. Eventually, if a serious problem persists, the body politic demands action. In some respects Congress's browbeating of China is turning into an uphill battle. As pointed out earlier, many of the economic arguments behind the anti-China case have weakened since 2005. The renminbi has appreciated by 35 percent versus the U.S. dollar, and China's broad measures of international imbalance—its current account as well as its multilateral trade surplus—have narrowed dramatically. Meanwhile, as noted in Chapter 8, the United States has successfully used the WTO dispute mechanism to address several of its complaints about Chinese trade practices.

Despite these developments, the U.S. economy remains weak, with middle-class workers still feeling considerable pressure. Persistently high unemployment and stagnant inflation-adjusted real wages cast a long shadow across the U.S. labor market. These problems are unlikely to improve in any material way for quite some time.

And all is not well on the U.S. trade front. America is still losing market share to foreign producers in key industries, exacerbating its trade deficit and putting unrelenting pressure on its factory workers. But the toughest sticking point is the persistence of an outsize trade deficit with China, which climbed to a record $315 billion in 2012. Never mind that bilateral trade deficits are a deceptive measure—politicians have no patience for analytics or theory. This one data point remains a lightning rod in the Washington economic debate.

Like much of the melodrama that drives the codependency between the two nations, resolution of the bilateral trade tensions has been left to the political arena. Washington is faced with two basic choices on economic policy that bear critically on its relationship with China—make good on its threat of trade sanctions, or face up to the imperatives of a new domestic agenda that alleviates the pressures of outsize trade deficits. More of the same is no longer a credible option.

While the United States is perfectly capable of solving its own economic problems, there is no real sign that it has the political will to do so. Tough problems require tough solutions, and that won't happen unless shared sacrifice has bipartisan support. Recent political polarization unfortunately points in the opposite direction.

There is, of course, another escape valve. A spontaneous, vigorous economic recovery would do wonders in healing the U.S. labor market and defusing U.S.-China tensions. The weight of postcrisis history and the still tough state of U.S. consumer balance sheets do not offer much hope of that. Yet anything is possible.

Given the range of options—from the homegrown cure to a further escalation of political pressure—it makes sense to take the analysis one step farther and consider the worst-case consequences of a U.S.-China trade war. That's not to say it will happen. But a failure to ponder the unthinkable smacks of complacency, heightening the risk that it might actually come to pass.

A Bad Dream

The United States and China are poised at the top of a very slippery slope. Creatures of two very different systems, they have much in common as they face what is perhaps the greatest test of their codependency. Both economies are at critical transition points—old growth models have been taken to excess and must be replaced by rebalanced new models. The mounting economic tensions between them could boil over, sparking a trade war.

Every war has its saga of the itchy trigger and the first shot. With America still licking its wounds several years after the Great Crisis and unemployment remaining unacceptably high, it has no shortage of itchy fingers. Let us assume that the first shot is, in fact, fired by Washington.[8] What happens next is pure conjecture but an important hypothetical illustration of how things could go terribly wrong.

A dark cloud hung over Camp David in December 2014, as U.S. President Barack Obama gathered his key advisers to ponder a bleak political landscape. Fiscal austerity had taken its toll, with cutbacks in federal government spending leading to another economic relapse. The dreaded second-term hex was increasingly evident, as the Obama Administration was rocked by a succession of scandals at home and in the foreign policy arena. Republicans had seized the moment with a stunning victory in the midterm elections the previous month, gaining control of both the Senate and the House. Desperate to avoid lame duck status for the final two years of his term, the president needed a policy gambit.

China was the answer, his advisers counseled. So, true to his word as a defender of the American middle class, Barack Obama issued an executive order in January 2015 declaring China guilty of currency manipulation.[9] In accordance with the Omnibus Trade and Competitiveness Act of 1988, that declaration triggered immediate high-level consultations between U.S. Treasury officials and their Chinese counterparts at the Ministry of Finance. The U.S. team demanded an immediate 20 percent appreciation of the renminbi against the dollar. China countered with zero change, noting the renminbi had already risen more than 35 percent against the dollar since 2005 and adding that it would not acquiesce to Washington's insistence on a Chinese fix for America's saving problem. Not surprisingly, the negotiations stalled and each party blamed the other in vitriolic press releases.

In early February, in his penultimate State of the Union address to the U.S. Congress, President Obama proclaimed, "Enough is enough. It is high time for China to play by our rules." Congress roared its approval, and within a week, overwhelming bipartisan majorities of both houses came to the support of the president. The Defend America Trade Act of 2015 (DATA), modeled after the currency manipulation remedies of countervailing tariffs first proposed by Senators Schumer and Graham in 2005, was signed into law on Presidents' Day, February 16, 2015. China was quickly deemed to be in violation of the new statute.

At that point, negotiations between the two countries took on a new urgency. But the leaders in both countries—with the U.S. delegation led by President Obama and the Chinese delegation led jointly by President Xi Jinping and Premier

Li Keqiang—were in no mood for compromise. The two economies were struggling with subpar growth and attendant pressures on their labor markets. Yet both leadership teams were determined to exhibit strength and determination to their anxious citizens at home. The negotiations failed and a postsummit joint press conference was canceled. In accordance with DATA, Washington then slapped immediate tariff increases of 20 percent on all Chinese products entering the United States.

In response, the Chinese export machine immediately screeched to a standstill. Amid howls of protest and plant shutdowns across China, Beijing declared this an act of economic war. It filed an immediate complaint with the World Trade Organization, arguing not only that Washington's currency valuation metrics were dubious but that using a currency to trigger broad-based countervailing duties was in violation of WTO rules, which were framed around commodity- or sector-specific protocols. As the National People's Congress (NPC) convened in March 2015, Premier Li Keqiang used the occasion of the his annual press conference to announce that China had no patience to endure a lengthy WTO dispute process that could take anywhere from two to five years to resolve.

Taking its cue from the premier, China's Ministry of Commerce immediately announced retaliatory tariffs of 20 percent on all U.S. shipments of goods to China. This hit growth-starved America right between the eyes. With $111 billion of American-made goods sold in Chinese markets in 2012, China had become the United States' third-largest and most rapidly growing export market. With American consumer demand stagnant and the fastest-growing segment of exports under new pressure from Chinese actions, an already weakened U.S. economy was suddenly in more serious trouble. Meanwhile, Walmart announced average price increases of 5 percent—pointing to sharp tariff-induced increases in import prices that it was only partly able to offset through reduced profit margins. Other retailers followed suit, and American consumers bought less in response. Talk of stagflation was in the air as forecasters lowered their sights on growth but raised predictions for inflation.

Financial markets swooned. The stock market was hit by the trifecta of reduced profit margins due to tariff increases, expectations of lower growth, and higher inflation. The bond market was clobbered by the sharp deterioration in inflationary expectations and by the realization that the Federal Reserve, with its seemingly never-ending zero interest rate policy, was woefully behind the curve with a hyperaccommodative monetary policy. A typically backward-looking Fed offered no comfort to shell-shocked market participants who were looking for higher interest rates to temper mounting concerns over inflation. After a regularly scheduled policy meeting in June 2015, the Federal Reserve reaffirmed its commitment to keep its benchmark policy interest rate near zero through 2016, and dangled the possibility that it even might up the ante on the size of the liquidity injections of quantitative easing that had been in effect since 2009. Yields on ten-year Treasuries moved back above 4 percent in response, and stocks came under further downward pressure.

Feeling the heat from financial markets, Washington turned the dial further on newly imposed anti-China trade sanctions. Senator Schumer went on national television on July 4, 2015, with a rousing Independence Day message: "Enough is enough. We've carried the big stick for years. Democrats and Republicans stand together in believing it is now time to use it." Building on Washington's newfound bipartisanship, President Obama agreed and called Congress back from holiday into a special session to consider the China problem.[10] By unanimous consent, the Congress quickly passed an amendment to DATA—upping the countervailing tariffs on China by another 10 percent. Borrowing from his 2007 book, Schumer commented after the action, "The United States is determined to fight for the middle class—if we have to, one family at a time."[11]

At that point, an indignant China turned to its own version of the Big Bazooka. The biggest foreign buyer of U.S. debt, owners of $1.3 trillion of Treasury securities, was nowhere to be seen at Treasury's August 2015 "quarterly refunding" auction. Treasury had announced intentions to sell $25 billion of ten-year notes and was counting on China to purchase at least $4 billion of the offering. China had been given special direct-dial privileges by Treasury officials, allowing it to circumvent Wall Street dealers and go directly to the issuer. When the line was activated in the Treasury dealing room on August 8, 2015, it went dead. Long-term interest rates spiked, taking yields on ten-year Treasuries above 7 percent within days, and the dollar plunged. The U.S. stock market, which had already sold off by 20 percent in the first half of 2015, went into free fall.

Just like that, the "exorbitant privilege" of the safe haven asset had vanished into thin air with the fall of the dollar.[12] Incredibly, Washington hadn't seen this coming. At a congressional hearing a week earlier on the China problem, Bob Corker, the new Republican chairman of the Senate Foreign Relations Committee, was asked whether he thought there was a risk of China balking at the upcoming Treasury auction. "Where else would they go?" he replied. Washington was smug in its belief that China wouldn't dare undermine the value of more than $2 trillion in Treasuries and other dollar-based holdings. Yet when asked at a press conference the day after China had answered that same question quite differently in the markets, Zhou Xiaochuan, the governor of the People's Bank of China, said, "This is not about risk-adjusted portfolio returns. We are defending our people against an act of economic war." When queried further as to whether China would move beyond its "buyer strike" and actually begin to sell its massive position in U.S. Treasury bonds, Zhou replied, "Only if we have to."

By the autumn of 2015, there was little doubt of the severity of the renewed recession in the United States. Lacking in savings, it found its trade sanctions on China backfiring. Ever needy of foreign capital, the country redirected its purchases of Chinese goods to other foreign producers. Most were higher-cost producers than China, effectively adding a tax on long-struggling middle-class families. The horrific policy blunder was a painful confirmation of a truth that should have been obvious—that there is no bilateral fix for the multilateral trade problems of a savings-short U.S. economy. The unemployment rate shot back up above 11 percent, surpassing earlier post–World War II highs hit in 1982 (10.8 percent) and 2009 (10.0 percent).

In China, Beijing went on high alert in the face of the ultimate economic disaster scenario, a major shortfall in economic growth. Exports had collapsed in light of the renewed weakness in U.S. consumption and the collateral damage that shortfall in demand had triggered in Europe, Japan, and other major economies around the world. With China unable to find new sources of foreign demand for its products and unwilling to slow down production and assembly lines for fear of putting millions of Chinese workers out of work, inventories of unsold goods piled up. Finally the overhang of production was too much and gave way in the absence of external demand support. Chinese GDP sagged immediately, flirting with the dreaded 4 percent threshold—far weaker than the trough growth rate of 6.6 percent in the Great Recession of 2008–9 and in fact the weakest reading on economic growth since the hard landing of the late 1980s in the aftermath of the tragedy in Tiananmen Square. Layoffs surged and social tensions spread like wildfire.

China quickly found itself backed into a corner. Contrary to its well-advertised rebalancing ambitions, it had dragged its feet in promoting internal private consumption, meaning that the sharp weakness in external demand was all the more disconcerting. Out of desperation, Beijing went back to the same old script that it first wrote in the aftermath of the Asian financial crisis of the late 1990s and rolled out yet another proactive investment stimulus, relying once again on accelerated infrastructure spending and property investment to plug the shortfall in GDP growth. But this time, there was an ominous twist: The external demand shortfall was so severe that it took considerably more investment and state-directed bank lending to address the growth problem than was the case in 2008–9. At the same time, the escalating outbreak of social unrest by newly unemployed workers in the cities raised serious questions about the urbanization strategy that China had long counted on to support the investment piece of its growth equation.

The Four Uns of Wen Jiabao came back to haunt China in a way the former premier had never dreamed of. An unbalanced and unstable Chinese economy had come off its moorings. Bad loans piled up in the Chinese banking system, prompting the People's Bank of China to reverse course and finally join other major central banks in embracing what Chinese leaders called the dreaded zero interest rate strategy. Structural reforms were put on hold and China's long-awaited pro-consumption rebalancing plan was put back on the shelf. With Chinese GDP growth slipping farther and now at risk of piercing the 3 percent threshold, the thirty-five-year growth miracle seemed all but over.

The severe shortfall in Chinese GDP growth proved to be a devastating development for the rest of the world. The major economies of East Asia—Japan, South Korea, and Taiwan—immediately lapsed into recession as their export-led growth lost the largest source of demand, China. Similar developments unfolded in China's resource supply chain—from Australia and New Zealand to Canada and Brazil. Export-led Germany, hugely dependent on Chinese capital equipment demand, also turned down, taking the rest of an otherwise sclerotic European economy with it. That sealed the fate of a once complacent world. The global economy plunged back into renewed recession, and the Great Crisis and Recession of 2008–9 suddenly looked like child's play.

It all began with seemingly innocent trade skirmishes between two codependent economies, the tough talk of political bluster. But it was a slippery slope to start with. And Globalization 2.0 was teetering on the edge, just like its predecessor in the early 1930s.

Then and Now

This bad dream comes with a lesson: Both economies, the United States' and China's, continue to struggle—trapped in antiquated growth models that are not delivering the prosperity that politicians and leaders continue to promise. In these circumstances it is far easier to assure one's constituents that they are not to blame than to tell them to lower their expectations and make sacrifices. True to the pathology of codependency, it is especially easier to blame one's problems on foreigners than on oneself. Still, the history of the Cold War shows that rhetoric can grow heated—far more heated than what prevails today—without either side taking the fateful next step. But sometimes wrong-footed steps are taken, and they can just as easily be taken by accident as by design.

Bad dreams can come true. In 1930, Senator Reed Smoot and Representative Willis Hawley did indeed fire the first shot in a catastrophic global trade war. Before dismissing the bad dream depicted above, it is worth

drawing a sharper contrast between the what-if of 2015 and the real thing—
the Great Depression of the 1930s, when trade policy became a live weapon
in what turned out to be a very unstable global environment.

Douglas Irwin's penetrating and richly detailed history of the Smoot-
Hawley Tariff Act of 1930 explains how the naïveté of politicians can spark
a global trade war.[13] It is a history that also reveals what is really at stake
today on the trade policy front as frictions build between the world's two
leading economies, the United States and China. Four key conclusions
stand out:

First, Smoot and Hawley were not antitrade isolationists. They were both
caught up in the domestic politics of protecting U.S. agriculture during and
immediately after the presidential election of 1928. At the time, the agricultural sector employed nearly 25 percent of the U.S. population, and unlike
manufacturing, which had bounced back smartly from a downturn in the
early 1920s, the farm sector remained depressed. Ironically, it was struggling not because of foreign competition—a point that was entirely lost in
the rush to higher tariffs—but because of speculative overhangs of excess
supply and high debt.

In accepting the Republican nomination for the presidency, Herbert
Hoover proclaimed that "the most urgent economic problem in our nation
today is in agriculture."[14] And that's where politics took the wrong fork in
the road—operating under the erroneous presumption that tariffs were the
means to renewed prosperity in farming. At that point in American history
it was not uncommon to view tariffs as a major instrument of economic
policy. Support was largely along party lines. Republicans from the North
typically favored tariffs as a means to provide support for industry, whereas
Democrats, beholden to exporters from the South, felt the opposite. After
the election, which Hoover and the Republicans won by a landslide, Congress moved quickly to deliver on a party platform that had affirmed un-
equivocal support for tariffs as "a fundamental and essential principle of
the economic life of this nation . . . and essential for the continued prosperity of the country."[15]

And then one thing led to another. After long and arduous hearings in
Congress in the early months of 1929, the Republican majority caved in to
the pressure brought by its manufacturing support base and broadened the

scope of its efforts from agriculture to industry. Previously, tariffs on farm products had been set at about half the level of those for manufactured goods. A call for "tariff equality" soon became a guiding principle of the legislative process. As lobbyists fought successfully to raise protection on some agricultural products above the levels prevailing in industry, manufacturers then insisted on maintaining an ever-rising parity—ultimately driving up tariffs even farther on farm and factory products alike. The log-rolling of special interests took on a life of its own. In the end, Smoot-Hawley led to tariff increases on almost nine hundred of America's thirty-three hundred dutiable imports.

Today, there is a much broader political constituency in the United States actually in favor of using trade policy to support American workers. In contrast with Republican-led efforts in 1929, there is now broad bipartisan support for such actions. Moreover, manufacturing, not agriculture, is leading the charge for such protection. Both major candidates in the 2012 presidential election campaign were avowed "fair traders"—recognizing the economic gains that have come from trade liberalization and tariff reduction, but warning that nations that didn't play by the same rules as the United States would have to face "the big stick."

Second, when the Smoot-Hawley bill began working its way through Congress in early 1929, the U.S. economy was still booming, moving toward a business cycle peak that occurred later that year. After a sharp recession in 1921, industrial production doubled between 1922 and 1929. The unemployment rate stood at just 3 percent as trade legislation was being considered by Congress. Import penetration was low, exports were surging, and the United States had nearly a $1.5 billion surplus in merchandise trade in 1929. The depressed agricultural sector was not enough to detract from a strong performance elsewhere in the U.S. economy. The Roaring Twenties stock market famously added to the froth.

Notwithstanding the Great Depression that was soon to follow, today's U.S. economy is in many respects in worse shape than it was in the late 1920s. Postcrisis aftershocks have had lasting impacts on output growth and job creation, headwinds not evident in the pre-Depression period. The 7.6 percent unemployment rate of 2013 was more than double that prevailing in 1929. And the United States is currently a large net debtor, with massive current account and trade deficits—not the saver and net creditor with external surpluses it was in the 1920s. During the run-up to the enactment of Smoot-Hawley in 1928–29, the overall state of the U.S. economy was really not the issue. This time it is, and that puts more pressure on Congress to come up with a policy fix.

Third, Smoot-Hawley tariffs were not targeted at any particular adversary. Amazingly enough, congressional leaders in 1929 hardly took international reactions into consideration when framing this legislation. Astonishingly, they argued, instead, that tariffs were a "domestic matter."[16] America's trading partners, of course, saw it differently—especially Canada, Cuba, Europe, and the United Kingdom. They all countered with reciprocal measures—either explicit retaliation or, more frequently, thinly veiled discrimination against American-made goods. This added to a worldwide outbreak of protectionism that deepened the downturn in global trade in the early 1930s and exacerbated the Great Depression.

While Smoot-Hawley had broad international repercussions, that outcome was not intentional and was more a result of politicians' naïveté and ignorance. The mindset is very different today. Unlike the Trade Act of 1930, which raised tariffs on a broad cross section of America's trading partners, current trade actions are aimed directly at country-specific objectives—focusing on Japan in the late 1980s and China today.

What's similar, however, is the failure to appreciate these actions' unintended consequences. In the 1930s, the possibility of foreign retaliation was simply not on Washington's radar screen. Today's mindset is equally reckless. It presumes that the surgical strike of a bilateral currency "fix"—despite its fatal flaw as the wrong answer to a multilateral trade deficit—can succeed without having blowback effects on U.S. exports or foreign capital inflows that savings-short America relies on.

Fourth, deflation in the early 1930s seriously exacerbated the increase in U.S. tariffs. As Irwin points out, a large portion of the existing U.S. tariff structure was set in fixed-dollar terms—say $1 per pair of shoes—that were independent of the absolute price of dutiable items. When prices started falling in the early 1930s, these fixed amounts added a far more onerous

tax on foreign imports. By Irwin's estimate, fully two-thirds of the total increase in U.S. tariffs from 1929 to 1932 can be attributed to this deflationary force.[17]

There is a deeper lesson to take from this point. The sharp recession
of the early 1930s was made worse by the confluence of several factors—
financial panic, banking failures, Fed policy blunders, and a 61 percent
plunge in global trade from 1930 to 1932. The collapse in trade was exacerbated by two developments—Smoot-Hawley-inspired protectionism and a
crisis-induced outbreak of deflation. While today's U.S. economy has yet to
slip into deflation, it has certainly come close in the past decade—after the
bursting of the equity bubble in early 2000, and again in the aftermath of
the Great Crisis of 2008–9. As Ben Bernanke warned over a decade ago,
"it" (deflation) could very well happen again.[18] The combination of anti-
China protectionist risks, together with the wrenching Great Crisis, bears
an eerie similarity to the twin forces at work in the early 1930s.

The most important difference between then and now concerns the
mechanisms of vulnerability. Yes, the U.S. economy was about to topple
into a catastrophic Depression in the 1930s, and with the benefit of hindsight it is wrong to say things were in good shape before that devastating experience. But from the standpoint of a current assessment of macro
vulnerability—namely a lack of savings, a bubble-dependent real economy,
and mounting systemic risks in the financial system—it is not a stretch to
claim that America's economic climate is just as precarious today as it was
in 1929, if not more so.

The same is true of the world economy. With trade having hit a record 32
percent of world GDP in 2008 versus 9 percent in the late 1920s, today's
global economy is far more interdependent than it was back then. Moreover, with the surge in global trade accounting for fully 42 percent of the cumulative increase in world GDP between 2001 and 2008, the vulnerability
of the global growth dynamic to a sharp reversal in the trade cycle is all the
more problematic.[19] The impact of a "trade accelerator" can cut both ways,
probably taking away as much on the downside of a global growth cycle as
it contributed on the upside.

This leads us to what is perhaps the toughest conclusion of all: The world
of Globalization 2.0 would have an especially tough time surviving without

the high-octane fuel of cross-border trade. The lessons of Smoot-Hawley need to be seen from that perspective. A major blunder on trade policy today actually has the potential to unleash comparable impacts on global growth. That underscores the risk of a treacherous outcome for the co-dependent U.S. and Chinese economies—as well as for the rest of an interdependent world—if the unthinkable were to become thinkable. A trade war in that context would be the worst possible outcome.

Prisoner's Dilemma

History is filled with the ebb and flow of political and economic cycles. But the intersection of the two has always presented especially interesting and at times daunting challenges. That's even more so when cross-border considerations are added to the equation, as they are with the codependent economies of the United States and China. And that's especially the case when both political and economic cycles are near their extremes, as they are today in an era of political polarization (U.S.), leadership transition (China), and postcrisis economic challenges (U.S. and China).

In assessing the validity of any prediction, it pays to examine the extremes of conceivable outcomes, in this instance, the Rosy Scenario of a spontaneous revival of the global economy or the Armageddon of a trade war. The best any honest forecaster can do is to assess relative probabilities of these alternatives. That gives a sense of where the risks lie—ultimately the most critical consideration for policy makers, politicians, businesspeople, and even the average citizen.

The optimistic scenario understandably has great appeal. And there have been several such periods since the end of World War II. None of them, however, arose out of thin air. They came instead from seismic shifts in the underlying macroclimate—postwar reconstruction, the taming of inflation, the fall of the Soviet Union, the emergence of China and India, or the advent and spread of a powerful new technology. Each of these breakthroughs was followed by a period of great prosperity, in some cases spreading from one nation to many.

Yet each of these sparks was lit at a time of great angst and uncertainty. The world was devastated and seriously in debt at the end of World War II.

A raging double-digit inflation seemed intractable in the late 1970s. In the 1980s, the United States was suffering from an unexpected and inexplicable twenty-year shortfall of productivity growth. The Chinese economy was in shambles after the Cultural Revolution. Yet in all of these occasions, tough times were followed by much better ones, as human ingenuity and sheer determination ultimately triumphed.

Today, the macroclimate is laced with a comparable atmosphere of darkness. Beginning in 2008, a series of wrenching crises took the developed world to the brink of collapse. As Japan—possibly the laboratory for the future of the United States and Europe—has known for a generation, the aftershocks from those crises do not fade quickly.[20] That makes it very hard on persistently unbalanced emerging and developing economies, which themselves remain heavily dependent on external demand from the crisis-battered developed world.

The most likely outcome that emerges from this chain of events does not offer much encouragement for those counting on the return of Rosy Scenario. In forecasting jargon, the risks on the downside outweigh those on the upside by a considerable margin. It would probably take another of those unforeseen magical sparks to shift the risks back to the upside.

With the macro risks skewed to the downside during a period of unrelenting pressures on workers and family incomes in the developed world, an increase in trade tensions between China and the United States is certainly conceivable. Sure, there is the boy-crying-wolf mentality noted above, fueled by the frequent saber rattling of Washington politicians who always seem to back away from the edge at the last minute. The cynic maintains that the Bad Dream would just be classic election-year politics. And there has, indeed, been a clear pattern in recent years of intensified China bashing leading up to presidential (and midterm) elections, followed by a more constructive posture in the postelection period.[21]

To the extent Washington conforms to this predictable pattern and lowers the anti-China decibel level after our fictitious 2014 midterm election, the odds don't favor the darker extremes of the Armageddon outcome, either. But painful memories of election-year politics in 1928–29 sound a cautionary note in extrapolating this tendency in perpetuity.

For China, the risk-assessment exercise takes on just as much importance as it does in the United States. The dream analysis presented above undoubtedly makes for sleepless nights in Beijing. Mindful of Washington's time-honored penchant for election-year trade bashing, there is certainly sentiment to let it all blow over this time as well. But with a more recent history of chaos and turmoil and a level of development that pales in comparison to American prosperity, the Chinese have a thin margin of error. China's new leadership team can hardly afford to be complacent in the face of Washington's tough rhetoric.

Like America's students of history, the Chinese also have a keen appreciation of the lessons of the 1930s. But this appreciation is more intellectual than practical. They certainly understand that a trade war would be an unmitigated disaster—risking an outbreak of social unrest that could well topple the Party from power. Those are not risks that modern China's leaders seem willing to take. In the same sense, their perceived sense of 150 years of humiliation at the hands of the West does not provide them with an easy way to back down without risking a major backlash from a strongly nationalistic populace.

In many respects this is a classic "prisoner's dilemma"—a game-theoretic framework that lays out the possibility of uncooperative behavior between two parties even when both know full well it is in their best interest to resolve the dispute between them.[22] On the surface, China and the United States do, indeed, appear to be trapped in just such a predicament.[23] And while the consequences of a bad outcome are severe for both "prisoners," China's inclination to operate strategically, as stressed in Chapter 5, may serve it well in understanding what's at stake and how to avoid the classic wrath of betrayal that the prisoner's dilemma ultimately offers.

The advice of the game theorist is to recognize that the rewards of betrayal are always greater than those of collaboration and cooperation. The only possible escape from the dilemma—and it is a temporary one, at best—is for one prisoner to learn from the actions and behavior of the other prisoner and tailor his or her moves to fit the history of counterparty responses to the common dilemma. China seems to have done exactly that several times in recent years—frequently sending a delegation of high officials and business leaders to the United States to buy items such as Boeing aircraft ahead of a Strategic and Economic Dialogue session, or allowing the renminbi to appreciate in advance of other U.S. decision points such as the release of the Treasury's semiannual foreign exchange report or a key congressional vote on currency or trade issues. While China may have bought a little bit of time with these actions over the years, it must still worry that it has not forestalled the endgame of the Bad Dream. U.S. politicians, for their part, seem more intent on saber rattling than on figuring out a strategy of extrication from this dilemma.

China's big strategic response is one we take up shortly—forging a rebalancing of its economy toward personal consumption and away from external demand and the potential repercussions of trade frictions and protectionist actions from the United States or other nations. But this shift will, of course, take time, time that hardly provides an expeditious escape from the prisoner's dilemma and the related risks of a Smoot-Hawley-type accident on trade policy. America has similar strategic options available to it in the form of a rebalancing away from excess consumption, but the likelihood of prompt and meaningful progress on this front seems lower than it does for China. In the end, neither party can afford to lose sight of the ultimate downside of entrapment, if and when its codependent partner moves from belligerence to betrayal and the Bad Dream comes true. That is the toughest lesson of all from the 1930s. Never say never.

PART V

RESOLUTION

LEFT UNTREATED, CODEPENDENCY can become a destructive psychological force that leads to identity crises and mounting frictions between partners. For the United States and China, the economics of codependency offers the possibility of a different endgame, especially if rebalancing brings new identities. For China, this will entail a transformation from the producer model to an emerging consumer society. The United States must move in the opposite direction, pulling back from excess consumption and rediscovering its competitive prowess by tilting its growth model toward capital spending, human capital, and export-led growth. America must wean itself from a deficit savings culture, while China needs to absorb its overhang of surplus savings.

These shifts offer extraordinary opportunities for both nations. Outward-facing American companies—goods producers and services providers alike—stand to reap a windfall from the expansion of Chinese consumption. But that comes only if corporate America wins the battle for market share the old-fashioned way, through competitive zeal. The United States risks squandering that opportunity if it fixates on a belligerent approach to China and relies instead on trade sanctions to address perceived competitive inequities.

For its part, China has much to gain from drawing on American experience in building a consumer society. The United States has taken the consumer-led growth model to unparalleled heights as a source of prosperity and economic hegemony. While it pushed this model to dangerous excess, it still provides China with a template for rebalancing—large-scale service and distribution networks in conjunction with a wide range of product choices. China has much to gain by drawing on American companies and expertise in these critical areas.

Of course, there are no guarantees that both nations will rebalance at the same pace—China's consumer may well start to emerge before America's producers are rejuvenated. An asymmetrical rebalancing could prove especially vexing for the United States, with its large and growing dependence on foreign capital. If a consumer-led China begins to draw down its surplus savings before America prunes its public and private sector deficits, financial markets could be roiled by sharply higher U.S. interest rates and a significant weakening of the dollar.

Structural change never occurs in isolation. While it can be driven by economic imperatives, it has enormous implications for the politics and sociology of any nation. This interplay won't be easy for either the United States or China. Widening income inequality and political ossification represent a tough combination for both. The Next China faces the challenge of realigning economic growth with a new set of political and social values. The Next America faces an equally daunting challenge of rewriting its social and political contracts. The world's most important economic relationship hinges on critical adaptations in both countries—and on a commitment to resolve structural imbalances without another wrenching crisis, a trade war, or something worse.

There are many moving parts to the structural transformation of any economy. Powerful new technologies often lead to unexpected twists and turns during these transitions. Today, the Internet offers a wide range of such possibilities, from breakthrough connectivity and networking to disruption of traditional businesses and job security. It provides both an opportunity and a challenge.

For China, even a censored Internet is the means toward greater unification of a long-fragmented society—with important implications for the establishment of national norms of consumer behavior as well as for the transparency of its long-opaque political system. This does not come without risk. As China pivots toward consumer-led growth, it will need to embrace the aspirations of a consumer society—upward mobility, property ownership, and free and open communication. The political consequences of those developments could be one of the biggest unknowns in a new era of connectedness. With the largest and most rapidly growing Internet user community in the world, the Chinese state may be forced to rethink its deeply entrenched rules of political engagement.

The Internet has played a different role in the United States. While it has facilitated new efficiencies of online distribution, it has also become an instrument of divisiveness. By enabling the dissemination of extreme views at both ends of the political spectrum, it has contributed to an unprecedented polarization of American politics. That makes it difficult for Washington to frame and win acceptance for the policy strategies that structural rebalancing of the U.S. economy requires. Long the global leader in innovation and new technologies, the United States risks falling behind China in converting the breakthroughs of the Internet into a positive and unifying force.

Identity crisis is the ultimate risk of codependency, and both countries seem to be in its early stages. Who is China? A significant portion of
China's thirty-year growth miracle was driven by exports of Chinese subsidiaries of Western multinationals. Was this at China's initiative to seek
foreign capital, technology, and know-how, or did it represent a conscious
effort of global companies to use cheap Chinese labor to solve their cost
problems? Who is America? So much of the recent U.S. growth bonanza
was supported by cheap Chinese goods and by especially cheap financial
capital. Could American consumers have gone to excess without their Chinese enablers?

Each nation deluded itself into a false prosperity that distorted its economic sense of self. America pushed its consumer model too far, and
China did the same with its producer model. Mirror images of each other's
insatiable appetite for growth, they turned codependency from a supportive
to a potentially destructive force. Just as a psychologist would argue that it
is now time for the cure, the economist must reach the same conclusion.

11

Rebalancing

Breaking bad habits is a struggle for any economy, but the United States and China no longer have any choice. While strong on the surface, they suffer similar maladies: They are the most unbalanced major economies in the world today. As opposite sides of the same coin, China and the United States are in a league of their own.

No unbalanced economy is ultimately sustainable. It is just a matter of how and when that message finally sinks in. The most dramatic wake-up call of modern times—the Great Crisis and Recession of 2008–9—sends a very strong message that the time for rebalancing is at hand.

Yet as the dust hopefully settles in the postcrisis era, rebalancing is not assured in either country. In part, that reflects the very human emotion of denial—the belief that crises are aberrations and what has worked in the past will work again in the future. But it's also a testament to the difficulty of structural change. It is extremely tough and often times painful for an economy to reinvent itself.

Temptations notwithstanding, neither the United States nor China can afford to risk doing nothing. Of the two economies, China seems to get it. While its Twelfth Five-Year Plan is a blueprint for structural rebalancing, the United States seems far more reluctant to accept the need for rebalanc-ing, let alone to formulate a plan to do so. Yet the two countries have been symbiotic in their historical imbalances, and the coming rebalancing of their economies needs to be equally complementary. The fate of codepen-dency rests on whether they can find common ground in addressing their joint challenges and opportunities in the years ahead.

The Heavy Lifting of Structural Change

Structural change goes hand in hand with global rebalancing. If rebal-ancing is defined as a shift in the macro structure of an economy that allevi-ates the sources of its underlying imbalances, the same idea can be applied to groups of economies—or even to the entire global economy. The key is a tempering of unsustainable imbalances. Changing an economy's major sources of growth unlocks a broad menu of reforms, incentives, and policy strategies that bear critically on both the stability and sustainability of eco-nomic growth.

This is, of course, easier said than done. Structural change takes time and immense effort; it is extremely difficult for any economy to achieve. The presence of compelling reasons to rebalance doesn't guarantee that it will happen. Deeply embedded structural characteristics define the core values of societies and political systems. Dislodging all that—even in the name of stability, growth, and sustainable prosperity—is not easy.

The Japanese economy is the laboratory of modern-day struggles with structural change. Its long-entrenched mercantilist model led to unsustain-able bubbles that brought it two lost decades of economic growth—and counting. Rebalancing signals don't come any more powerful than that. Japan's newly elected Prime Minister Shinzo Abe seized on this imperative with aggressive policy initiatives in early 2013 aimed at bringing fifteen years of deflation to a quick end. The "three arrows of Abenomics"—aggressive monetary easing, fiscal stimulus, and a regulatory reform agenda—offer encouragement that the government finally gets it. But Japan continues to drag its feet in embracing a long list of neglected items on its structural reform agenda—especially more flexible employment and immigration policies, aggressive corporate restructuring and bankruptcy provisions, information technology–enabled productivity enhancement in its services sector, a postnuclear energy strategy, and reforms of its gargantuan postal saving system.[1] Without pushing ahead on structural change, Japan's temporary boost from monetary and fiscal stimulus will quickly fade. Both the United States and China should heed the lessons of Japan very seriously.

For purposes of discussion, it helps to put numbers on the rebalancing imperatives of the United States and China. The U.S. economy should reduce the personal consumption share of GDP from its current record high of around 69 percent to a more sustainable 63–64 percent by 2015, the average that prevailed in the final quarter of the twentieth century. That would free up resources worth 5–6 percentage points of GDP to be directed at increasing exports, business capital spending, or both.

The Chinese economy needs to make comparable shifts. Its combined share of exports and investment is currently more than 70 percent of GDP; meaningful rebalancing would imply a reduction of at least 5 percentage points over the next three to five years. The proceeds, in this case, should be applied toward an increase in China's lagging sector—internal private consumption.

Timing is obviously a key consideration in formulating and implementing rebalancing agendas. The sooner the better, from the standpoint of macroeconomic management. But structural change, almost by definition, entails a major unwinding of deeply embedded habits, incentives, and values. It would be unrealistic to expect either the United States or China to shift its output shares by as much as 5 percentage points in anything less than three to five years.

Inertia is, of course, the enemy of change. China will undoubtedly be tempted to stick with its old model—which after all has given it a remarkable record of growth and development for more than three decades. Several possible outcomes might keep China in its comfort zone and thereby prevent rebalancing: An unexpectedly vigorous rebound in global demand might lull China back into a reliance on exports; or a major outbreak of political instability or social unrest might force it to put rebalancing on hold.

China's legacy as a centrally planned economy also creates stiff resistance to structural change. While the old State Planning Commission has been dismantled, its successor, the NDRC, still dominates state-directed economic decision making. Since 1979, the national mantra of "reforms and opening up" has been almost exclusively directed at strengthening China's producer culture. Entrenched provincial and local party power blocs, in conjunction with equally powerful state-owned enterprises—both operating under the NDRC umbrella—only deepen that imprint on the national psyche. To the extent structural change needs to buck these powerful forces, forces that intensified in the aftermath of the massive postcrisis stimulus in late 2008, Chinese rebalancing could face stiff resistance.

Yet the old model has fallen out of favor for good reasons. That's what Premier Wen's Four Uns were all about.

The United States, too, is deeply reluctant to accept its rebalancing imperatives. In large part, that's because American consumers are steeped in a culture of excess.[2] Not only has consumption long been the dominant segment of the U.S. economy, but it personifies the ethos of the body politic. Since at least 1958, when John Kenneth Galbraith published his landmark book, the United States has been known as the affluent society.[3] In the years that followed, consumerism has come to personify the self-image of a nation—for many, the American identity.

Partly in reflection of this strong pro-consumption bias, today's U.S. fiscal and monetary authorities seem intent on resurrecting the old unbalanced growth model. The Federal Reserve's experimental liquidity injections of quantitative easing, commenced in the depths of the Great Crisis of 2008–9, are focused on boosting asset markets. By doing so, the U.S. central bank is attempting to dangle newfound wealth creation arising from higher stock and home prices in front of battered consumers in the hope of reversing an unprecedented postcrisis shortfall of personal consumption.

It appears, however, that American families are smarter than Washington policy makers. They have so far opted to resist the bait and have chosen instead to repair crisis-damaged balance sheets by paying down debt and rebuilding saving. Progress has been slow but healing is now under way. Yet if American consumers cling too tenaciously to old habits—as they are certainly being tempted to do by the Fed—consumers will remain predisposed toward allocating their limited incomes toward spending, with little likelihood of a meaningful revival in personal saving. Ultimately, that could be a very serious problem for deficit-prone America and a major stumbling block to rebalancing. Meanwhile, the shift toward export- and investment-led growth remains exceedingly difficult for a U.S. economy that is chronically short of savings.

It is not clear which country's rebalancing agenda faces the biggest hurdle—whether it is harder to curb the excesses of a producer model or those of a consumer society. Neither will be easy, yet both are essential.

The Next China

China's Twelfth Five-Year Plan, formally enacted in March 2011 to run through early 2016, features a major shift toward personal consumption. The private consumption share of Chinese GDP had fallen from 53 percent in the early 1980s to about 35 percent by 2008, where it has remained ever since. That gave China the dubious distinction of having the smallest consumption sector of any major economy in the world.

A falling consumption share should not be equated with declining personal consumption. Instead, it means that consumer demand has been growing more slowly than the rest of the Chinese economy. That underscores a critically important aspect of the modern Chinese growth miracle: The Chinese consumer has played only a secondary role in powering China's 10 percent annual GDP growth over the past thirty years. The main drivers have been, as we have stressed repeatedly, China's massive surge of exports and fixed investment.

The Twelfth Five-Year Plan makes the Chinese consumer the centerpiece of the Next China.[4] There are many aspects to this story, but they revolve around two objectives—first, boosting personal income, and second, persuading families to spend this new income rather than save it.

The Chinese economy suffers major deficiencies on both of these counts. In 2011, disposable personal income was only about 45 percent of GDP—below the nearly 50 percent share recorded in 2002 and far short of the 77 percent portion in the U.S. economy.[5] There are many causes: subpar employment growth, lagging real wages and benefits, and financial repression of yields on household saving balances that limits personal interest income. All of these factors must be addressed if subpar Chinese consumer purchasing power is to increase as a share of GDP.

Before getting to the details, it is important to stress a conceptual point: While increasing personal income is a necessary condition for stronger consumption, it is not sufficient. High and rising personal saving stands between income and consumption growth. To the extent that China's household saving motives reflect fear—a reasonably accurate assessment, given the state of flux arising from massive urbanization, the decline of the cradle-to-grave benefits of the old Communist system, and the country's woefully deficient social safety net—that has the potential to soak up most or even all of any surge in personal income.

The Twelfth Five-Year Plan, a monumental undertaking with many moving parts, attempts to tackle all of these aspects of China's daunting consumption problem. If it succeeds, China may well hit the target outlined above and boost the consumption share of its GDP by 5 percentage points by the end of 2015. The pro-consumption plan has three main building blocks:

Jobs. China does not generate enough jobs. Overall employment growth has averaged just 0.5 percent per year in the decade ending 2011—making the country Asia's laggard in net job creation. Employment growth in urban areas has been far more impressive, averaging 4.1 percent over the same period and sending a strong signal as to where Chinese job opportunities lie. That has led to a massive migration to the cities, taking the urban share of China's overall population above 52 percent. But a significant portion of the growth in urban jobs has been offset by a decline in rural employment of some eighty-two million over the ten-year period 2001–11.[6]

China's sluggish overall employment growth stems from one of its greatest structural anomalies. The export- and investment-led growth model rests on a foundation of manufacturing and construction. As China has moved up the value chain and encouraged the growth of profit-driven private companies, its manufacturing model has come to resemble that of other, more advanced economies—boosting productivity by substituting technology for people, capital for labor. This has left China with a capital-intensive, labor-saving growth dynamic.

A labor-saving growth model is especially challenging given China's continuing need to absorb surplus rural labor as the means toward poverty reduction and increases in per capita incomes for the country's entire population. The flow of rural-to-urban migration is now about fifteen million to twenty million people a year. This would create a huge labor absorption problem even if China were running a labor-intensive economy. But it no longer is—or at least, not to the degree that it once did. Putting it another way, China is not generating enough jobs per unit of output, and to compensate, it has to generate more units of output. That means it needs to run faster and faster on the treadmill of output growth in order to absorb enough labor to maintain social stability.

That goes a long way in explaining China's addiction to double-digit GDP growth and in unmasking a critical oversight of China's vaunted economic stewards, Zhu Rongji and Wen Jiabao. In the old days—as recently as the late 1990s—China could hit its labor absorption target with around 6 percent annual GDP growth. But now it needs closer to 9 percent or even 10 percent to achieve the same result. That extra growth of 3–4 points per year, a result of the economy's shift toward more capital-intensive, labor-saving manufacturing businesses, has enormous consequences. Hypergrowth in the 9–10 percent range was a recipe for mounting internal imbalances. Without it, China would have had a much easier time dealing with excess resource consumption, environmental degradation and pollution, and even mounting income inequalities. Premiers Zhu and Wen, architects of the modern development miracle, failed to fully appreciate this major structural anomaly and its profound implications for China's rebalancing imperatives.

Services are the antidote for much of China's missing job creation. For starters, services—or the so-called tertiary sector—generated about 30 percent more jobs per unit of output in 2011 than did manufacturing and construction, the secondary sector.[7] A services-led Chinese economy would thus need only about 7 percent GDP growth to hit the same labor absorption target that requires 10 percent growth in a manufacturing- and construction-led economy. That slower growth would also help relieve many of the above-noted internal strains that have arisen from decades of hypergrowth.

China has the most undeveloped services sector of any major economy in the world today. At 43 percent of GDP, Chinese services are well below the 55 percent of India and Asia's other developing economies. And of course it is far from the 75 percent share of the United States, the world's quintessential services economy. This underscores one of the key structural opportunities for China relative to other major economies. Its undersized services sector is ripe for expansion.

The Twelfth Five-Year Plan has targeted a 4–percentage point increase in the services share of the Chinese economy, from 43 percent in 2010 to 47 percent by 2015. The abundance of low-hanging fruit in Chinese services suggests that this target could easily be surpassed. China has very small footprints in wholesale and retail trade, domestic transportation, and the overnight delivery and logistics systems required of China's supply chains; the scale of its services sector is also substandard in leisure and hospitality, as well as in healthcare and finance. Unlike more advanced knowledge-intensive professional services, where staffing requires massive investments in human capital, these transactions-intensive pieces of Chinese services could be staffed relatively quickly through three- to six-month worker training programs.

A comparison with the services sector of the United States underscores the potential for development of Chinese services. Currently, private services account for 68 percent of total employment in the United States, well above the 44 percent share in China's urban units.[8] Four segments of private services—wholesale and retail trade, leisure and hospitality, healthcare, and professional and business services—collectively account for 50 percent of total employment in the United States, but just 16 percent in China. If the Chinese share were to equal the American share, China would have to add the equivalent of 49 million jobs, surpassing the government's target of 45 million new jobs in urban areas. If China were to close half the gap with the United States in just the wholesale and retail trade sectors, that alone would boost its services jobs by 5.5 million.

In short, a shift to labor-intensive services is an important piece of the Chinese rebalancing equation. While certain services are beyond the reach of a still relatively poor developing economy like China—especially those offered by professionals such as lawyers, accountants, and consultants—there are many basic services that could fit right in with the rising Chinese standard of living. The consumer culture of the Next China can't come to life without the infrastructure of distribution and transactions processing that a services sector provides. To the extent that a shift to services could also alleviate some of the side effects of China's persistent imbalances, the case is all the more compelling.

Wages. Employment is the foundation of personal income and consumer purchasing power. But the price of labor, or the wage rate, is the key factor in converting job creation into labor income. Economic theory tells us that labor ultimately receives its just reward as its contribution is measured by a worker's marginal productivity.[9] It is not a coincidence that high-productivity economies such as the United States are also at the upper end of the pay scale. The productivity imperative, and the real wage gains it would foster, remains one of China's greatest challenges.

Boosting subpar wages has long been a focus of Chinese policy. Minimum wages were first introduced in 1993, and the labor reform legislation of 2004 required that they be boosted every two years. Further reforms in 2008 were aimed at protecting the rights of Chinese workers through mandatory employment contracts, arbitration and mediation of labor disputes, and such safety net programs as unemployment insurance and re-training. Partly as a reflection of these policies, labor wages have been rising steadily since 2004. Hourly compensation rates in Chinese manufacturing increased at a 17 percent average annual rate between 2004 and 2008, with gains approaching 30 percent in 2007 and 2008.[10] Yet this surge hasn't really made a dent in boosting the personal income share of Chinese GDP. In large part, that's traceable to two factors—the low starting point of Chinese wages, and the move toward capital and away from labor in the increasingly advanced manufacturing sector.

The Twelfth Five-Year Plan places considerable emphasis on rising wages as a means to boost Chinese personal income and consumption. A number of explicit provisions are directed at boosting productivity and wages in rural agriculture, which still accounts for nearly 55 percent of all Chinese employment. These include financial support for farmers, as well as expanded subsidies for agricultural production and farming communities. Apart from direct subsidies to existing programs, the plan also stresses rural productivity enhancement through a variety of other new initiatives, ranging from rural infrastructure and water conservation projects to rural electrification and new financial vehicles.[11]

But the most powerful boost to Chinese wages comes from urbanization—specifically, the government's unrelenting focus on rural-urban migration as the principal means of absorbing surplus labor and providing an antidote to poverty. According to the OECD, 316 million Chinese citizens are projected to move from the countryside to newly urbanized areas between 2011 and 2030—close to 16 million per year over a twenty-year period.[12]

That's where the other key variable in the personal income equation—wages—comes into play. The OECD also calculates that urban workers' per capita income is currently 3–3.25 times that of their rural counterparts.[13] Provided that newly relocated rural workers can find employment in urban areas—the big "if" in the labor calculus of the Next China—there is good reason to be optimistic that personal income will rise as a share of Chinese GDP. Matching up job creation with urbanization is far from easy. But it is essential for Chinese rebalancing. The services sector is key. The expansion of China's deficient footprint in services is the most effective means to reconcile rural-urban migration with the need to increase employment, per capita wages, and ultimately personal income.

If rural-urban migration matches the OECD's projection and the urban-to-rural wage differential holds, a back-of-the-envelope calculation suggests that the personal income share of Chinese GDP could be boosted by 5 percentage points by 2020 and another 10 points by 2030.[14]

There are certainly other factors on China's personal income agenda—not the least of which would be an end to the financial repression that has kept down the personal interest income of Chinese savers. Liberalization of interest rates on saving deposits would be very important. Some estimates suggest that this action alone would boost the personal income share of Chinese GDP by 5–10 percentage points.[15] The Twelfth Five-Year Plan alludes to such reforms, but there has yet to be meaningful follow-up.

Financial security. It is one thing to boost labor income by policies that promote employment growth and higher worker pay. But as noted above that income is unlikely to be translated into discretionary spending if Chinese families are uncertain and insecure about their future welfare. Fear-driven precautionary saving will absorb any windfalls of income—thereby defeating a pro-consumption strategy. Evidence suggests that this has been one of the most powerful drags on Chinese consumption.[16]

The Chinese social safety net has long been inadequate. While this problem is prominently featured in the Twelfth Five-Year Plan, it won't be easy to solve. Shortfalls in the funding of retirement income are especially troubling. The paucity of assets in China's various pension plans underscores the challenge. As of 2011, the National Social Security Fund had just 869 billion renminbi of assets under management; local government social security funds had 1.5 trillion renminbi (a 2010 estimate), and balances in private pension plans totaled just 300 billion renminbi.[17]

Combining the three sources of retirement funding and spreading the total assets of about 2.7 trillion renminbi over China's huge workforce, we see that the so-called retirement safety net contains assets of just USD $1,690 per worker for the 257 million who were actually covered by such plans in 2010. If the same amount is spread over all of China's 764 million workers—not unreasonable in terms of the nation's ultimate liability—it shrinks to just $565 of assets per person to cover lifetime retirement benefits.[18] Money goes a long way in China, but not that far. The nation's provisioning for lifetime retirement falls woefully short of providing a reasonable standard of living for its rapidly aging population. Little wonder that Chinese families put their money away in the bank rather than spend it.

The Twelfth Five-Year Plan speaks forcefully about this problem. So far, however, the talk has not been followed by meaningful action. With an economy awash in surplus saving, China has ample leeway to transfer public funds to retirement pensions, either at the central government or provincial and local levels. The longer it delays addressing retirement security, the harder it will be to jump-start consumer demand.

Healthcare presents a similar challenge. In 2009, China enacted major healthcare insurance reforms. As in its retirement funding strategy, China's healthcare plan focused more on the number of enrollees (close to 95 percent of the population) than on benefit levels. It turns out that the plan's total funding—850 billion renminbi spread out over three years—provides benefits equaling just $30 per year for each of China's 1.3 billion citizens. Such amounts don't even begin to address people's needs in an area that is key to their financial security.[19] Again, China's surplus savings economy has the potential to invest considerably more in funding its safety net. The time to do that is now.

Adding up. The Twelfth Five-Year Plan represents a major turning point in the long-awaited rebalancing of the Chinese economy. It is particularly strong in laying out a blueprint for the development of the embryonic services sector and for emphasizing a massive rural-urban migration that leverages services development into a meaningful increase in labor income. But it falls short in providing funding for the social safety net—not only in recognizing the need to instill greater financial security by addressing key issues of retirement and medical care, but also in drawing on the nation's vast surplus savings to deliver on that recognition. Until that piece falls into place, the Chinese consumption story will remain incomplete.

The Next America

It would be unfair to call 2013 the year of America's 238th one-year plan. As the bastion of free-market capitalism, the United States has a deep aversion to anything that smacks of planning. But the year did mark a turning point in the postcrisis journey of the U.S. economy—a long overdue recognition that the United States was in desperate need of new sources of growth.

That realization was brought home by an American consumer in the grip of an enduring balance sheet recession, with still-high liabilities continuing to put the squeeze on households, especially those with "underwater" collateral that had been decimated by the bursting of the property bubble. With inflation-adjusted consumer spending having grown by just 1.1 percent a year since early 2008—a fraction of the 3.6 percent gains that prevailed in the dozen years before the onset of the crisis in 2007—the U.S. growth model was broken. The 69 percent of the U.S. economy currently earmarked for personal consumption has been incapable of delivering anything close to its historical contribution to growth.

And so a fundamental rethinking of the American economy is in order. Long possessed of the dominant economy in the world, the United States finds this tough new reality hard to accept. But denial is no longer an option. It is time for an introspective assessment of what it might take to recapture the magic. With balance sheet–constrained consumers likely to stay in a deep freeze for years, the Next America requires something very different.

The other 30 percent. At one level, looking beyond the 70 percent consumption share for America's new growth recipe is a straightforward exercise. By process of elimination, four sectors emerge as potential candidates: residential construction, government spending, net exports (exports less imports), and business capital spending. Which will it be?

The odds don't favor homebuilding, or residential construction. While a case can be made that the U.S. housing market has finally hit bottom after the worst contraction in the post–World War II era, the subsequent expansion in this sector has come from a very low base. With residential construction activity only about 3 percent of GDP in 2013—less than half its 6.6 percent peak share in 2005—even a vigorous and sustained recovery of the sector would barely make a dent in offsetting what promises to be a chronic shortfall of consumer demand.

But it's not just the astonishing shrinkage of the homebuilding sector that impairs its role as a new engine of economic growth; a number of other factors compound the problem. The mortgage loan foreclosure backlog of distressed property is still some 1.3 million units, and it will take more time for this overhang of supply and its attendant downward pressure on home prices to work its way through the system.[20] Meanwhile, despite the Fed's extraordinary efforts to subsidize the cost of mortgage credit through its zero interest rate policy and quantitative easing aimed at direct purchases of more than $1.3 trillion in mortgage-backed securities since early 2009, persistently high unemployment and related pressures on personal income continue to constrain potential homebuyers.

Nor does the government sector emerge as a viable candidate as a new engine of U.S. economic growth. With record deficits and debt at the federal level, it is widely accepted that spending restraint is increasingly urgent. In an era of fiscal discipline, with federal government purchases having fallen from a cycle peak of 8.8 percent of GDP in mid-2010 to 7.5 percent by mid-2013, a sharp reversal is exceedingly unlikely—especially with the federal government now locked into the automatic spending constraints of "sequestration."[21] The same can be said of state and local governments, where extremely tight budgets are forcing major retrenchment in many jurisdictions. Spending by these government entities has declined in fifteen of the twenty-two quarters from early 2008 to mid-2013, and its share in the economy is down 1.9 percentage points from its mid-2009 peak of 13.1

percent of GDP. Barring a spontaneous revival of revenues—not likely in a persistently weak recovery—the state and local government sector should continue to be a drag on overall economic activity for years.

That leaves two sectors—net exports and business capital spending—as the strongest candidates for economic leadership in the Next America. Collectively, exports and capital expenditures accounted for 25.6 percent of GDP in 2012, while imports made up 16.9 percent. Significantly, the export share, at 13.5 percent, is already at its all-time high, making significant further growth a challenge. Capital expenditures, at a little over 12 percent of GDP, remain well below their peak of 14.5 percent in 2000. The formula for revival would thus entail some combination of a sharp rebound in business capital spending and further growth in exports, in conjunction with a reduction in imports. That poses the ultimate question for the Next America: What will it take to achieve this?

Competitiveness. One important aspect of the answer can be found in the imperative of America's competitive challenge. With internal, or domestic, demand unlikely to provide anything close to the needed support for the American growth machine, focus must shift to external demand. While exports are an important aspect of the challenge, so, too, is the need to turn back the tide of import penetration. None of this can occur in a vacuum—especially with a U.S. economy that remains deficient in saving and therefore must import surplus saving and goods from abroad in order to grow. That issue will be addressed shortly, but saving can't do it alone. Nations must also compete effectively to capture—or in America's case, recapture—global market share.

The United States has lost its competitive edge. That's the verdict of the World Economic Forum's (WEF) Global Competitiveness Index, which saw the United States slip into seventh place in 2012–13—down from fifth place in 2011–12 and continuing a downward trend that has been evident since 2005, when the United States was last number 1.[22] The latest tally finds the United States behind Switzerland (number 1), Singapore (2), Finland (3), Sweden (4), the Netherlands (5), and Germany (6). Moreover, the United States scored only fractionally higher than the United Kingdom, Hong Kong, and Japan, underscoring the risk of further slippage in this widely followed measure of competitiveness.

The WEF metric draws on some 113 indicators in its assessment of global competitiveness. It breaks down its composite index of overall competitiveness into three subindexes: *basic requirements*—institutions, infrastructure, macroclimate, and health and primary education; *efficiency enhancers*—higher education, efficiency in labor, product and financial markets, technological readiness, and market size; and *innovation and business sophistication*. These subindexes allow us to pinpoint the most important sources of America's competitiveness problem.

The United States scores highest in "efficiency enhancers"—number 2 behind Singapore and well above China (30). Within this category, the United States ranks number 1 in market size—hardly surprising for the biggest economy in the world—sixth in labor market efficiency, and eighth in higher education and training; but its rankings in other parts of this category are much lower—especially gauges of technology availability and absorption (11), financial market development (16), and goods market efficiency (23).

In "innovation and sophistication factors," the United States is seventh, behind Switzerland, Japan, Finland, Germany, Sweden, and the Netherlands, and again well above China (34). This subindex ranks the United States much better in innovation (6), especially in its emphasis on research and development collaboration between universities and private industry; but its ranking on "business sophistication" (10) is held down by disappointing scores on production processes and supply chain management, including the quality of local suppliers—an especially worrisome result in light of the increasing sophistication of Asia's China-centric supply chains.

The most serious problem comes in "basic requirements," where the United States ranked number 33. It not only trailed most developed economies but was also behind many large developing economies, including China (31). A ranking of 111 on "macroeconomic climate" was clearly the most disturbing aspect of this low ranking. That reflected the country's public sector debt and deficits and the brinksmanship of dealing with them, its shortfall in domestic saving, and its reckless bubble-prone flirtation with false prosperity beginning in the late 1980s. But the United States also received low rankings on healthcare and primary education (34) and business confidence in public and private institutions (41). Surprisingly, it does somewhat better on infrastructure; but here its number 14 ranking is inflated by excess passenger airline capacity, which masks significant weakness in other infrastructure metrics such as those pertaining to roads, rail, ports, airports, energy supply, and mobile phone subscriptions.

Over the years, more has been written on competitiveness than on almost any other subject in global economics. It cuts to the heart of many of the globalization issues we have been discussing and also bears critically on several aspects of U.S.-China codependency—especially the two nations' different approaches to state involvement in their economies, and to macroeconomic strategy. Much of the literature on competitiveness is highly subjective, laced with strong opinions and deeply held ideological allegiances. The WEF metrics are helpful in providing a more objective assessment of the problem. But it is important not to take the metrics too far—to keep in mind that there is an art, as well as a science, to understanding the global competitive challenge that the United States now faces.

The WEF competitiveness rankings reveal a rich menu of issues that the United States must address if it hopes to shift its growth model from domestic to external support. It must remedy deficiencies in both the human and physical dimensions of capital formation—particularly in primary and secondary education and in replacing and upgrading its antiquated infrastructure. Addressing the pitfalls of macro management is also high on the list, as is deepening corporate America's expertise in supply chain management—the new industrial model of globalization.[23]

As important as these issues are, however, they don't do justice to the biggest elephant in the room—the growing disconnect between competitive prowess and job creation. It is no longer true, though it is still often considered a given, that improved competitiveness equals massive new numbers of jobs. Apple, arguably one of America's most successful innovation and competitive success stories, generates nearly ten times as many jobs offshore (especially in China) as it does domestically.[24] What good does it do for a nation to succeed in the global competitive sweepstakes if the reward for success is increasingly hollow companies that create more jobs offshore than onshore? That goes back to the question in Chapter 6 that David Ricardo could not answer.

Saving. Can America afford to compete? In normal times, no one would have had to ask such a question. But these are not normal times. When we are saving nothing—or at least nothing beyond the saving that covers depreciation, or the wear and tear of existing facilities—it becomes necessary to ask where we will find the money for a broad array of urgent national priorities from national defense and entitlements to infrastructure and educational reform.

What will it take to get America saving again? Credible and sustainable federal government deficit reduction is obviously at the top of the list. But this can has now been kicked to the end of the road. A bipartisan resolution of fiscal gridlock is obviously the only way out—on both the revenue and expenditure sides of the equation. Taking the budget deficit from 7.5 percent of GDP in 2012 back to its 1980–2007 average of 3.3 percent would, all other things being equal, boost America's gross domestic saving by more than 4 percentage points of GDP. That windfall wouldn't permit the United States to commit to everything on its competitiveness menu, but it would be a major step in the right direction.

Deficit reduction should not be the only item on America's savings agenda. We also need to provide enhanced saving incentives for U.S. families, many of whom squandered their income-based savings on the false dreams of the property bubble. With the excesses of asset-based saving no longer an option, Washington needs to address the financial insecurities of crisis-battered families and come to grips with America's long-neglected saving agenda. Several possibilities come to mind: an expansion of existing IRA and 401(k) programs; targeted retirement saving incentives for low- and middle-income families, half of whom have no retirement plan whatsoever; tax reform that moves from an income to a consumption tax (such as a value-added tax or national sales tax) in order to tilt incentives toward future consumption; and a normalization of the Federal Reserve's zero interest rate policy that artificially depresses yields on saving accounts—in effect, ending a financial repression that bears an eerie resemblance to a similar condition in China.[25]

The enactment of such incentives should be phased in over three to five years. A more immediate push might be counterproductive in inhibiting consumer demand and recovery in the broader economy—consistent with the "paradox of thrift" noted in Chapter 7. But time should not be lost in addressing the longer-term concerns that most Americans share about saving and financial security. Unless America deals with its chronic savings shortfall, Washington will forever be tempted to compensate for that deficiency by resorting to policies that encourage risky financial engineering in order to extract purchasing power and saving from volatile asset markets. This didn't work in the late 1990s or 2000s and it won't work in the future. But with the Federal Reserve still intent on restarting the asset economy with the liquidity injections of unconventional monetary policy, there is certainly no lack of effort to convince people that they don't have to save the old-fashioned way—out of their paychecks rather than out of assets and the bubbles that often plague asset-dependent economies.

Stability. In keeping with the World Economic Forum's assessment of U.S. competitive challenges, the Next America will also need to get much better at macro policy management. That won't happen if policy makers don't tackle the destabilizing imbalances that have all but crippled the global economy.

This goes back to the basic point of Chapter 1—a political culture that has long been biased toward the seduction of a false prosperity. A key aspect of the problem is the politicization of monetary policy. Central banks, especially in the developed world, have become caught up in the search for growth and have strayed from their core missions of maintaining price stability and (in the case of the Fed) full employment. They have taken huge risks in leveraging monetary policy as an unsustainable source of growth.

The policy mandate of America's Federal Reserve needs to be formally revised to take account of this dangerous tendency. In the aftermath of the Great Crisis, senior Fed officials now claim to recognize that they need to take financial stability more seriously than they did in the past. But the operative view in the central bank is that this is a matter for "macroprudential" regulation—the setting of industry-wide standards for banks and markets aimed at avoiding "systemic" risks—and not a proper subject for monetary policy.[26]

Steeped in denial, the Fed is basically absolving interest rates and monetary policy of any blame for the excesses that caused so much damage to the financial markets and the real economy during the Great Crisis. In effect, it holds that excess liquidity, fostered by a highly stimulative monetary policy that encouraged reckless borrowing, had nothing to do with the profusion of equity, property, and credit bubbles that almost brought down the U.S. economy. It also condones the ideological capture of the monetary policy decision making—a serious problem, as we saw, in both the Greenspan and the Bernanke eras. While senior Fed officials have now promised to take financial stability more seriously, experience suggests they cannot be trusted to resist the ever-enticing political economy of false prosperity.

The only way to resolve this problem is for Congress to hardwire financial stability into the Fed's legal mandate. This follows the modifications to the mandate that were made with the Full Employment Act of 1946 and the Humphrey-Hawkins amendment to that act in 1978—the former aimed at codifying the goal of full employment and the latter making the Fed explicitly accountable for price stability.

Financial stability should be added as a third leg of the Fed's policy mandate.[27] As with the first two targets, the operative definition of financial stability should be left to the Board of Governors of the Federal Reserve System, but it should take into account the rate of change in major asset and credit market indexes, growth in aggregate leverage, and any asset- and credit-related distortions to the real economy. Finally, coincident with its biannual submission of a Monetary Policy Report to Congress and in cooperation with the newly established Financial Stability Oversight Council, the Fed should also be required to submit a Financial Stability Report to Congress that details its compliance with the new mandate.

There is no foolproof way to mandate high-quality performance from any economy. But the current approach has failed, and the Next America needs greater accountability from its policy makers. A renewed focus on competitiveness, saving, and stability will give the United States a much better chance at uncovering new sources of sustainable growth and prosperity.

Balance

The rebalancing of an unbalanced world will take time and enormous effort. The United States and China have an opportunity to lead by example. And they should, since they have not only the largest economies in the world but the most unbalanced.

In one sense, the choices are black and white. Imbalances are bad, balance is good. One is sustainable—the other is not. One is more crisis-prone than the other. The fix seems so obvious. But is it?

Rebalancing poses a special challenge for two codependent economies such as the United States and China. Joined at the hip in so many ways over the past thirty years, they have not been attentive to the toll that mounting imbalances has taken on their seemingly symbiotic relationship. If they move in tandem to address these issues, the risk of destabilizing repercussions seems low. But what if they don't?

The crises of recent years are warnings to both of the consequences of inaction. The goals are not in dispute: The Next China must become more of a consumer-led economy, and the Next America must once again become more of a producer-led economy. What is in dispute is whether they have the political will to pull it off. Rebalancing and the structural change it requires do not come without pain and sacrifice. This is where politicians invariably stumble—whatever system they represent.

12

The Next America
Meets the Next China

The rebalancing of two codependent economies will require a role reversal. If all goes according to the script presented in the previous chapter, the United States will change from a consumer into more of a producer. China will experience the opposite conversion.

Yet the shifts will not be black and white, complete switches from one model to another. Rebalancing is a far more subtle transformation. The U.S. and Chinese economies should emerge from this process with broader and more solid foundations of sustainable growth—drawing support from both consumption and production, from internal as well as external demands.

Given the strong ties that bind them, the coming role reversals are enormous opportunities for both economies. For a growth-starved United States, China's nascent consumer markets offer great potential as a new source of demand. That might be the perfect spark for a reemergent American export machine. Similarly, a rebalanced China has much to draw on from the world's quintessential consumer—goods, services, systems, and managerial expertise. A consumer culture could be China's ultimate import. The trick will be for each nation to take advantage of the other's rebal-

ancing rather than get swept up in the fears of the unknown, misconstru-
ing the need to change as yet another threat.

That won't always be easy. With postcrisis aftershocks likely to linger
for years, each country will be sensitive to any development that appears
to challenge its growth aspirations. While these concerns are understandable, they are probably overblown. That is especially the case with respect to
the trade frictions that have intensified in recent years between the United
States and China. In theory, rebalancing should temper trade frictions
rather than worsen them, yet misreading that remains a key risk. Nor will
it be easy to orchestrate the rebalancing of both economies in unison. Their
respective transformations will most assuredly move at different speeds,
leading to asymmetrical adjustments and destabilizing repercussions that
might prove challenging to manage.

While it is unrealistic to expect rebalancing to be perfectly synchronous
and seamless, the directional shifts in the two countries are clear. That's
the basic point that both nations must seize. Of necessity, growth remains
the all-encompassing objective. But the strain that results from rebalancing
is likely to be quite different from the strains of the past. It will be driven
more by a focus on the quality of growth than by a simple fixation on the
top-line magnitude of the quantity of GDP growth.

We have stressed earlier the key role that leadership has played in shaping economic management in China and the United States. An even bigger leadership lesson could be at hand. Successful rebalancings by these
codependent economies would allow China and the United States to lead
by example—something a crisis-prone world sorely needs.

America's Ultimate Export

For most of the post–World War II era, the United States has been at or
near the top of the global export sweepstakes. That changed in 2006, when
China moved into first place. But the United States is still holding its own
in the number two position—technically third, if all the countries in the
European Union are lumped together—so it is hardly an also-ran in global
trade.

But number two is not the point. The race, itself, is less important than the opportunity to run. America does not need to beat China in the export business. Instead, a growth-starved U.S. economy needs to draw on China as a major lever for a renewal of its export business. With American consumers tapped out after the Era of Excess, exports have the potential to fill an important void in the U.S. growth calculus. There is no better solution for a struggling American economy than to parlay its codependent relationship with China into an important new source of economic growth.

China is well positioned to help. It is now America's third-largest export market. At $111 billion in 2012, it remains far behind Canada ($292 billion) and Mexico ($216 billion), which benefit not just from the NAFTA free-trade zone but from close geographic proximity and an integrated North American supply chain. While China doesn't enjoy the NAFTA and supply chain synergies of Canada and Mexico, it has become an increasingly important destination for American products. China has not only widened the lead considerably on the United States' fourth-largest export market—Japan ($70 billion)—but it is closing the gap with Mexico and Canada.

That's because China is by far America's fastest-growing major export market. From 2005 to 2012, U.S. exports to China expanded at a 16.2 percent average annual rate—more than double the 7.5 percent combined growth of U.S. exports to Canada and Mexico over the same period. U.S. exports to Japan over that time grew at just 4.3 percent a year. Moreover, given that the growth of European demand is likely to remain sluggish, new pressure will probably emerge in a number of other major U.S. export markets: the United Kingdom (the fifth-ranked U.S. export market), Germany (6), and the Netherlands (9). The United States will want to lean on China all the more in light of likely shortfalls in its exports to Europe.

The current mix of U.S. exports to China doesn't come as a much of a surprise. U.S.-made power generation equipment is at the top of the list, and with the exception of the agricultural category of oil seeds and oleaginous fruits (mainly soybeans), which is number 2, the rest of the top ten consists of either capital equipment or natural resources. These include electrical machinery and equipment (3), nonrail motor vehicles (4), and aircraft (5). Exports of optical and medical equipment are the sixth-largest U.S. export to China, followed by four resource-based or commodity exports—plastics (7), pulp and paper (8), copper (9), and organic chemicals (10). Collectively, the top ten accounted for $63 billion, or 60 percent of total U.S. exports to China in 2011.[1]

With the possible exception of some $5 billion of U.S. exports of optical and medical equipment, which has obvious ties to healthcare, the bulk of America's export business in China has been closely aligned with the investment- and export-led character of the nation's economic model. In a detailed tally of Chinese purchases of American-made goods, consumer products barely show up. In 2011, all of these items added up to just $2 billion, or 1.9 percent of total U.S. exports to China. The top ten U.S. exports to industrial China were worth thirty times more than the small subset going to the Chinese consumer.

Still, it is worth understanding the types of American-made consumer products that are currently being exported to China. It gives a sense of the starting point in what could well be an important growth opportunity. Excluding $1 billion of pharmaceutical exports, the top ten exports of American-made consumer goods to China are, in order of importance, toys, games, and sporting goods (1), writing and art supplies (2), records, tapes, and disks (3), televisions, VCRs, and other video equipment (4), toiletries and cosmetics (5), household appliances (6), books and printed matter (7), jewelry (8), furniture and household goods (9), and artwork, antiques, and stamps (10).[2] The amounts in these largely low-end consumer products categories are tiny, the largest being $600 million in toys and sporting goods. In the coming rebalancing of the Chinese economy, not only will consumers play a more active role in driving economic growth but they can also be expected to move up the value chain and expand their demand for more sophisticated foreign-made products. All this underscores the considerable opportunities for U.S. exporters in a consumer-led rebalancing of the Chinese economy.

The United States is clearly punching well below its weight in mapping its global trade structure on to China. Nonauto consumer products currently account for about 12 percent of total U.S. exports, or roughly six times the share these items have in the export mix to China. If the structure of U.S. exports to China resembled the norms of America's other trading partners, foreign shipments of consumer goods would be about $10 billion higher.

Shifting the mix of U.S. exports to China from industrial products and resources to consumer goods is of course just another way of slicing pie. If the share of the latter goes up, shares going to other products will, by definition, go down. The challenge for the United States is to expand the overall size of its export pie. The pro-consumer transformation to the Next China offers just such an opportunity. For China, this is a transformation about demand, not supply, one that should provide a powerful impetus to the overall volume of global trade. For the Next America to tap that impetus it will need to bring its export businesses into close alignment with the coming expansion of domestic Chinese markets. This is one of the ultimate dreams of codependency.

There are three aspects to this challenge for U.S. exporters—competitiveness, market access, and vision. The first issue, America's increasingly tough competitive challenge, was addressed in Chapter 11. One can only hope that the United States rises to meet this challenge head on in the years ahead. Conceptually, *market access*—making certain that U.S. companies have a fair shot in conducting business in Chinese markets—should not be a problem. As noted in Chapter 2, China is very open economy. The import share of its GDP has averaged 28 percent since 2002, not only three times Japan's historical ratio but well above that of most of the world's major economies.

In recent years, however, market access has become a contentious issue between the United States and China. It is now a prominent item on the agenda in the high-level summitry of the Strategic and Economic Dialogue (S&ED) that takes place annually between the two nations. As well it should be. For far too long, the S&ED has been dominated by the currency debate. To the extent the Chinese currency issue has been marginalized by reality—namely, a 35 percent appreciation of the renminbi versus the U.S. dollar since 2005, a sharp reduction in China's international trade and current account imbalances, as well as a recognition of the fallacious bilateral fixation on America's multilateral problem—attention needs to be directed at the removal of tariff and nontariff barriers that distort trade flows in both directions. Those are code words for market access.[3]

The tough economic climate since 2008 has made market access an issue for both the United States and China. That was especially the case after the U.S. stimulus program of 2009, which featured a "Buy American" provision.[4] China countered with similar actions of its own.[5] The result was a conscious effort by the Chinese to alter government procurement practices so as to favor domestic production and so-called indigenous innovation. Some progress has been made in removing these barriers, but more efforts are needed. America's competitive revival will ring hollow if its newly energized companies are unfairly closed out of markets like China.

Vision is far trickier. But the key in this sense is for the United States to be forward looking—aiming the export potential of the Next America toward the shifting economic structure and needs of the Next China. While that future is of course not precisely known, the Chinese have offered some important hints for the Next America to ponder.

For example, as noted earlier, the Twelfth Five-Year Plan is quite explicit in identifying seven "strategic emerging industries" (SEIs) that will be featured prominently in China's industrial policies over the next ten years: energy conservation, new generation information technology, biotechnology, high-end equipment manufacturing, alternative energy, alternative materials, and autos running on alternative energy. The government plans to increase the GDP share of these SEIs from 3 percent in 2010 to 15 percent by 2020.[6]

The SEI focus could be an important export opportunity for American companies, especially if they get their act together on competitiveness and are assisted by negotiated improvements in access to Chinese markets. These are all cutting-edge industries where rapid growth is heavily dependent on state-of-the-art research and development, together with commercially viable technologies and processes—all of which play to America's strengths. Whether those gains are realized by U.S. exporters, partnerships with China's companies, or some combination of the two, there is enormous upside in this area—provided, of course, that upside is not marginalized by the outbreak of Chinese cyberhacking noted in Chapter 8.

The export opportunities afforded by the Next China will go well beyond its SEIs. As the consumer base broadens and becomes wealthier, demand for sophisticated goods and services will increase. There is no wish list of what that might entail, but as the world's quintessential consumer society, the United States needs only to look in the mirror to make some educated guesses. Think shelter, furniture and appliances, motor vehicles, electronics, and other trappings of modern consumer societies. Chinese consumers will aspire to all of them—and to the quality and product safety that American brands offer.

One thing we can be sure of is that consumer demands in the Next China will present opportunities for U.S. exporters that go well beyond the current product mix, which is heavily skewed toward low-end toys, sporting goods, and apparel. Nor are the Chinese overly parochial in their brand preferences. Foreign brands have enormous appeal in China—certainly in luxury products, where Chinese sales are expected to account for 20 percent of the world market by 2015.[7] While the buying habits of wealthier Chinese may not translate to those in the middle of the income distribution, where the bulk of the growth in Chinese consumption will be concentrated, it speaks to the openness of the nation's untapped consumer tastes. The world's consumer product producers have a vast opportunity: China must have the greatest reservoir of pent-up consumer demand in history.

China's Ultimate Import

Even a state-directed economy like China's can't just push a button and bring its dormant consumers to life. Not only does it have to promote growth in jobs, wages, and the social safety net, as stressed earlier, it also needs to learn the habits of consumption from others. Who better to teach that than the United States? That America took its consumer model to excess doesn't mean that it has nothing to offer. To the contrary, there is much that China can draw on from the world's largest consumer—not just goods and services but expertise in the systems, institutions, and distribution networks that underpin consumer markets. This could be China's ultimate import—and an equally important opportunity for the Next America.

Modern consumer societies encompass far more than demand for material products. Services play equally important roles in shaping lifestyles. Services are also, as we saw in the last chapter, among the keys to China's rebalancing as envisioned in the Twelfth Five-Year Plan. The services share of the Chinese economy, now just 43 percent of GDP, should be at least in the mid-50 percent range of comparable developing nations like India. That it is not underscores the opportunity for those who can help the Chinese make this transition. The United States is at the top of that list.

The case for Chinese services is compelling for many reasons: As an essential new source of job creation, services are critical to the labor absorption required of rural-urban migration. Urbanization on the scale that China is experiencing simply won't work without rapid growth in labor-intensive services and the new employment possibilities this development implies. Services also underpin the infrastructure of consumer demand—providing the distribution and transactions processing functions that modern consumer societies require. And to the extent that increasingly services-led growth allows for slower expansion of Chinese GDP, as well as reduced resource demand and environmental degradation, the Next China stands a much better chance of becoming more manageable, greener, and more sustainable.

Services could also be the most global piece of the Next China's development strategy. This is at odds with the historical role of the services sector as largely domestic industries clustered around major population centers.[8] Not easily transportable, let alone tradable, service providers needed geographic proximity to the markets they served. But the fragmented, localized services model has been overturned by two related developments: new IT-enabled technologies and the emergence of vast networks of multinational services providers. Beginning in the 1990s, these trends, in conjunction with deregulation in such services as finance, telecoms, and utilities, have led to a restructuring of services companies around the world.[9] A new global services industry has emerged as a result, driven by large-scale networked companies that deliver localized output to markets around the world.

China is a part of the array of services markets that are now being targeted by these globalized services enterprises. With China's domestic services sector uncompetitive and underdeveloped, the major service providers around the world are increasingly well positioned to seize this opportunity.[10] The United States, whose services sector accounts for about half the services outlays of the major advanced economies in the world, is in a prime position to benefit the most from this development.[11]

China's Services Bonanza

How large is this opportunity? The economic forecasts of the International Monetary Fund provide a starting point for estimating the scale of the coming surge in Chinese services. IMF estimates put China's GDP at roughly $9 trillion in 2013 as measured in current U.S. dollars, or 56 percent of America's $16.2 trillion economy. IMF forecasts call for this dollar-based measure of nominal Chinese GDP to expand at roughly a 10.6 percent average annual rate over the five years ending in 2018. That's basically double the 5.4 percent current-dollar growth rate they assume for the U.S. economy over the same period. On that basis, in 2018, Chinese GDP would be about 71 percent of that of the United States.[12]

For the years that follow, we engage in creative but hopefully reasonable extrapolation, an extrapolation based on current-dollar GDP rather than the real, or inflation-adjusted, metrics used for most of the analysis in this book. For China, we presume that annual GDP growth will gradually decelerate by a little less than 1.5 percentage points from 10.3 percent in 2019 to 9 percent by 2025. This is consistent with the point made earlier, that an increasingly services-led Chinese economy can hit its labor absorption target with slower GDP growth because it will have shifted from the capital-intensive, labor-saving manufacturing of the old model toward the capital-saving, labor-intensive, services-driven character of the new model.[13] That would still make China a $28 trillion economy in 2025, or about 94 percent the extrapolated size of the United States, the latter based on a 5.25 percent average annual growth rate assumed for U.S. nominal GDP from 2019 to 2025. A further extrapolation at a slightly slower 8.5 percent annual growth pace for China would result in full convergence of nominal GDP between the United States and China in 2028.[14]

To this baseline GDP extrapolation we then add in a gradual shift in the mix of the Chinese economy toward services. The Twelfth Five-Year Plan calls for a 4–percentage point increase in the services share of the Chinese GDP, from 43 percent in 2011 to 47 percent by 2015. In this exercise, we take the official planning target as a given, even though as we noted in the previous chapter there is a good chance that China could do better. Over the following ten years, 2016 to 2025, we allow for further expansion in the services share averaging an additional 1 percentage point of GDP per year. That would take China's services share to 56 percent by 2025—on a par with present-day India and 13 percentage points higher than what it was in 2012.

This leads us to a very powerful conclusion: If these extrapolations are even approximately right, the Chinese services sector will increase more than fourfold, from $3.5 trillion in U.S. dollars in 2012 to $15.9 trillion by 2025. The difference—slightly more than $12 trillion—is a good first-order approximation of the potential bonanza likely to be generated by the sharp expansion of Chinese services in the next twelve years.

The last piece of this puzzle is to figure out the portion of that bonanza that may actually be accessible to foreign businesses. As in any country, foreign participation in Chinese services can take place either onshore or offshore. The onshore option can take a range of forms, from wholly owned subsidiaries to minority stakes in joint ventures. The offshore option relies on cross-border connectivity, either through physical travel and in-person service delivery or IT-enabled dissemination of services from one remote desktop to another.

There is also a regulatory aspect. Historically, nations are very protective of their domestic services markets. Consistent with the implications of Ricardian comparative advantage noted in Chapter 6, services have long provided an important shelter for workers who lose out to international competition in tradable manufacturing. If China fears such a displacement and attempts to stave it off through regulations aimed at restricting the operations of foreign services providers, the global opportunities of China's services led rebalancing will be limited.

There are metrics that allow us to examine this possibility. The World Bank maintains a comprehensive database that measures restrictions in global services trade across five sectors (telecommunications, finance, transportation, retail, and professional services) in 103 countries.[15] On a scale of 0 to 100, where 0 is totally unrestricted and 100 represents a completely closed services sector, China does not fare badly. Its overall score of 36.6 is considerably better than the 65.7 score given to India, although not as good as those of Japan (23.4), South Korea (23.1), the United States (17.7), or Europe (26.1). Since the turn of the twenty-first century, Beijing has steadily been relaxing foreign ownership restrictions in a broad array of joint ventures and partnership arrangements. Barring a trade war, there is little reason to believe this trend will be reversed in the years ahead.

Putting this all together is more art than science. It is impossible to know with any precision how much of the $12 trillion services bonanza

China might make available to foreign services providers. It would prefer, of course, that its own companies lead the charge. But for a nation lacking in experience and scale in services, that is not a realistic option. World Bank metrics offer encouragement that China will allow foreign participation. The question is, how much?

A helpful benchmark comes from the creative research of J. Bradford Jensen of Georgetown University, who has developed tools to measure the "tradability" of U.S. services in global markets.[16] His estimates suggest that a large portion of workers in the U.S. services sector are now employed in tradable occupations; in the broad business services category, for example, he calculates that this applies to roughly 70 percent of all workers. That is probably a good proxy for the tradability of U.S. services output as well.[17]

Of course, China is not the United States—either in terms of the development of its services sector or its willingness to allow tradability in services. The World Bank's metrics on services trade restrictions suggest that China is about half as open as the United States. Using that estimate would suggest cutting Jensen's employment-based tradability measure of 70 percent for the United States in half to around 35 percent as a first approximation of the tradability of China's $12 trillion services bonanza. At the same time, as China continues to deregulate and reform its own services sector—continuing trends seen over the past decade—there is every reason to believe that its services trade restriction metrics will begin to converge on those of the United States; in coming years it is quite possible that the 35 percent tradability factor could rise toward 50 percent, or even higher.

In sum, the minimum opportunity for onshore and offshore foreign services companies in China could be in the $4 trillion range (35 percent of $12 trillion). More optimistically, it could be as high as $6 trillion if the Chinese government moves toward further opening up, through reforms and deregulation, of its embryonic services sector.

If these estimates are in the ballpark, this is a very big deal, especially for developed economies struggling to uncover new sources of growth. Nowhere is that opportunity greater than in the United States, which, as the world's largest services provider, currently accounts for 14 percent of global services exports—twice the share of the next largest exporter.[18] In contrast to its chronic deficits in merchandise trade, the United States has maintained consistent surpluses on services trade—strong validation of its comparative advantage in services. America is well positioned to benefit from the tailwinds of rapid growth in global services trade—worldwide trade in services expanded at a 14 percent average annual rate over the pre-crisis 2004–8 interval, almost as fast as the 15 percent trend surge in trad-able goods over the same period. But the United States is especially poised to benefit from the coming bonanza in China. This could well be one of the most extraordinary economic opportunities the Next China offers the Next America.

China has much to gain as well. American services companies have ad-vantages in process design, scale, and professional and managerial exper-tise that China's nascent services industries lack. It would take decades for China to develop an indigenous services culture of its own, especially one with the scope and scale that its enormous economy requires. Partnering with the United States would be an important shortcut for a nation that is determined to move quickly on the road to rebalancing.

As noted previously, there are immediate opportunities for U.S. services companies to expand and partner in China, especially in wholesale and retail trade, domestic transportation, and the overnight delivery systems of supply chain logistics—as well as in the processing segments of finance, healthcare, and data warehousing. These are the low-hanging fruit of Chi-na's services bonanza, and U.S. services companies are well positioned to do the picking. Recent high-level discussions in the Strategic and Economic Dialogue between the United States and China have made significant prog-ress in opening up Chinese financial services to increased foreign invest-ment. The negotiators should now turn to nonfinancial services as well.

A Confluence of Forces

Producer economies don't have the habits of consumer societies. While China's highly refined production model has had extraordinary success for more than thirty years, it has come at the expense of the Chinese con-sumer, who has been largely an afterthought in the country's economic development. The Twelfth Five-Year Plan represents the first major effort at change—but it is a destination, not a detailed road map.

How does China become a consumer? The basic recipe is clear: services-led jobs plus urbanization-driven increases in average incomes. Add to that the funding of a comprehensive social safety net, and presto—awash in newfound income, the increasingly secure Chinese consumer springs to life. It's a great story, well grounded in analytics and macroeconomic theory. But it will take more than that for China to pull it off. Generations of Chinese have known little of the norms and habits of modern consumer societies. Providing them with a windfall of discretionary purchasing power is one thing. Sparking an attitudinal shift toward discretionary consumption is another matter altogether. Rebalancing is not behavioral reengineering.

Polling data underscore the impediments to such an attitudinal shift. A recent McKinsey survey of Chinese consumer behavior shows that despite more than thirty years of rapid development, household buying habits remain very conservative. Only 28 percent of all Chinese consumers confess to impulse buying—well below the 49 percent who admit to it in the United Kingdom.[19] Scarred by the Cultural Revolution, fearful of job insecurity in an era of state-owned enterprise reform, and facing inadequate income support in retirement, middle-aged and elderly Chinese consumers are understandably cautious. Their attitudes also reflect the norms of moderation that underpin the Confucian value system.

Moreover, the emerging Chinese consumer is trapped between two powerful forces—rural-urban migration and high-speed aging. New consumers from the countryside—fifteen million to twenty million per year—enter cities with a subsistence income and almost no discretionary spending power. Meanwhile, the demographic profile of a rapidly aging Chinese population is tilted increasingly toward a further absorption of discretionary income: Without a safety net, soaring old-age dependency ratios will force each working-age family to fund the retirement of two sets of parents.[20] The combination of these developments makes it exceedingly difficult to envision a spontaneous liberation of the Chinese consumer.

What magical spark will convert these producers into consumers? The same question, of course, could have been asked in the late 1970s in the aftermath of the Cultural Revolution, when the Chinese economy was in shambles. But there was a powerful spark back then that offers China important lessons today. It came in the form of a basic survival instinct that was converted into the aspirations of sustained development.

The transition from survival to growth was a key piece of the earlier puzzle. Two words say it all—"opening up." By encouraging foreign direct investment and the technology transfer that comes with the influx of capital and expertise from abroad, China built and learned how to operate a state-of-the-art production, assembly, and distribution platform. This was the true miracle of the ultimate producer.

It has a similar opportunity today in services. The transition is not as urgent as it was in the tumultuous late 1970s. But as Wen Jiabao's Four Uns warn, the consequences of inaction could be grave—a possibility underscored by mounting internal imbalances as well as by the tendency of China's two largest external markets, the United States and Europe, to suffer repeated crises and extended aftershocks. Just as it imported Western technology and processes to bring its producer culture quickly up to speed, China needs to do precisely the same with the modern trappings of a consumer society.

Opening up its $12 trillion growth bonanza in services to foreign companies would be a decisive step in that direction. Inexperienced in the art and practices of modern services, China needs to build working relationships with well-established companies from the West. It already has an impressive track record to draw on.

A pilot project in financial services is a case in point. In the mid-1990s, Premier Zhu Rongji came to the realization that China could not implement an aggressive program of state-owned enterprise reform without the capital-raising capabilities of a global investment bank. But there were no such companies in China. Morgan Stanley, in partnership with China Construction Bank, was invited in to develop such a financial services capability. Within ten years, China had built a new joint venture company, China International Capital Corporation (CICC), into a world-class investment banking capability.[21]

Similar examples can be taken from a wide range of subsidiary and franchise networks—from operators in the fast-food restaurant and beverage industry (KFC, McDonald's, and Starbucks) and hotels (St. Regis, Shangri-La, and Hyatt) to airlines (Dragon Air, aka Cathay Pacific) and consulting (McKinsey, BCG, PWC, and Ernst and Young). In all of these cases, China has followed the CICC pilot initiative approach—leveraging the expertise of a foreign services provider to build a scalable domestic services capability.[22]

This is why the coming services bonanza could end up being so important for Chinese consumers. By opening up and partnering with the world's leading service providers, China can import the expertise in distribution, systems solutions, marketing, and skills development that can bring its own services sector to life surprisingly quickly. This is the same approach it took in manufacturing—converting foreign-sponsored ventures into rapidly growing domestic enterprises that led to the extraordinary successes in competitive leapfrogging noted earlier.

There is no reason the same approach wouldn't work in services. Moreover, there is a voracious appetite among foreign companies to participate in this transformation—few global services firms today would pass up the chance to establish operations in China. Admittedly, this addresses only one side of the Chinese consumer equation—it expands the menu of choices for personal spending. There is still no guarantee that Chinese consumers will step up and make those choices. But as we will see in the final chapter, there are good reasons to think they will.

The Asymmetrical Push

The rebalancing of two codependent economies entails risks as well as opportunities. One major risk mentioned earlier is "asymmetrical rebalancing," where one economy gets on with structural change before the other does.

China will be first to adjust. In part, that's because China thinks and acts strategically—and the Twelfth Five-Year Plan lays out its rebalancing strategy very clearly. But it is also because the Chinese leadership excels in implementation. Once committed to a strategy—and arriving at that commitment often entails a drawn-out internal debate—China invariably delivers ahead of expectations. The growth and development record of the past thirty years speaks for itself. Now, there is every reason to believe that China's newly installed fifth generation of leaders,[23] focused on maintaining social stability and conditioned by pragmatism, recognizes the importance of shifting from an economic model supported by external demand to one that draws much greater sustenance from internal demand. There were strong signs in early 2013 that China's new leaders were, in fact, willing to accept slower economic growth. Their imposition of greater discipline to monetary and fiscal policies stands in sharp contrast to the proactive hyper-growth strategies of the past. Yet slower growth works in China only if the economy becomes more services-led, more consumer-led.[24]

Just as the external shocks of 2008–12 have been wake-up calls for China, the rebalancing of the Chinese economy could also be the wake-up call for the Next America. That's *not* because the United States is engaged in a strategic battle for economic supremacy and wants to match China step for step. It's more a question of necessity: America's wherewithal to fund its savings-short economy.

With China redeploying its surplus savings to support internal private consumption, the United States will start to lose its largest external source of capital. Washington needs to take this possibility seriously. The musings in the Bad Dream of Chapter 10 are worrisome in that regard, underscoring a very real disbelief by the U.S. political consensus in the possibility that China might reduce its demand for dollars and deploy its surplus assets elsewhere. The quip, "Where else would they go?" is actually a verbatim quotation of a senator (not Bob Corker) I encountered in one of my appearances in front of the U.S. Congress. That xenophobic retort misses a key point: For China, "elsewhere" is not a shift in its foreign exchange reserve portfolio into euro- or yen-denominated assets. It is instead a redirection of surplus saving into the funding of a social safety net and all the other trappings of a Chinese consumer society. The Next China will have less demand for dollars than it has had in the recent past.

Under such circumstances it will be very difficult for an unbalanced U.S. economy to avoid sharply higher long-term interests or a much weaker dollar. Without a new generous donor of foreign capital to temper such pressures, the United States will have no choice but to plug its external funding gap by boosting domestic saving. While federal deficit reduction must be an important part of this response, a restoration of household saving will also be needed. Only by saving more and spending less will America finally begin to wean itself from the unsustainable excesses of its hyperconsumption growth model.

Painful as it sounds, an asymmetrical rebalancing in which China steps out first will thus seal the fate of the United States. America will have no choice other to accelerate the shift of its economy away from private consumption toward more promising and sustainable sources of future growth. As noted, this will require more saving and a focus on competitiveness, spurring new growth in business capital spending and exports. While this won't be easy to pull off, failure to do so would be self-destructive—it would deny the United States the very opportunities its unbalanced economy so desperately needs.

Muddling along—which has been America's preferred course of inaction in recent years—is really not an option in an asymmetrical rebalancing scenario. China's determination to rebalance must be taken as a given, a shift that will force its codependent partner to respond. The only real question is the nature of that response. The more the United States resists accepting its own strain of rebalancing, the more acute the pressures of a weaker dollar and higher interest rates are likely to be. From the standpoint of codependency, it boils down to a simple choice—whether the United States wants to be in control of its destiny and seize the opportunities of the Next China or abdicate control and squander those opportunities.

America should not view this as a Bad Dream along the lines of the fictional scenario depicted earlier. Yes, an asymmetrical rebalancing comes with likely pressures on interest rates and the dollar. If the United States stands still and does nothing in response—or even worse, attempts to strike back—it will, indeed, suffer the repercussions of those pressures. But more than that, a United States that stubbornly clings to the old model will miss the truly unique opportunities that a rebalanced Chinese economy is about to offer.

All roads thus lead to the same place. The only difference is how quick and painful the rebalancing will be for these two codependent nations. If it is asymmetrical, America's adjustment is forced on it from outside. From a strategic point of view—something China has and America doesn't—the scales are already tipped in that direction. China has an indelible impression of what can be gained through reforms and opening up. America doesn't seem to be so sure of where to go and how to get there. But there is one more critical piece to the story—an exogenous shock that provides an even a more compelling reason to believe that China is about to step out first and take a giant stride toward rebalancing.

13

Codependency, the Internet, and a Dual Identity Crisis

Globalization stands for connectivity and interdependence. It reflects an integration of economies and markets woven together by cross-border flows in trade, financial capital, technology, and information. Globalization implies growing assimilation—a blurring of distinctions in the economic roles and identities of nations, companies, and people.

But globalization can also breed a new economic disorder—the "relationship addiction" of codependency.[1] The relationship between the U.S. and Chinese economies, with the world's ultimate consumer locked in a tight embrace with the world's ultimate producer, exemplifies this syndrome—not just in the cross-border transfer of goods but also in the exchange of financial capital. Two large, dynamic economies, both plagued with unbalanced and unstable tendencies, have become very needy in what they ask and expect of each other. This relationship obviously brings important benefits but there are serious risks. Psychologists warn that codependency ultimately leads to identity crisis, denial of responsibility, and the tendency to blame others for problems.[2] China and the United States manifest many aspects of that mutual pathology.

The Internet could ironically turn out to be a new enabler for the identity crises of codependent nations. Like the physical globalization it helps connect, the Internet further obscures boundaries between nation-states, cultures, and different strata of economic well-being. For China and the United States, with the two largest Internet user communities in the world, it changes the rules and means of engagement between citizens (or *netizens*, as Internet users have been dubbed), businesses, and their governments. That's been especially evident recently in China. In 2007, China surpassed the United States as having the largest Internet user community in the world—yet another in a long list of examples of developmental leapfrogging.

But there is far more to this aspect of the story than scale and speed. By redefining connectivity within and across nations, the Internet has also challenged deeply entrenched perceptions of self-identity. It has given China something it has never had before—the national identity that comes with an increasingly connected user community. A new e-based connectivity is bringing together China's heretofore diverse and fragmented population. By itself, this one development has the potential to inject something that has long been missing: broad-based exposure to the cohesive norms of an emerging consumer society.

How this meshes—or doesn't—with the tight controls of China's one-party political system is one of the biggest question marks for the Next China. But for now, it is the connection that matters most—a connection that could provide a strong spark to the consumer-led impetus of the Next China. In the future, more will matter. Ultimately, a connected and rebalanced China will need to face deeper issues of personal freedom, political reform, and ultimately democracy.

Despite its codependent relationship with China, America has long failed to appreciate important transformations of the Chinese economy. This is nothing new; the United States is hardly alone in its blindness. Jonathan Spence famously argued that since the thirteenth century, the West has seen China largely as another version of itself.[3] This misapprehension only complicates the dual identity crisis—making it virtually impossible for nations like the United States to get out of their own skin in assessing ever-changing developments in China.

Those deeply entrenched biases permeate America's current impressions of the Chinese economy and cause many politicians, policy makers, academics, and other commentators to miss the sharp contrasts between the two systems. Yet China is still a poor developing economy, with a per capita income one-eighth that of America. It has a blended system of resource allocation, combining state-directed and market-based features, as well as a one-party political system, a stagnant and rapidly aging population, an unprecedented push toward urbanization, surplus saving, and the macro drivers of export- and investment-led growth. The United States is at the opposite end of the spectrum on nearly all of those counts. China cannot, and should not, be assessed in the same way that America sees itself. The optics of the two economies, as well as the lens by which they should be viewed, are very different. So much of Washington's China fixation misses that key point.

China suffers from a comparable set of biases. Since the Opium Wars of the mid-nineteenth century, the nation's feelings toward the West have been colored by a deeply wounded sense of humiliation. The normal give and take of external criticism has evoked a fierce backlash of Chinese nationalism, with collateral impacts on both economic and regional security policies—most recently manifested through aggressive territorial claims in the South China Sea, intensified frictions with Japan, and protectionist efforts to support indigenous innovation.

All this injects an almost personal animosity into the tensions between the United States and China. The combination of identity crises and biased assessments of each other is a tough one. Consistent with the psychologist's assessment of defense mechanisms, the risks of economic codependency are rising and could be nearing their most destructive state, when China and the United States turn on each other.[4] The Bad Dream of a trade war, or a clash over cyberhacking, could well arise from an escalation of such risks. Can the Next China and the Next America look inside themselves and convert the perils of codependency into the opportunities of coexistence? That is the ultimate test of resolution.

China's Big Bang

While a nation's core values may remain fixed, its economy rarely does. Over the past thirty years, the Chinese development clock has run three to four times as fast as those of other economies. Its more than thirty-fold increase in per capita GDP since 1980 is something that took today's developed economies more than a century to accomplish.

As fast as the journey has been, China's experience with the Internet breaks its own speed records. As of the end of 2012, China's Internet community was estimated at 564 million users—more than a fourfold increase in just six years.[5] In 2005, the United States had almost twice as many Internet users as China, but today the tables are reversed—the Chinese Internet community is more than twice the size of the American one. It is also nearly four times larger than India's, and it far exceeds that of any other developing country.

And there is plenty of room for further growth. At the end of 2012, only 42 percent of China's 1.3 billion people were connected—slightly more than half the penetration ratios in South Korea (82.5 percent), Japan (79.5 percent), and the United States (78.1 percent). If China closes just half of that gap and takes its penetration ratio to 60 percent, it would add 240 million additional users, an increment comparable to the existing Internet community in the United States, currently estimated at 245 million.

China's netizens are far from passive surfers. More than half its Internet users are regularly connected to microblogs or social networks. Participation in microblogging is a more intense, active experience than casual web surfing. Survey data reveal that the average Chinese netizen is online about 2.6 hours per day—a full hour more than the average fifteen- to forty-nine-year-old in China spends watching television.[6] As in most nations, growth in the usage of China's social networks and microblogs is exploding, up 24 percent in 2012 alone to include some 309 million individuals, or 23 percent of China's total population. Still, since microbloggers make up only 55 percent of China's Internet users, well below the global norm of 70 percent, there is significant potential for further migration to these more active platforms.[7]

This could be where the rubber meets the road for Chinese consumption. Scale and growth comparisons of commercial and economic activity nearly always come out dramatically in China's favor. That's certainly the case with its rapid embrace of the Internet. But now with more than 20 percent of China's vast population communicating intensively with each other through regular usage of microblogs, or *weibos* such as Sina Weibo, a new force is energizing the Chinese consumer. More passive surfing by the remainder of China's Internet users only adds to this impetus.

Online activity encourages a sharing of tastes, trends, and lifestyle habits. The assimilation of this knowledge in the form of collective tastes and preferences of a rapidly expanding user community has the potential to bring national norms of emerging Chinese consumers into much sharper focus than would have been the case in the days before the Internet. Young people in an up-and-coming city like Chengdu in China's inland Sichuan province now have a better sense of what their counterparts are buying and wearing in wealthy coastal cities such as Shanghai and Shenzhen. The same may even be true of their parents. As seen through the lens of the Four Uns, the new tools of the Internet can take China from uncoordinated to coordinated.

A recent McKinsey survey underscores the unique role that social media play in shaping consumer habits in China—especially when compared with other nations.[8] Given their basic distrust of such "formal institutions" as branded advertising, Chinese consumers place an especially high value on the kind of peer-to-peer recommendations that its weibos provide. McKinsey survey data show that China's consumers are more inclined to purchase products that are favorably mentioned on social media sites, especially those that received positive recommendations from friends or acquaintances. The latest trends in online shopping in China certainly underscore the potential of this trend. In just one year, the population of online shoppers soared by 43 percent to 242 million at the end of 2012, a huge acceleration from the 25 percent growth rate in 2011.[9]

There was always a missing piece to the Chinese government's conceptualization of consumption-led growth—the spark that would in effect rewire the human DNA and bring Chinese consumers out of the shadows. That spark could well come from the exogenous shock of a new technology, represented by the rapidly expanding Chinese Internet community. If so, it would be exquisitely timed—occurring at the same moment when the incentives and policies outlined in the pro-consumption Twelfth Five-Year Plan fall into place. Suddenly, courtesy of the Internet, the case for China's consumer-led rebalancing no longer looks like the abstract conjecture of macroeconomic theory.

This story has a familiar ring. History shows us that a narrow focus on industrialization is not enough for sustained economic development. Economic takeoffs are one thing, but they are likely to be fleeting without catalytic reinforcement from consumer demand. The reinforcements from personal consumption have come in different shapes and forms. In the United States, the post–World War II release of pent-up demand noted in Chapter 1 was an especially powerful example, with personal consumption expenditures rising from 49 percent of GDP in 1944 to 63 percent a decade later in 1954.[10] Going back farther in time, comparable, albeit less dramatic, gains were evident in Great Britain, parts of continental Europe, and Japan in the latter part of the nineteenth century as the early benefits of industrialization started to spread and take hold in the broader population.

The economics profession has been engaged in a seemingly endless and at times heated debate over the sources of economic growth.[11] But whatever the answer to the growth miracle—technological change, rising investment in human capital, the geographic dissemination of innovations, or reaction to external events following wars and revolutions—there is general agreement that sustainable growth can't happen without a spark from consumer demand. That spark has long been absent in China's producer-led development saga. The Internet Revolution could well provide the impetus to the next phase of this remarkable transformation.

Weibo, Political Reform, and the Modernization Thesis

But that impetus doesn't come without risk. For most countries, the implications of the Internet stretch well beyond economics. China is hardly an exception. The Internet not only shakes its norms of social engagement; perhaps even more important, it ups the ante on the political reform debate—long one of China's most sensitive issues. It's not just the open architecture of instant communication that is so germane to political risk, or even demands for the transparency of governance. It is also the Internet's ability to offer Chinese netizens a real-time aspirational narrative of upward mobility, freedom of expression, and government accountability. This dialogue raises one of the toughest questions of all for the Next China: Can a consumer society emerge and flourish without meaningful political reform?

This would not be an entirely new debate in China. Chinese history has long been known for the liveliness of intellectual protest by artists, scientists, and writers.[12] Tolerance was generally the rule—but to a point: as long as the protest didn't pose a serious threat to the state. That was true of earlier periods in Chinese history—namely, the tenacious protests against the late Ming dynasty emperors, the insurgence of Ming loyalists during the early Qing dynasty, the fall of the late Qing dynasty, and the May 4 movement of 1919. Each of these instances was disruptive but not a regime-threatening event. A restrained state was successful in making the distinction between the normal ebb and flow of discourse in a large society and the more serious risks of rebellion.

A similar mindset prevailed in contemporary times. Following the upheaval of the Communist Revolution, post-1949 China was also rife with political dissent and turmoil—from the Hundred Flowers movement of 1957 to the chaos and disruption of the Cultural Revolution. In both of these latter cases the turmoil was sponsored by Mao Zedong rather than inspired by those in opposition to his leadership. In those instances, as well as the pro-democracy movement of the late 1970s culminating in the "fifth modernization" wall posters of Wei Jingsheng in 1978, the government conformed to historical patterns and remained willing to put up with an active and at times intense debate over the role of politics in shaping Chinese society.[13]

This leniency came to a tragic end in Tiananmen Square in June 1989. While the Party initially tried to maintain China's historical inclination toward tolerance, ultimately it became a matter of survival, a threat to be suppressed at all costs. Suddenly, the normal give and take of protest and dissent was cast in a very different light. China's continuous history of social turmoil had gone from benign to malign, culminating in a regime-threatening event that has since seared the risks of instability into the minds of modern China's leaders. The debate over political reform now occurs in this context, obviously a very different mindset from that which prevailed before 1989.

This new mindset features stability as a goal of paramount importance in shaping the broad reach of policy and social norms in China. That's true of matters bearing on economic stability, as the first of Wen Jiabao's Four Uns—unstable—emphasizes. But it is especially the case regarding the risks of social and political instability. In keeping with this new point of reference, Beijing now moves proactively to address stability risks before they get out of hand.

This approach has become all the more important in the Internet era, when event-driven sparks in one isolated part of the country can instantaneously be transformed into outpourings of national concern. Those concerns triggered Beijing's proactive responses to the Falun Gong movement in 1999, as well to the outpouring of anger over the Sichuan earthquake in 2008, outbreaks of ethnic violence in Tibet and Xinjiang in 2008–9, a horrific high-speed train crash in Wenzhou in 2011, and the fall of Bo Xilai in 2012. In each of these cases, the government became unnerved about the vigor of exchange and debate that was occurring in weibo chat rooms and moved quickly to censor and ultimately suppress it.

The interplay between stability and political reform will change significantly in the Next China. The balancing act as it currently exists has been refined in the context of a producer model. The goals of production, assembly, and distribution were aimed largely at satisfying foreign demand. Internal instability posed a very different set of risks. That's not to say that frequent protests over land confiscation, shortages of key foodstuffs, and, more recently, environmental concerns were ignored. But rarely did they have serious and lasting consequences for China's externally dependent economic growth. As long as the producer model was continuing to deliver spectacular increases in economic output, the Party leadership and the Chinese people were satisfied. And China stayed the course.

The rules of engagement will obviously have to change as rebalancing takes aim on the emergence of a consumer society. As the burden of sustainability in the Next China shifts to internal demand, that, combined with the hypergrowth of the Internet user community, could create an entirely different mixture of stability risks. State control by a one-party system works very differently (or possibly not at all) when the economy is driven by internal demand. It is not clear what would occur if Chinese citizens, connected by the Internet in vast numbers, were to reassess the role of the government through the eyes of consumers.

This doesn't necessarily mean the pure form of democracy, freely elected representation, is the definitive answer for governance of China's consumer society—at least not right away. The Arab Spring of 2011–12 has been a lightning rod in focusing attention on this aspect of the rebalancing debate—especially since that extraordinary political upheaval was mobilized by the same Internet that is expanding so rapidly in China today. The Chinese government, to judge by the scant and largely negative attention given to the Arab Spring in the country's state-controlled media, feared that those uprisings might inspire something similar in China.[14]

A similar conclusion can be drawn from the widely accepted "modernization thesis" that maintains democracy is vital for economic prosperity.[15] Curiously, and controversially, recent research does not validate some of the more basic tenets of this notion. At least that's the verdict from a 2008 paper in the *American Economic Review* that examined the experience of 185 countries over the past five hundred years.[16] Daron Acemoglu and his coauthors argued that to some extent, a spurious link between political reform and economic development may be traceable to the "fallacy of the starting point"—that all countries at some point were very poor, nondemocratic societies. Adjusting for this, the empirical relationship between democracy and prosperity breaks down.[17]

That should not be interpreted as a negative judgment on the ultimate benefits of democracy. To the contrary, over the long sweep of history— hundreds of years rather than decades—the same researchers found that economic prosperity and political freedom go hand in hand. But they challenge the conventional wisdom of near-contemporaneous causality—that democratic reforms will pay quick economic dividends, or that prosperity can't be sustained without an immediate shift to democracy.

These findings obviously have important implications for China. Even if the Internet is playing a powerful role in spurring a rapid pro-consumption rebalancing, it would follow that China may still have plenty of time to implement political reforms. For the Chinese leadership, the challenge may be more evolutionary than revolutionary. Since Deng Xiaoping, the modern Chinese Communist Party has strongly embraced gradualism in moving away from the absolute power model of the Mao era and replacing it with a more adaptive system that allows for flexible constraints on political and social expression. In fact, consistent with the decentralization and localization of political authority that began with Deng's reforms of the early

1980s, the boundaries of government control in cities and townships have actually been relaxed as China moved up the development curve.[18]

That hardly means constraints on personal expression are unimportant in modern China. There are still tripwires, and as stressed above, when they are triggered and considered legitimate threats to stability, the government reacts strongly, as it did in 1989 and again in moving against Falun Gong in 1999[19] and Bo Xilai in 2012. But can China maintain this delicate balancing act? Cheng Li, of the Brookings Institution, who has dubbed this approach "resilient authoritarianism," now raises questions as to its sustainability.[20]

In an Internet-enabled era of pro-consumption growth, it is certainly possible that the increasingly vigorous freedom of expression that is spawned by the Internet will get snagged in the tripwires. In quashing weibo-based discussions of recent ethnic violence in Tibet and Xinjiang provinces, China's active cybercensorship efforts drive that point home.[21] The same, of course, can be said for China's aggressive censorship of dissenting voices in many diverse walks of life—from poetry (Liu Xiaobo), to art (Ai Weiwei), to the law (Chen Guangcheng). The Internet ups the ante on the tension between open discourse and political stability.

This is not a trivial matter for the Next China. Survey data reveal how seriously the Chinese people treat their online discussions. A McKinsey sampling suggests that more than 60 percent of the 270 million users of China's microblogs in 2011 viewed social media channels as "important places to express their opinions"—although only about 25 percent actually do this.[22] Weibos have become an increasingly important vehicle for intense discussions of a wide range of controversial social, economic, and political issues. Even when the censors step in and attempt to quash discussion, Chinese netizens have figured out how to keep the conversations going through the use of code words and alias usernames.

While China's censors continue to try and limit the extremes of weibo-expressed opinions, the government understands the porous nature of any such filtering and recognizes the limits of its ability to control the Internet. It is possible, and certainly desirable, that the Chinese government will come to appreciate the need for a more enlightened approach to the rapidly expanding exchange of e-based messaging, and permit ever-wider boundaries of expression. It is also possible that the government could do the opposite and shut down the Internet.

The draconian scenario is unlikely. While China is vilified in the West for being intolerant of dissent, the very existence of its Internet platform suggests, at a minimum, a more nuanced interpretation. The explosive growth of China's microblogging platforms reflects Beijing's willingness to let that growth happen—thereby providing strong hints of acceptance of the new technologies of connectivity and social expression. As in all such decisions, it boils down to costs and benefits. From the Chinese government's perspective, it may well be that the costs of fighting a losing battle over the control of information are far outweighed by the benefits of an Internet-enabled consumer culture.

Elections and Governance in China

Notwithstanding the research of Acemoglu and his colleagues, free and open elections are widely considered the first necessity of democracy—if not sufficient, then certainly necessary. The one-party Chinese state is a long way from accepting that type of radical shift in its political system. Moreover, with a painful history of ethnic strife, the government fears that multiple parties might simply replicate ethnic divisions. While political reforms, including elections, have been evident at the village and township levels since the 1980s, these experiments have been contained within the one-party CCP structure.[23] Still, that is an encouraging development given the country's serious corruption problems, which make it difficult to dislodge deeply entrenched local power blocs. It remains to be seen, however, whether local political reforms can percolate up to the national level.

If anything, the odds favor a continued shift toward "semicompetitive" intraparty elections rather than multiparty elections—building on a development that has already begun at the village level.[24] It would be a huge leap, however, for China to institute this process at the national level. It seems far more likely that the CCP would allow several candidates to compete for individual seats within the Party structure in the National People's Congress than it would let multiple political parties fight for control of the state legislature.

For China, as for any nation-state, political reform cannot occur in a vacuum. Unlike Russia, which following the collapse of the former Soviet Union opted to attempt political reform before economic reform, even the most progressive of Chinese reformers have argued that economic reforms should take precedence.[25] There is no appetite for shock therapy, for allowing political transitions to destabilize a weak and vulnerable economy. In today's China, sustained economic development is considered a vital precondition for political reform.[26]

At the same time, political theorists have long stressed that democracy requires far more than electoral accountability: State building and the rule of law are equally vital, and many argue that they need to take equal precedence in the sequencing required for a stable and robust democracy.[27] While China has made good progress in state building, it remains a laggard in creating a modern legal framework and fostering an independent judiciary.[28] Internet or not, the lack of a well-developed rule of law remains an enduring impediment to political reform in China.

To borrow from Marshall McLuhan, while the Internet is the medium, transparency could well be its most important message.[29] In China, early signs of progress in that direction are encouraging. The explosive growth of the Chinese Internet coincides with an important shift in the regulatory environment that occurred in 2008, the implementation of the Open Government Initiative (OGI).

The OGI framework, comparable in many respects to the U.S. Freedom of Information Act of 1966, requires basic disclosure of the Chinese government's work, with the exception of matters bearing on state security and social stability. The OGI also sets up administrative and appeal mechanisms in order to hear grievances and ensure compliance. But it has clear and important limits: OGI rules do not cover the political arms of the Chinese system—the CCP, the National People's Congress, or the judiciary. Instead, the focus is largely on the efficiency of the governance process itself. As such, China's OGI initiatives are best construed as baby steps on the road to a more robust transparency of the state.

To the extent these first efforts at transparency start to feed on themselves in China—as has been the case in other countries—they could also begin to creep into the government's broader political functions. Originating at the local level, the national version of OGI has been in place only since 2008, so it is premature to judge its impacts. Recent examples of regulatory modification and clarifications by Beijing and Hunan municipal governments, especially pertaining to contentious policies regarding land acquisition, are encouraging signs that this new feedback loop is working.[30]

Against the new OGI backdrop, the Internet has the potential to enable the shift to a more transparent Chinese state. Online access to the OGI platform opens up the regulatory debate to a broad swath of the nation's population, on issues ranging from the behavior of state-owned enterprises and urban land confiscation to environmental degradation and corruption. While this hardly puts China in the forefront of progressive governments, the interplay between the Internet and the new OGI framework changes the rules of engagement between the Chinese people and their adminis-trative overseers. That it dovetails with the emergence of Internet-driven consumer norms makes it all the more important.

While China's economic progress has been nothing short of extraordi-nary over the past thirty-plus years, it still has a considerable distance to go to establish a modern consumer society. The Internet's role as an acceler-ant to this process—from the twin standpoints of establishing consumer norms and of driving political reforms—injects a new and potentially pow-erful force into the equation. In addition to the macrostrategy agenda of job creation, wage increases, and the promised improvement of the social safety net, a new connectivity can be one of the most important catalysts of pro-consumption rebalancing. It addresses the third of Wen's Four Uns—uncoordinated—head-on by offering cohesion to a long fragmented Chi-nese society. It remains to be seen whether that can bring China's nascent consumers to life. But by embracing the Internet—censorship and all—the government has taken a bold step in that direction.

All of this should not be taken as an unrealistic picture of an enlightened Chinese political system that has seized on the Internet as a new instru-ment of personal freedom. Instead, it is best seen as another example of modern China's pragmatism that dates back to Deng Xiaoping, a pragma-tism that in this case that may well play an important role in the upcoming rebalancing of the Chinese economy. At the same time, a controlling state still has a long way to go in redressing the persistent asymmetry between economic progress and political development in China. It is a delicate and at times risky balancing act. And it will undoubtedly be an enduring source of tension for the Next China. For the time being, this is very much a work in progress.

The Internet and American Polarization

What about the other side of the codependent coin—the world's most powerful democracy? Sadly, it is not in the greatest shape right now. A myopic, polarized U.S. political system no longer stands as the shining beacon the rest of the free world has long sought to emulate. Nor is it much of a role model for nondemocratic societies, like China, that are contemplating new economic and political reforms. And when Washington succumbs to the pitfalls of codependency and blames others for its failure to address its own economic problems, it creates major complications in its important economic relationships, especially the one with China.

The recent litany of political dysfunctionality in the United States speaks for itself—especially in matters of economic policy. The problem is not just the lack of a strategy. It is also a Congress that has failed to pass a federal budget since 2009, engaging in a fiscal brinksmanship that raises the specter of draconian cutbacks in government operations and sovereign debt defaults. The government's dysfunctionality just scratches the surface of even deeper problems for a nation with a decaying infrastructure, mounting inequalities of incomes and opportunities, and a crisis in primary and secondary education. With a two-year election cycle, fund-raising and incumbency preservation have taken precedence over effective governance. If this is the best that democracy has to offer, Winston Churchill probably had it right: that it "is the worst form of government except all those other forms that have been tried from time to time."[31]

The United States certainly has difficult economic problems for which there are no easy solutions. Yet it is hardly alone in this. Just ask Europe, Japan, or China. But America is a restless and impatient nation. The two-year election cycle only encourages the desire for instant gratification—indeed, it makes long-term thinking almost impossible. Washington believes that a pampered and angry electorate has no tolerance for the heavy lifting of a serious reform of domestic economic policy—to say nothing of waiting out the years it would take to see concrete results. So it defers structural change and the incumbency risk it might engender and embraces short-term fixes that often make our problems worse. At the same time, the United States demands quick fixes from China as well, like large currency revaluations.

Sadly, this myopic and, at times, hypocritical approach deflects attention from one of America's greatest strengths—a long history of successes in the arena of global competition. The need to draw on those strengths is all the more urgent in a difficult postcrisis climate. As has been stressed earlier, the potential vigor of Chinese consumer demand should be seen as a welcome ray of hope, especially with the anemic internal demand of American consumers likely to persist. With China focused on a rapid expansion of its domestic consumer markets, U.S. companies—goods producers and service providers alike—could hardly ask for a better break. This is America's opportunity to seize, not to squander.

Ironically, America also risks mismanaging a key aspect of its technological prowess—long one of its strongest competitive attributes. Unlike China, where the Internet offers a new connectivity for a historically fragmented society, the United States has allowed the Internet to become a medium of polarization and political dysfunction. Virtually nonexistent barriers to entry have led to a proliferation of websites—well over 600 million of them in early 2013.[32] But in one important respect the explosion of online information has pushed the nation apart rather than brought it together. A Pew Research poll conducted during the U.S. midterm election of November 2010 supports that conclusion. Three key findings were especially pertinent: (1) Fully 73 percent of all Internet users in the United States (54 percent of the adult population in late 2010) went online in search of election insights; (2) 54 percent of America's netizens indicated that the Internet makes it easier for them to connect with those of like-minded political views; and (3) 55 percent of the U.S. user community felt that the Internet increases the impact of political extremists.[33] This doesn't exactly paint a picture of a freethinking and open-minded American electorate as one of democracy's greatest virtues.

The confluence of Internet-based fund-raising, widely available extremism via the Internet, cable TV, radio, and real-time Twitter-like feedback has made an important contribution to the cacophony of polarization and dysfunction that is now so pervasive in American politics.[34] Political myopia has been taken to a new level. Politicians now frame strategies based on feedback loops that have been compressed into nanoseconds.

With further apologies to Marshall McLuhan, it's important not to shoot the medium. The Internet and its profusion of extreme websites are, of course, reflective of divisions that have festered in the United States for many decades. But the powerful amplification mechanism is very important. As the so-called ultimate instrument of democracy, the Internet has the capacity to allow one captivating or well-funded voice to become very loud very quickly. In that important respect, it has become a breeding ground for a pervasive extremism. It is hard to believe this is all a coincidence—that the explosion of the Internet and the polarization of American politics have only by chance occurred at the same point in time.[35]

This is a worrisome development for the United States—not just for its people but also for its economy. To the extent that the solution of America's economic problems requires a consensus of shared responsibility, the polarization of American society risks giving us precisely the opposite. It will be extremely difficult for Washington to come to its senses in this climate. That highlights perhaps one of the biggest challenges for the codependent U.S.-China relationship: In a persistently tough economic climate, it will be that much harder for America's hyperreactive body politic to resist the temptations of China bashing.

This underscores the great irony of the contrasting roles the Internet is playing in shaping the two economies. In China, the Internet is bringing a fragmented society together over consumer norms and more transparent governance. In the United States, the Internet encourages polarization and divisiveness, contributing to an increasingly dysfunctional government. America, long known for its technological prowess, risks falling far short of China in converting this era's dominant technological breakthrough into a constructive force of economic growth and sustained prosperity.

The Mirrors of Codependency

Psychologists raise grave doubts over whether codependency is sustainable; the economist is more ambivalent. But both social scientists make important points. The corrosive symptoms of psychological disorder are already creeping into the economic relationship between China and the

United States. Both nations suffer from classic identity crises that risk turning destructive. The psychological disorder needs an economic cure. Rebalancing, the macro fix for an economic identity crisis, is that cure.

The rebalancing prescription is grounded in the economic imperatives facing both nations—pro-consumption in the case of China, and pro-saving in the case of the United States. The structural changes that drive this rebalancing will not be painless for either side. But the endgame provides enormous opportunity for each. The challenge is for both to see it. For a growth-starved United States, China can become a new and important source of demand. For China, the United States offers both the products and the services expertise of the world's quintessential consumer society. With the economics of a shared rebalancing should also come the psychological benefits of healing a troubled relationship—namely, avoiding trade frictions and protectionism that lurk on the dark side of codependency.

Politics is the weakest link in the U.S.-China economic relationship. Mustering political support for rebalancing certainly won't be easy, especially since incentives for new sources of economic growth invariably put pressure on old sources of growth. Acceptance of such a transitional growth sacrifice could be the most vexing aspect of the collective challenge. The political disconnect in both systems complicates the problem. Just as an antiquated one-party Chinese state is struggling to keep up with its dynamic blended economy, a dysfunctional and polarized U.S. democracy is woefully out of step with a sluggish free-market economy. Neither economy is well aligned with its political system. China needs an agenda for political reform, but so does the United States.

In many important respects, China and the United States have become reflections of each other. The ultimate producer is the mirror image of the ultimate consumer, and the surplus saver the mirror image of the deficit saver. Internet-enabled connectivity fits with China's pro-consumption rebalancing while it fosters tension and extremism in the U.S. political climate. The experience of one offers insight into the challenges facing the other. Not only must each nation take a careful look in its own mirror but it must also study carefully the lessons and experiences of the other. Only then can the United States and China own their codependency and convert it into a positive force of shared economic prosperity.

Wen Jiabao, modern China's most reflective premier, was candid in describing what China sees when it looks in the mirror. The Four Uns of an unbalanced, unstable, uncoordinated, and ultimately unsustainable Chinese economy paint a fairly accurate picture of its emerging pitfalls, as well as the agenda that defines opportunities for the future. China's self-image is laced with pride and a fragile sense of confidence, but, most important, with a strong determination to stay the course of development and rising prosperity. In embracing the imperatives of rebalancing, China owns up to the self-criticism of the Four Uns. It frames its future consumer society very much as the mirror image of the highly successful producer model of the past thirty years. The early read on its fifth generation of leaders points to a China that is now embracing that future.[36]

What does the United States see when it looks in the mirror? Ironically, voters appear to have a more realistic self-image than their elected leaders. Owning up to the circumstances of a wrenching crisis and recession, most Americans look to the future with trepidation. But like their leaders, they have yet to embrace a meaningful reordering of growth priorities as a solution. Conditioned by an era of unbridled prosperity, and with memories of tough experiences on the 1930s and 1940s having faded, the U.S. body politic now treats sacrifice as the antithesis of the American way. The American vision of the future remains more a return to the way it was than a fundamental rethinking of the road that ultimately led to a false prosperity. Unless that changes, America's future is unlikely to match its vibrant past.

Curiously, neither nation seems able to look into the other's mirror—to understand how the other sees itself. Caught up in its own pathologies of economic distress, each allows self-interest to trump collective interest. This is where the psychologists' insights into codependency ring true. No two major economies are more intertwined than those of the United States and China. They have played powerful roles in shaping each other's economic journeys over the past three decades. Where would China have been without the open-ended demand of the American consumer? Where would the American consumer have been without cheap goods and low interest rates made in China? The short answer is that each would have been lost without the other.

One of the tragic ironies of codependency is that partners often subsume their sense of self into an increasingly destructive relationship. China and the United States both have the opportunity to break the bonds of a destructive codependency. Their economies will change out of necessity. Their relationship, and especially the political forces that drive it, must adapt to these new economic realities. A failure to adapt risks collision—the Bad Dream of a trade war, or worse.

Trust is key to resolving the political disconnect between the two. Yet distrust is deep on both sides. For China, it is woven into the fabric of humiliation dating back to the Opium Wars. For the United States, it is rooted in the Cold War fears of Red China and the historical aversion to socialism as the antithesis of democracy. These impressions have arisen not out of thin air but from painful experiences in the not-so-distant past—invasions by Europe and Japan in the case of China, and a Chinese-sponsored hot war in Korea, as well as its support for North Vietnam in the 1960s, in the case of the United States. Future leaders in both nations will need to confront this historical baggage head-on in framing a more trustful relationship between their countries. But as a decade of trade-related tensions attest, trust issues are not just about the past. The cyberhacking dispute adds a new and important dimension to the Sino-American trust deficit.

The stakes are global. Codependency between the United States and China is one of the most salient features of the new globalization. Frictions could undermine not only the two countries' relationship but the entire global economy. The imbalances of codependency will drive the economic agendas of the United States and China. Rebalancing will define their future—separately and collectively.

NOTES

1. The Political Economy of False Prosperity

1. U.S. President Lyndon B. Johnson was crystal clear in articulating the central role played by the Full Employment Act of 1946. In his words, "The principles of our policies emerge from that Act." See *Economic Report of the President: Transmitted to the Congress January 1966* (Washington, D.C.: United States Government Printing Office, 1966), 5.

2. See John Maynard Keynes, *The General Theory of Employment, Interest, and Money* (London: Macmillan, 1936).

3. See Arthur M. Okun, *Political Economy of Prosperity* (Washington, D.C.: The Brookings Institution, 1970).

4. See Barry Eichengreen, *Globalizing Capital: A History of the International Financial System* (Princeton: Princeton University Press, 1996).

5. See Alan S. Blinder and Jeremy B. Rudd, "The Supply-Shock Explanation of the Great Stagflation Revisited," CEPS working paper no. 176, presented at the National Bureau of Economic Research conference on the Great Inflation, Woodstock, Vt., November 2008.

6. See Barry P. Bosworth, *The Decline in Saving: A Threat to America's Prosperity?* (Washington, D.C.: Brookings Institution Press, 2012).

7. See International Monetary Fund, "The Globalization of Labor," in *World Economic Outlook* (Washington, D.C., 2007).

8. Nobel laureate Franco Modigliani is widely credited for introducing the wealth effect as a determinant of personal consumption. See, for example, Franco Modigliani and Richard H. Brumberg, "Utility Analysis and the Consumption Function: An Attempt at Integration," in *Post-Keynesian Economics,* ed. Kenneth K. Kurihara (Rutgers, N.J.: Rutgers University Press, 1954); and Albert Ando and Franco Modigliani, "The 'Life Cycle' Hypothesis of Saving: Aggregate Implications and Tests," *American Economic Review* 53 (March 1963).

9. See John Cassidy, *Dot.con: How America Lost Its Mind and Money in the Internet Era* (New York: Perennial Currents, 2003); and Robert J. Shiller, *Irrational Exuberance*, 2nd ed. (Princeton: Princeton University Press, 2005).

10. See Stephen S. Roach, "The Perils of False Prosperity: China, America, and a New Globalization," Jackson Institute Lecture, Yale University, April 14, 2011.

11. See Michael Mandel, "The Triumph of the New Economy," *Business Week*, December 30, 1996.

12. See Barry Naughton, *The Chinese Economy: Transitions and Growth* (Cambridge: MIT Press, 2007).

13. See Jonathan D. Spence, *The Search for Modern China*, 2nd ed. (New York: Norton, 1999).

14. See Frank Dikötter, *Mao's Great Famine: The History of China's Most Devastating Catastrophe, 1958–62* (New York: Walker, 2010).

15. See Spence, *The Search for Modern China*, 572.

16. The Four Modernizations appear to have been first mentioned by Zhou Enlai and Deng Xiaoping in the mid-1970s, and were subsequently noted by Hua Guofeng at the First National Conference on Learning from Dazhai in Agriculture, held in Shanxi province in September and October 1975; see Spence, *The Search for Modern China*.

17. Huang points out the great confusion that exists over the ownership structure of TVEs. Western analysts have long presumed that TVEs were modern offshoots of earlier collectives, and as such were owned jointly by workers and local Party governments. In a careful examination of TVE ownership records, Huang finds that the bulk of these companies were privately owned—underscoring his key conclusion that they represent modern China's best example of private sector entrepreneurialism at work. See Yasheng Huang, *Capitalism with Chinese Characteristics: Entrepreneurship and the State* (New York: Cambridge University Press, 2008).

18. See Supachai Panitchpakdi and Mark L. Clifford, *China and the WTO: Changing China, Changing World Trade* (Singapore: John Wiley and Sons [Asia], 2002).

19. International Monetary Fund, *World Economic Outlook* database, April 2013.

20. See Chapter 12 for a more precise estimate of the timing of this likely convergence.

21. The conversion to international prices is based on purchasing power parity (PPP) rates that adjust for disparities in price levels across counties. These measures are expressed in constant 2005 PPP dollars in order to adjust for inflation. Given the wide disparities between repressed prices of many nontradable Chinese goods and services relative to a comparable basket of goods and services in other countries, the IMF estimates that per capita GDP in China as measured on a PPP basis in current dollars was $10,011 in 2013, fully 50 percent higher than the U.S. dollar–based estimate of $6,629. See IMF, *World Economic Outlook* database, April 2013.

22. See Barry Eichengreen, Donghyun Park, and Kwanho Shin, "When Fast Grow-

ing Economies Slow Down: International Evidence and Implications for China," National Bureau of Economic Research working paper no. 16919, March 2011.

23. International Monetary Fund, *World Economic Outlook* database, 2012.

24. See James Kynge, *China Shakes the World: A Titan's Rise and Troubled Future—and the Challenge for America* (New York: Houghton Mifflin, 2006).

25. See Jayati Ghosh, "Poverty Reduction in China and India: Policy Implications of Recent Trends," United Nations Department of Economic and Social Affairs, DESA working paper no. 92, January 2010. World Bank "Development Indicators" put China's poverty reduction at closer to 600 million since 1980.

26. University of California professor Chalmers Johnson is responsible for first articulating Japan's self-image as a developmental state. See Chalmers A. Johnson, *MITI and the Japanese Miracle: The Growth of Industrial Policy, 1925 to 1975* (Stanford: Stanford University Press, 1982).

27. See Stephen S. Roach, "The Japan Syndrome Goes Global," speech before the World Knowledge Forum, Seoul, South Korea, October 12, 2010.

28. The capital spending share of Japanese GDP went from 18 percent in 1983 to 25 percent in 1991 before plunging back to 13 percent by 1996; source: Japan Statistics Bureau, Ministry of Internal Affairs and Communications.

29. See Ben S. Bernanke, "The Great Moderation," remarks at the meetings of the Eastern Economics Association, Washington, D.C., February 20, 2004.

30. Harvard professor Benjamin Friedman has stressed the destabilizing consequences—economic, social, and especially moral—of misguided quests for economic growth; see Benjamin M. Friedman, *The Moral Consequences of Economic Growth* (New York: Knopf, 2005).

31. See Pöyry Management Consulting (Norway), "Marriages of Convenience: A Comparative Study," Norwegian Directorate of Immigration, 2010.

32. The arguments for a new and sustainable symbiosis between the United States and China have been framed as a "new" Bretton Woods system of international finance; see Michael P. Dooley, David Folkerts-Landau, and Peter Garber, "The Revived Bretton Woods System," *International Journal of Finance and Economics* 9 (October 2004).

33. See Shiller, *Irrational Exuberance*.

2. Who Depends on Whom?

1. International Monetary Fund, *World Economic Outlook* database, 2012.

2. International Monetary Fund, *World Economic Outlook,* May 2007.

3. International Monetary Fund, *World Economic Outlook* database, 2012.

4. As noted in Chapter 7, new research from the Organization of Economic Cooperation and Development (OECD) and the World Trade Organization (WTO) suggest that the U.S.-China bilateral trade deficit would have been 33 percent lower in 2009 if it were corrected for this bias. See "What Can the TiVA Database Tell

Us?" available on Measuring Trade in Value Added: An OECD-WTD Joint Initiative, May 2013, at www.oecd.org.

5. *China Statistical Yearbook 2011*, National Bureau of Statistics, PRC.

6. Others have focused on statistical distortions to the bilateral U.S.-China trade data, noting the Chinese trade figures point to a considerably smaller imbalance than the U.S. data. These discrepancies appear traceable to two conceptual differences in the data—valuation disparities at the point of entry and reexporting through third-party locations such as Hong Kong. Irrespective of the dataset, however, both the U.S. and the Chinese statistics point to a comparable widening in the bilateral imbalance since 2005. See Michael E. Martin, "What's the Difference—Comparing U.S. and Chinese Trade Data," Congressional Research Service, April 21, 2010.

7. Bureau of Economic Analysis, U.S. International Trade Statistics, U.S. Department of Commerce.

8. This was the unfortunate title of a World Bank opus on the region published in the mid-1990s just before the wrenching pan-regional crisis; see World Bank, *The East Asian Miracle: Economic Growth and Public Policy*, A World Bank Policy Research Report, September 30, 1993.

9. See Carla A. Hills, Peter G. Peterson, and Morris Goldstein, *Safeguarding Prosperity in a Global Financial System: The Future International Financial Architecture*, Report of an Independent Task Force Sponsored by the Council on Foreign Relations, 1999.

10. *China Statistical Yearbook 2012*, National Bureau of Statistics, PRC, and International Monetary Fund.

11. Based on the Federal Reserve's real effective index of the broad trade-weighted value of the dollar, the cumulative depreciation totaled 24.5 percent from February 2002 to June 2013 (see Chapter 4, n. 39).

12. China does not release official estimates of the composition of its foreign exchange reserves. Official U.S. statistics put Chinese holdings of longer-term U.S. government securities at $1.3 trillion in May 2013; see Department of the Treasury, Federal Reserve Bank of New York, and Board of Governors of the Federal Reserve System, "Major Foreign Holdings of Treasury Securities," July 14, 2013. The remainder of about $700 billion is generally thought to be broadly distributed in other dollar-denominated assets such as agency and corporate debt instruments; see Nicholas E. Lardy, *Sustaining China's Economic Growth After the Global Financial Crisis* (Washington, D.C.: Peterson Institute for International Economics, 2012), 141–42.

13. This quickly became a major factor in the policy debate in the early 2000s—whether low long-term U.S. interest rates were an outgrowth of external factors like China's saving glut, as successive Federal Reserve chairmen Alan Greenspan and Ben Bernanke argued in their efforts to exonerate the Fed of any culpability, or whether this phenomenon could be more an outgrowth of the Federal Reserve's easy monetary policy, as Maurice Obstfeld and others have stressed.

See Ben S. Bernanke, "The Global Saving Glut and the U.S. Current Account Deficit," Remarks at the Sandridge Lecture, Virginia Association of Economists, Richmond, Va., March 10, 2005; Alan Greenspan, "Testimony Before the Financial Crisis Inquiry Commission," Washington, D.C., April 7, 2010; and Maurice Obstfeld, "The Immoderate World Economy," *Journal of International Money and Finance* 29, no. 4 (2010).

14. See Kenichi Ohmae, *The Borderless World: Power and Strategy in the Interlinked Economy* (New York: HarperCollins, 1991).

15. See Jonathan Cummings, James Manyika, Lenny Mendonca, Ezra Greenberg, et al., "Growth and Competitiveness in the United States: The Role of Its Multinational Corporations," McKinsey Global Institute, June 2010; and Economist Intelligence Unit, "Multinational Companies and China: What Future?" November 2011.

16. Curiously, there is an enormous disparity on how each country values the cumulative investment by U.S. companies into China over the years. Chinese statisticians calculate the stock of such foreign direct investment at a mere $4.9 billion as measured in U.S. dollars in 2010. This number seems woefully understated. The U.S. Commerce Department's $60.5 billion estimate of this stock for 2010 represents a $10.7 billion increase from the investment position in 2009—more than double the cumulative stock that Chinese statisticians credit U.S. companies with in more than three decades of such investments. This only underscores the flawed metrics of China's foreign direct investment statistics.

17. The flip side of that benefit shows up in claims of exploitation of low-wage Chinese labor that many believe has been exacerbated by the so-called Walmart effect in China. See Yu Xiaomin and Pun Ngai, "Walmartization, Corporate Social Responsibility, and the Labor Standards of Toy Factories in South China," in *Walmart in China*, ed. Anita Chan (Ithaca, N.Y.: Cornell University Press, 2011).

18. These estimates, taken from international compensation comparisons maintained by the U.S. Department of Commerce, are detailed in Chapter 7, note 31.

19. Ironically, while senior Federal Reserve officials were quick to pin the blame on China for suppressing U.S. interest rates via the savings-glut mechanism noted above, they were unwilling to accept Chinese sourcing as a major source of U.S. disinflation—preferring, instead, to explain this development as more an outgrowth of the stunning successes of monetary policy in achieving the so-called Great Moderation. See Ben S. Bernanke, "The Great Moderation," speech before the Eastern Economic Association, Washington, D.C., February 24, 2004. A more balanced perspective can be found in a paper given by Bank of England Deputy Governor Bean; see Charles Bean, "The Great Moderation, the Great Panic and the Great Contraction," Schumpeter Lecture, Annual Congress of the European Economic Association, Barcelona, Spain, August 25, 2009.

20. See Chan, *Walmart in China*.

21. See, for example, Dorinda Elliott, "Wal-Mart Nation," *Time*, June 19, 2005.

22. See Joe Studwell, *The China Dream: The Elusive Quest for the Greatest Untapped Market on Earth* (London: Profile, 2002).

3. The Boss and the Maestro

1. See Bob Woodward, *Maestro: Greenspan's Fed and the American Boom* (New York: Simon and Schuster, 2000).
2. See Cheng Li, *China's Leaders: The New Generation* (Lanham, Md.: Rowman and Littlefield, 2001).
3. See Jonathan D. Spence, *The Search for Modern China,* 2nd ed. (New York: Norton, 1999).
4. See "An Interview with the Wall Street Journal," April 2, 1999, in *Zhu Rongji Meets the Press* (Oxford: Oxford University Press, 2011).
5. See Edwin Lim et al., *China: Long-Term Development Issues and Options: The Report of a Mission Sent to China by the World Bank* (Baltimore: published for the World Bank by Johns Hopkins University Press, 1985).
6. See Ezra F. Vogel, *Deng Xiaoping and the Transformation of China* (Cambridge: Belknap Press of Harvard University Press, 2011).
7. See Laurence J. Brahm, *Zhu Rongji and the Transformation of Modern China* (Singapore: John Wiley and Sons [Asia], 2002).
8. See "*Business Week* Interviews the Vice Premier about China's Economic Plans," January 15, 1994, in *Zhu Rongji Meets the Press.*
9. See Brahm, *Zhu Rongji and the Transformation of Modern China,* xxix.
10. See "Premier Zhu's Briefing at the First Session of the Ninth National People's Congress," March 19, 1998, in *Zhu Rongji Meets the Press.*
11. See Joseph Fewsmith, "China and the WTO: The Politics Behind the Agreement," National Bureau of Asian Research, December 1999.
12. Ibid., and *Zhu Rongji Meets the Press,* 364.
13. See Nicholas R. Lardy, *China's Unfinished Economic Revolution* (Washington, D.C.: Brookings Institution, 1998).
14. As a longtime participant in the China Development Forum, I remember well the final session of the 2001 meetings—the audience with Premier Zhu at the Great Hall of the People. In that meeting I argued that the U.S. economy was moving into a mild recession in the aftermath of the bursting of the dotcom bubble—a view few shared at the time—and that this could have important implications for the export-led Chinese economy. At the end of the meeting, the premier said to me in perfect English, "I hope you are wrong, but we are planning as if you are right." I have had a standing invitation ever since.
15. See Woodward, *Maestro.*
16. See Alan Greenspan, *The Age of Turbulence: Adventures in a New World* (New York: Penguin, 2007), 86.
17. Greenspan took advantage of the election of Jimmy Carter in 1976 to return to graduate school. He received his Ph.D. in economics from New York University

in 1977, combining three of his previously published articles into the requisite dissertation.

18. Herbert Stein was appointed by President Nixon as the ninth chairman of the Council of Economic Advisers and served in that capacity from 1972 to 1974, before being succeeded by Greenspan; Donald Rumsfeld was head of the Economic Stabilization Program, charged with administering wage and price controls in the early 1970s; and Dick Cheney was Rumsfeld's deputy. For Rumsfeld and Cheney, it was just the beginning of long careers in public service, whereas for Herb Stein, the Council chairmanship marked the end of his road in Washington.

19. As Greenspan notes, his Senate confirmation hearing was held on the afternoon of August 8, 1974; that same evening President Nixon resigned. That gave Gerald Ford, America's first unelected president, the opportunity to go with a different economic team. He didn't, and Greenspan was sworn in about a month later, on September 4, 1974. See Greenspan, *The Age of Turbulence,* 64.

20. Ibid.

21. Ibid., 40.

22. See Alan Greenspan, "The Challenge of Central Banking in a Democratic Society," speech at the Annual Dinner and Francis Boyer Lecture of the American Enterprise Institute for Public Policy Research, Washington, D.C., December 5, 1996.

23. See Alan Greenspan, "The Economic Outlook," testimony before the Joint Economic Committee, U.S. Congress, June 9, 2005.

24. See Alan Greenspan, "The State of the Banking Industry," testimony before the Committee on Banking, Housing, and Urban Affairs, U.S. Senate, April 20, 2004, and "Consumer Finance," remarks at the Federal Reserve System's Fourth Annual Community Affairs Research Conference, Washington, D.C., April 8, 2005.

25. See William McChesney Martin, Jr., address before the New York Group of the Investment Bankers Association of America, October 19, 1955.

26. See Greenspan's testimony before the Oversight and Government Reform Committee of the U.S. House of Representatives, October 23, 2008.

27. See, for example, George A. Akerlof and Robert R. Shiller, *Animal Spirits: How Human Psychology Drives the Economy, and Why It Matters for Global Capitalism* (Princeton: Princeton University Press, 2009).

28. See Greenspan, *The Age of Turbulence,* 33.

29. My first position as a professional economist was on the research staff of the Federal Reserve Board in Washington, D.C., from 1973 to 1979. I started out as the capital spending analyst, and quickly found out that the senior Fed staff and policy makers—especially Chairman Burns—were interested mainly in comparative cyclical analysis of U.S. capital spending and its determinants. Forecasts of the future, a key input into the monetary policy decisions that the Fed was charged with, were invariably couched in a meticulous assessment of business cycles of the past.

30. It was Ben Bernanke, speaking in his earlier capacity as a governor serving under Chairman Greenspan, who actually articulated the Fed's first formal endorsement of the Great Moderation as an apt depiction of the Greenspan era. See Ben S. Bernanke, "The Great Moderation," remarks at the meetings of the Eastern Economics Association, Washington, D.C., February 20, 2004.

31. See Alan Greenspan, "Risk and Uncertainty in Monetary Policy," speech at the Annual Meetings of the American Economic Association, San Diego, January 3, 2004.

32. See Justin R. Pierce and Peter K. Schott, "The Surprisingly Swift Decline of U.S. Manufacturing Employment," NBER working paper 18655, December 2012.

33. See Greenspan, *The Age of Turbulence*, 294.

34. See *Zhu Rongji Meets the Press*, 383, and Brahm, *Zhu Rongji and the Transformation of Modern China*, 282.

4. The Great Stability Debate

1. See Wen Jiabao's October 25, 2011, speech to an audience of fifteen hundred at his high school alma mater, Nankai High School in Tianjin.

2. See Barry Naughton, "The Emergence of Wen Jiabao," *China Leadership Monitor* 6 (Spring 2003).

3. See Cheng Li, *China's Leaders: The New Generation* (Lanham, Md.: Rowman and Littlefield, 2001).

4. See ibid.

5. As is the case in most Western government transitions, new leadership teams in China typically "clean house" and put in their own loyalists in key staffing positions. Wen was a clear exception, serving as head of the General Office of the Chinese Communist Party Central Committee for Party Secretaries Hu Yaobang, Zhao Ziyang, and Jiang Zemin; Jiang, however, did finally replace Wen early in his leadership tenure in 1993; see Naughton, "The Emergence of Wen Jiabao."

6. Mishus, as Chinese call personal secretaries, have long played a critical role as key administrators in earlier dynasties and more modern Chinese governments; see Li, *China's Leaders*.

7. See Joseph Fewsmith, "China's Response to SARS," *China Leadership Monitor* 7 (Summer 2003).

8. Wen's favorite foreign books, which he often took with him on his travels, were Adam Smith's *The Theory of Moral Sentiments* (1759) and Marcus Aurelius's first-century treatise on Stoic philosophy, *The Meditations;* see transcript of CNN interview with Wen Jiabao, broadcast on *Fareed Zakaria GPS*, October 3, 2010.

9. See Jonathan Spence, *The Search for Modern China*, 2nd ed. (New York: Norton, 1999), 624–30.

10. See Sharon LaFraniere, "Chinese Premier Offers a Tribute to a Reformer," *New York Times*, April 15, 2010.

11. See Malcolm Moore, "Wen Jiabao Promises Political Reform for China," *Telegraph*, October 4, 2010.

12. See Michael Wines and Sharon LaFraniere, "Chinese Article Seems to Chide Leader," *New York Times,* October 27, 2010.

13. See Stephen Roach, "China's Stability Gambit," *Project Syndicate,* March 26, 2012.

14. Only later were murder charges revealed against Bo Xilai's wife, Gu Kailai, who was tried and convicted in August 2012 for the poisoning death of a British businessman, Neil Heywood.

15. See "Premier Wen Jiabao Meets the Press," March 14, 2012, published on the occasion of the premier's annual press conference in the Great Hall of the People following the conclusion of the 2012 National People's Congress.

16. The next day, on March 15, Bo was formally removed as Chongqing Party secretary, and on April 10 the government announced that he was under formal investigation for "serious disciplinary actions" and had been suspended as a member of the Politburo; see Alice Miller, "The Bo Xilai Affair in Central Leadership Politics," *China Leadership Monitor* 38 (Summer 2012).

17. See John Garnaut, "The Revenge of Wen Jiabao," *Foreign Policy,* March 29, 2012.

18. See Ben S. Bernanke, *Essays on the Great Depression* (Princeton: Princeton University Press, 2000).

19. See Ben S. Bernanke, "Long-Term Commitments, Dynamic Optimization, and the Business Cycle," Ph.D. diss., Massachusetts Institute of Technology, 1979.

20. See Milton Friedman and Anna Schwartz, *A Monetary History of the United States, 1867–1960* (Princeton: Princeton University Press, 1963).

21. For a compendium of Bernanke's research papers on the Great Depression, see his *Essays on the Great Depression.*

22. See the testimony of former U.S. Treasury Secretary Henry Paulson before the Banking Committee of the U.S. Senate on July 15, 2008.

23. A good summary of Bernanke's views on the financial accelerator can be found in Ben S. Bernanke, "The Financial Accelerator and the Credit Channel," speech before the Conference on the Credit Channel of Monetary Policy in the Twenty-First Century, Federal Reserve Bank of Atlanta, June 15, 2007.

24. Bernanke's first and largely unadulterated critique of the Bank of Japan can be found in Ben Bernanke, "Japanese Monetary Policy: A Case of Self-Induced Paralysis?" in *Japan's Financial Crisis and Its Parallels to the U.S. Experience,* ed. R. Mikitani and A. S. Posen (Washington, D.C.: Institute for International Economics, 2000); for a kinder and gentler version presented after he became a Fed governor, see Ben S. Bernanke, "Some Thoughts on Monetary Policy in Japan," speech before the Japan Society of Monetary Economics, Tokyo, May 31, 2003.

25. According to the controversial findings of this research, the so-called financial frictions associated with widespread U.S. banking failures contributed only to the early stages of the Great Depression; more lasting impacts are traceable to weakened productivity and policy-induced frictions in the labor market; see V. V. Chari, P. J. Kehoe, and E. R. McGrattan, "Business Cycle Accounting," *Econometrica,* May 2007.

26. See Ben Bernanke and Mark Gertler, "Monetary Policy and Asset Price Volatility," NBER working paper 7559, February 2000.

27. As noted in Chapter 3, Alan Greenspan's "mission accomplished" statement after the bursting of the equity bubble in 2000 appears to have given the Fed a false sense of security in relying on the same strategy to deal with mounting property and credit bubbles later in the decade. See Alan Greenspan, "Risk and Uncertainty in Monetary Policy," speech at the Annual Meetings of the American Economic Association, San Diego, January 3, 2004.

28. There were a few, however, who were warning Chinese leaders of the mounting risks of global imbalances and their potential repercussions on an unbalanced Chinese economy; that was the thrust of a paper that I had just presented at the annual China Development Forum on March 22, 2007. See Stephen S. Roach, "China's Global Challenge," in *The Next Asia: Opportunities and Challenges for a New Globalization* (Hoboken, N.J.: John Wiley and Sons, 2009).

29. As a personal witness to the premier's remarks that day—at least through a video feed into a nearby Beijing meeting room—I was quick to jump to a similar conclusion, as was a senior Chinese policy maker who sat alongside me as we collectively gasped at the significance of the Four Uns; see Roach, *The Next Asia*.

30. See Roach, "China's Stability Gambit."

31. See Stephen S. Roach, "China's 12th Five-Year Plan: Strategy vs. Tactics," a paper presented to the twelfth annual China Development Forum, March 20–21, 2011.

32. Nominated by President George W. Bush in May 2002, Ben S. Bernanke was initially sworn in as Fed governor on August 5, 2002.

33. See Ben S. Bernanke, "On Milton Friedman's Ninetieth Birthday," remarks at the Conference to Honor Milton Friedman, University of Chicago, November 8, 2002.

34. His original argument of this point can be found in Ben S. Bernanke, "Nonmonetary Effects of the Financial Crisis in the Propagation of the Great Depression," *American Economic Review*, June 1983.

35. Anna Schwartz, Friedman's longtime collaborator and coauthor, was, in fact, highly critical of Bernanke's depiction of the role of monetarism, and she came out publicly against his reappointment as Fed chairman in 2009; see Anna Jacobson Schwartz, "Man Without a Plan," op-ed, *New York Times*, July 26, 2009. Another minority view against the Bernanke reappointment can be found in Stephen Roach, "The Case Against Bernanke," op-ed, *Financial Times*, August 26, 2009.

36. See Bernanke, "On Milton Friedman's Ninetieth Birthday."

37. See Ben S. Bernanke, "Deflation: Making Sure 'It' Doesn't Happen Here," remarks before the National Economists Club, Washington, D.C., November 21, 2002.

38. Through 2013, the Fed's official target was a federal funds rate in the 0 percent to $^1/_4$ percent range and a commitment to hold it there for "at least as long as the unemployment rate remains above $6^1/_2\%$." The December 2012 policy statement goes on to stress that this outcome-based policy directive is "consistent with its earlier date-based guidance," which was to hold the funds rate at the zero bound

though mid-2015. See "Statement of the Federal Open Market Committee," December 11–12, 2012, available at www.federalreserve.com.

39. Based on the Federal Reserve's Price-Adjusted Broad Dollar Index, which has declined by 24.5 percent from its peak in February 2002 (112.8170) to June 2013 (85.1231); available at www.federalreserve.com.

40. See Richard C. Koo, *The Holy Grail of Macro Economics: Lessons from Japan's Great Recession* (Hoboken, N.J.: John Wiley and Sons, 2009); and Paul Krugman, "It's Baack: Japan's Slump and the Return of the Liquidity Trap," *Brookings Papers on Economic Activity,* 2001.

41. See the Papers of John Maynard Keynes, Janus Repository, Cambridge University, speeches and lectures given outside Cambridge University, PS/6.

42. See Koo, *The Holy Grail of Macro Economics.*

43. U.S. Congressional Budget Office, "The Budget and Economic Outlook: Fiscal Years 2013 to 2023," Washington D.C., February 2013, and *The Annual Report of the Council of Economic Advisers,* Washington D.C., March 2013.

44. The policy trap—where misguided attempts to mask a policy blunder with a new strategy gives rise to ever greater imbalances and macro risks—has long been viewed as one of the more powerful forces behind Japan's prebubble excesses, as yen suppression was followed by bubble-inducing monetary ease; see Akio Mikuni and R. Taggart Murphy, *Japan's Policy Trap: Dollars, Deflation, and the Crisis of Japanese Finance* (Washington, D.C.: Brookings Institution Press, 2002).

45. In 2012, Ben Bernanke grudgingly gave a little ground in recognizing the Fed's need to focus on financial stability by conceding, "Going forward, for the Federal Reserve, as well as for other central banks, the promotion of financial stability must be on an equal footing with the management of monetary policy as the most critical policy priorities." While that is a step in the right direction, it still preserves the firewall between the Fed's core monetary policy functionality and the tool kit that can be used to address matters of financial stability. See Ben S. Bernanke, "Some Reflections on the Crisis and the Policy Response," speech at the Russell Sage Foundation and the Century Foundation Conference on Rethinking Finance, New York, April 13, 2012. Bernanke has since moved a bit farther; see Chapter 11, n. 26.

46. In a rare interview on the television show *60 Minutes,* on March 15, 2009, Ben Bernanke actually taped a segment in his hometown of Dillon and spoke at length of the impact of the financial crisis on small-town America; one of the highlights was an on-camera stroll past his childhood home, which had been sold at a foreclosure auction earlier that year as the housing crisis took its toll on Dillon.

5. Two Takes on Strategy

1. That's actually putting it mildly. The U.S. Senate has failed to pass a formal budget resolution since 2009, meaning that the federal government has effectively

been running on the basis of "continuing resolutions" for more than four years. See Bill Heniff Jr. and Justin Murray, "Congressional Budget Resolutions: Historical Information," *CRS Report for Congress*, Congressional Research Service, Washington, D.C., March 13, 2012.

2. See Barry Naughton, *The Chinese Economy: Transitions and Growth* (Cambridge: MIT Press, 2007).

3. See, for example, *A Study of the Soviet Economy*, published jointly by the International Monetary Fund, the World Bank, the Organisation for Economic Cooperation and Development, and the European Bank for Reconstruction and Development (Paris, 1991).

4. See Jonathan D. Spence, "Planning the New Society," chapter 20 of *The Search for Modern China*, 2nd ed. (New York: Norton, 1999).

5. In 1956, the planning function was split into two ministries—the original SPC, which had responsibility for plan design, targets, interindustry flows, and pricing and a newly established State Economic Commission (SEC), which was charged with implementation and production coordination. The SPC and the SEC were merged again in 1988. See Lance L. P. Gore, "China's Mini-State Council: National Development and Reform Commission," EAI Background Brief no. 614, April 2011.

6. See Naughton, *The Chinese Economy*.

7. For a discussion of the evolutionary characteristics of the modern planning function in China, see Gregory C. Chow, "Economic Planning in China," Princeton, CEPS working paper 219, June 2011.

8. As is detailed in Chapter 12, a new focus on what the NDRC calls strategic emerging industries (SEIs) in the recently enacted Twelfth Five-Year Plan is an important exception to this trend in that it provides goal-oriented detail for a specific set of innovations-based, technology-intensive industries. Seven SEIs have been singled out—energy conservation, new generation information technology, biotechnology, high-end equipment manufacturing, alternative energy, alternative materials, and autos running on alternative energy. See National Development and Reform Commission, *Report on the Implementation of the 2011 Plan for National Economic and Social Development and on the 2012 Draft Plan for National Economic and Social Development*, presented at the Fifth Session of the Eleventh National People's Congress, March 5, 2012.

9. A case in point is the recent elevation of Liu He to vice chairman of the NDRC. Liu, who played an active role in drafting the Twelfth Five-Year Plan and in leading the China team that coauthored the China 2030 report with a team of researchers from the World Bank, is one of China's most progressive macro thinkers. Even more significant, he was also promoted to director of the Office of the Central Leading Group on Financial and Economic Affairs, a high-level group that provides support to economic policy of China's State Council and the Party Central Committee. Educated in China and the United States, Liu also has deep knowledge of global macrostrategic issues; see He Liu, *A Comparative Study of Two Global Crises* (Beijing: China Economic Publishing House, 2013).

10. See Chalmers A. Johnson, *MITI and the Japanese Miracle: The Growth of Indus-trial Policy, 1925 to 1975* (Stanford: Stanford University Press, 1982). With a head count of more than twelve thousand employees, MITI was a much larger bureau-cracy than China's NDRC; see http://www.wtec.org/loyola/polymers/ac_miti .htm#fa_3.

11. See Gore, "China's Mini-State Council."

12. The NDRC also houses a number of internal think tanks designed to provide research and analytical support for its wide-ranging functionality. Its Office for Policy Research provides direct support for its senior leaders, while its Academy of Macroeconomic Research supports a variety of longer-term investigations in areas ranging from energy and transportation to land resources and social devel-opment. See ibid.

13. See Janos Kornai, *The Socialist System* (Oxford: Clarendon, 1992).

14. In fact, there have been several times in recent years when protests and even riots erupted over the mispricing and associated shortages of essential foodstuffs such as cooking oil and pork. In 2007, three people were killed and thirty-one injured in Chongqing during the cooking oil riots. In 2011, there were violent protests in Xinjiang province over soaring pork prices.

15. In recent years, however, the NDRC has opened up the planning debate by solic-iting opinion from foreign experts. U.S. professors Michael Spence, Peter Dia-mond, and Paul Romer—the first two, Nobel laureates—played such a role in the development of the Twelfth Five-Year Plan. See He Liu, "Increasing the Propor-tion of Middle-Income Earners and Enlarging the Domestic Market: The Basic Logic of the Proposal for the 12th Five-Year Plan," Office of the Leading Group of Finance and the Economy, CPC Central Committee, 2010.

16. See Barry Naughton, "Economic Policy in 2004: Slipping Behind the Curve?" *China Leadership Monitor* 13 (January 2005).

17. Based on metrics that go back to 1879, party polarization in the United States, as derived from an analysis of party divergences in Democratic and Republi-can voting patterns in Congress, rose in 2011 to its highest on record in both the Senate and the House of Representatives; see Nolan McCarty, Keith Poole, and Howard Rosenthal, "Polarized America," at www.voteview.com/polarized _america.

18. See U.S. Executive Order 12835, "Establishment of the National Economic Coun-cil," January 25, 1993.

19. Within a few months after the NEC's inception, the Clinton administration rec-ognized that the large size of the council's membership made it unwieldy as a policy advisory body. Accordingly, a Principals Group was established that con-sisted of a core subset of council members, including the secretaries of the Trea-sury, Commerce, and Labor, together with the budget director and the chairman of the Council of Economic Advisers; see Kenneth I. Juster and Simon Lazarus, *Making Economic Policy: An Assessment of the National Economic Council* (Wash-ington, D.C.: Brookings Institution Press, 1997).

20. The ever self-effacing Rubin, of course, begged to disagree. In his words, "I had no

idea what to do"; see Robert E. Rubin and Jacob Weisberg, *In an Uncertain World: Tough Choices from Wall Street to Washington* (New York: Random House, 2003).

21. See N. Nohria, R. Kaplan, and N. Davison, "Robert Rubin," Harvard Business School Case Study 9-407-064, January 2007.

22. Beginning in 1972, a team of Brookings Institution researchers (led by Alice Rivlin and Charles Schultze) published an annual assessment of the U.S. federal budget entitled *Setting National Priorities*. It quickly became the definitive and most widely anticipated assessment of U.S. fiscal policy, only to be supplanted eventually by the research of the Congressional Budget Office, of which Rivlin was the first director, from 1975 to 1983.

23. In fact, the last time both houses of the U.S. Congress passed a so-called concurrent budget resolution and its requisite spending bills on time was back in 1996; see David M. Walker, "Our Make-Believe Federal Budget," *Politico*, February 13, 2012.

24. See Chris Edwards, "Number of Federal Subsidy Programs Tops 1,800," *Tax and Budget Bulletin*, April 2009.

25. The United States is not alone in producing consistently optimistic budget forecasts. An analysis of a sample of thirty-three countries over the 1985–2009 period shows a consistent bias toward overoptimistic GDP growth and budget forecasts; see Jeffrey Frankel, "Over-Optimism in Forecasts by Official Budget Agencies and Its Implications," Harvard Kennedy School, June 2011.

26. The OMB's latest long-term budget forecasts show the ever-present influence of Rosy Scenario, with average deficits of 7.8 percent of GDP in 2011–12 projected to decline to 2.6 percent by 2017 and then ease further to 2.1 percent by 2023. See Office of Management and Budget, *Fiscal Year 2014 Midsession Review, Budget of the U.S. Government* (Washington, D.C.: U.S. Government Printing Office, 2013).

27. In his 1982 opus that extolled the virtues of Japanese industrial policy in driving that economy's high-growth miracle, Chalmers Johnson concluded that the United States could well benefit from an American-style MITI; see Johnson, *MITI and the Japanese Miracle*, 323.

28. Nor should strategy be confused with the short-term objectives of "operational effectiveness," or cost-cutting; see Michael E. Porter, "What Is Strategy?" *Harvard Business Review*, November–December 1996.

29. Both Greenspan and Bernanke remain insistent that monetary policy played little or no role in fostering precrisis excesses in the U.S. housing market or the broader economy; they pin the blame, instead, on inadequate regulatory oversight and do admit to some Fed culpability in that area. These views are best summarized in Ben S. Bernanke, "Monetary Policy and the Housing Bubble," speech at the Annual Meeting of the American Economic Association, Atlanta, January 3, 2010; Alan Greenspan, "The Crisis," *Brookings Papers on Economic Activity*, Spring 2010; and Ben S. Bernanke, "Causes of the Recent Financial and Economic Crisis," testimony before the Financial Crisis Inquiry Commission, Washington, D.C., September 2, 2010.

30. Three NEC chairmen share the responsibility for this passive approach to mounting prebubble excesses in the U.S. economy—Stephen Friedman (2002–5), Alan Hubbard (2005–7), and Keith Hennessey (2007–9). They all served under President George W. Bush.

31. See Ben S. Bernanke, "Semiannual Monetary Policy Report to the Congress," testimony presented before the Financial Services and Banking Committees of the U.S. House of Representatives and the U.S. Senate, respectively, on July 13–14, 2011.

32. The American Recovery and Reinvestment Act of 2009 contained approximately $50 billion in federal spending initiatives on highways, bridges, mass transit, and rail. Implementation lags seriously delayed the short-term impacts of the shovel-ready approach, and political gridlock prevented several follow-up initiatives proposed by the Obama administration from being passed by Congress.

33. While export growth did, in fact, account for 40 percent of the anemic 2.4 percent annualized recovery in U.S. real GDP in the first three years after the crisis, the bulk of that impetus can be traced to cyclical rebounds in emerging markets—especially in China-centric Asia and Brazil-centric Latin America. With both of these engines of pan-regional activity slowing down in 2012–13, the same was the case for the U.S. export revival. See Stephen S. Roach, "The Great American Mirage," *Project Syndicate*, June 2012.

34. See Congressional Budget Office, "Final Sequestration Report for Fiscal Year 2013," Washington, D.C., March 27, 2013.

35. Nor was the sequestration of 2013 unique in the annals of statutory rules-based federal budget control efforts—the first being the so-called Gramm-Rudman-Hollings Act of 1985; see Megan Suzanne Lynch, "Statutory Budget Controls in Effect Between 1985 and 2002," CRS Report for Congress, Congressional Research Service, Washington, D.C., July 1, 2011.

6. A New Globalization

1. See Angus Maddison, *The World Economy: A Millennial Perspective,* Development Centre Studies of the OECD, 2001, 27.

2. See Alfred D. Chandler, Jr., *The Visible Hand* (Cambridge: Belknap Press of Harvard University Press, 1977).

3. See Kevin H. O'Rourke and Jeffrey G. Williamson, *Globalization and History: The Evolution of a Nineteenth-Century Atlantic Economy* (Cambridge: MIT Press, 2000).

4. See Harold James, *The End of Globalization: Lessons from the Great Depression* (Cambridge: Harvard University Press, 2001).

5. See Maddison, *The World Economy.*

6. See International Monetary Fund, *World Economic Outlook* database, October 2012.

7. Niall Ferguson calculates that by 1913, European empires encompassed 52 per-

cent of the world's total land mass and included 51 percent of all the global populace; see Niall Ferguson, *The War of the World: History's Age of Hatred* (London:
Penguin, 2006).

8. See James Anderson, "Borders, Fixes, and Empires: Territoriality in the New
Imperialism," Centre for International Borders Research, Queen's University,
Belfast, 2005.

9. See O'Rourke and Williamson, *Globalization and History*.

10. See Mary Meeker and Chris DuPuy, *The Internet Report*, Morgan Stanley Research, December 1995.

11. In January 1918, ten months before the end of World War I, U.S. President
Woodrow Wilson reaffirmed his commitment to a removal of trade barriers and
free cross-border exchange in the third of the so-called Fourteen Points he enu-
merated in an important address before a joint session of the U.S. Congress. See
James, *The End of Globalization*.

12. See Gary Clyde Hufbauer, Jeffrey J. Schott, Matthew Adler, Claire Brunel, and
Woan Foong Wong, "Figuring Out the Doha Round," Peterson Institute for International Economics, Washington, D.C., 2010.

13. See Anne Siebert, "Quantitative Easing and Currency Wars," European Parlia-
ment's Committee on Economic and Monetary Affairs, Brussels, 2010.

14. See Catherine Mann, *Accelerating the Globalization of America* (Washington, D.C.:
Institute for International Economics, 2006).

15. See Peter K. Schott, "The Relative Sophistication of Chinese Exports," *Economic
Policy* 23, no. 53 (2008).

16. According to the U.S. Bureau of Labor Statistics, a full accounting of blue-collar
workers would also include another forty-six million Americans, or 32 percent
of the total workforce, employed in the following occupations: service workers
(maintenance and cleaning staffs); construction and extraction industries; instal-
lation, maintenance, and repair; and transportation and material moving occupations. Unlike their production worker counterparts toiling on factory assembly
lines, however, these workers are not exposed to global competition.

17. See J. Bradford Jensen, *Global Trade in Services: Fear, Facts, and Offshoring* (Washington, D.C.: Peterson Institute for International Economics, 2011).

18. See Alan S. Blinder, "How Many US Jobs Might Be Offshorable?" *World Economics* 10 (April–June 2009).

19. There is nothing new about the antiglobalization sentiment of the U.S. workforce. One of the first studies to systematically identify and measure this sentiment was published in 2001, well before the recent intensification of such concerns; see Kenneth F. Scheve and Matthew J. Slaughter, *Globalization and the
Perceptions of American Workers* (Washington, D.C.: Institute for International
Economics, 2001).

20. In 2007, the World Economic Forum—long the closest thing to an official platform for the globalization debate—established a new annual meeting in China.

The official title of what has since become the summer Davos: "The Annual Meeting of the New Champions."

21. See David Ricardo, *The Principles of Political Economy and Taxation* (1817; Homewood, Ill.: Irwin, 1963).

22. See, for example, Jagdish N. Bhagwati, "Don't Cry for Free Trade," Council on Foreign Relations, October 15, 2007; Thomas L. Friedman, *The World Is Flat: A Brief History of the Twenty-First Century* (New York: Farrar, Straus and Giroux, 2005); and Martin Wolf, *Why Globalization Works* (New Haven: Yale University Press, 2004).

23. See Joseph A. Schumpeter, *Capitalism, Socialism, and Democracy* (London: Routledge, 1943).

24. See Ralph E. Gomory and William J. Baumol, *Global Trade and Conflicting National Interests* (Cambridge: MIT Press, 2000).

25. Ibid., 15.

26. A similar point was made a few years earlier with respect to Japan and the multiple equilibria possibilities offered by its large-scale industrial *keiretsus* such as Mitsubishi, Mitsui, and Sumitomo; see Takatoshi Ito, "Japan and the Asian Economies: A 'Miracle' in Transition," *Brookings Papers on Economic Activity* 2 (1996), 206.

27. See Paul A. Samuelson, "Where Ricardo and Mill Rebut and Confirm Arguments of Mainstream Economists Supporting Globalization," *Journal of Economic Perspectives* 18 (Summer 2004).

28. See "Response from Paul A. Samuelson," *Journal of Economic Perspectives* 19 (Summer 2005), 243.

29. Those words are not entirely idle conjecture. In 2006, the Woodrow Wilson Center invited me, along with Paul Samuelson, William Baumol, Ralph Gomory, and a few others, to participate in a forum on new critiques of classical Ricardian trade theory. Samuelson was very direct in warning of the growing risk of U.S.-China trade frictions. The proceedings of the presentations and discussion can be found in Lynn Sha and Kent H. Hughes, eds., *New Thinking in International Trade: Global Competition and Comparative Advantage* (Washington, D.C.: Woodrow Wilson International Center for Scholars, 2009).

30. See, for example, Dani Rodrik, *The Globalization Paradox: Democracy and the Future of the World Economy* (New York: Norton, 2011); and Joseph E. Stiglitz, *Globalization and Its Discontents* (New York: Norton, 2002).

31. Columbia Professor Jagdish Bhagwati, who remains one of the staunchest defenders of free trade, has been highly critical of the new critics of globalization; see Jagdish Bhagwati, "The Consensus for Free Trade Among Economists—Has It Frayed?" Lecture before the World Trade Organization, Geneva, October 8, 2007.

32. See Baumol's opening remarks at the 2006 conference at the Woodrow Wilson Center in Sha and Hughes, *New Thinking in International Trade*.

33. The IMF estimates that world GDP, in U.S. dollar terms, will hit $77.8 trillion in

2014; see International Monetary Fund, *World Economic Outlook* database, April 2013.

34. See, for example, Thomas L. Friedman, *The World Is Flat: A Brief History of the Twenty-First Century* (New York: Farrar, Straus and Giroux, 2005).

35. In November 2009, nine months after the U.S. stimulus bill was enacted with its "Buy American" provisions, three Chinese agencies—the Ministry of Science and Technology, the Ministry of Finance, and the all-important National Development and Reform Commission—jointly issued Directive 618, the National Indigenous Innovation Products Accreditation Program.

36. The Tyson quotation is taken from Karen Pennar, "The Gospel of Free Trade Is Losing Its Apostles," *Business Week,* February 27, 1989, 89. Tyson went on to publish a major study of the trade conflicts the United States was facing—a study that catapulted her into senior economic policy positions in the Clinton Administration; see Laura D'Andrea Tyson, *Who's Bashing Whom: Trade Conflict in High Technology Industries* (Washington, D.C.: Institute for International Economics, 1992).

37. See Niall Ferguson and Moritz Schularick, "Chimerica and the Global Asset Market Boom," *International Finance* 10, no. 3 (2007), and "The End of Chimerica," Harvard Business School working paper 10-037, 2009.

38. There is growing concern inside and outside of China about recent backpedaling on state-owned enterprise reform that has pushed China farther away from a market-based system; see The World Bank and the Development Research Center of the State Council, the People's Republic of China, *China 2030: Building a Modern, Harmonious, and Creative High-Income Society* (Washington, D.C.: International Bank for Reconstruction and Development, 2012).

7. Bilateralism in a Multilateral World

1. World Trade Organization, International Trade Statistics 2009, http://www.wto .org/english/res_e/statis_e/its2009_e/its2009_e.pdf, 2.

2. These are annual estimates. In the third quarter of 2011, the net domestic saving rate hit plus 0.3 percent—the first positive quarterly reading following thirteen consecutive quarters in negative territory; see U.S. Department of Commerce, Bureau of Economic Analysis, "National Income and Product Accounts," table 5.1.

3. From 1960 to 1976, for example, the U.S. current account was in surplus for all but two years—the exceptions being relatively small deficits in 1971–72. The first signs of the big imbalances to come came in 1977–78, when the current account recorded deficits of 0.7 percent of GDP; small surpluses in 1981–82 quickly turned back into deficits in most of the years that have since followed. See U.S. Department of Commerce, Bureau of Economic Analysis international and national databases.

4. India is estimated to have had the second-largest current account deficit in 2012 at $93 billion, followed by the United Kingdom at $85.5 billion; see International Monetary Fund, *World Economic Outlook* database, April 2013.

5. It is important to note that there are several conceptual differences between trade and current account balances. The largest one reflects the balance on international income flows—namely, receipts of income from foreign assets owned by U.S. companies and citizens minus payments to foreigners for assets they own in the United States. Another difference comes from "unilateral transfers" to overseas governments—mainly taxes paid overseas by U.S. citizens. In recent years, there has been a sharp expansion of the surplus of the international income balance—increasing from $25.3 billion in 2002 to $227.0 billion in 2011. That swing toward a rapidly expanding international income surplus has pushed the current account deficit below the trade deficit for three of the four years since 2007. Source: Bureau of Economic Analysis, U.S. Department of Commerce.

6. The U.S. State Department currently recognizes 195 independent states in the world, whereas there are currently 193 member states in the United Nations.

7. Edward Denison first noted the seemingly trendless pattern of private saving in the United States in the decades immediately following World War II. This became a subject of great consternation and debate in the economics profession. See Edward F. Denison, "A Note on Private Saving," *Review of Economics and Statistics* 40 (August 1968); and Paul A. David and John L. Scadding, "Private Savings: Ultrarationality, Aggregation, and 'Denison's Law,'" *Journal of Political Economy* 82, no. 2 (1974), 225–49.

8. For example, in the precrisis 2000s (2000–2007), American households had been saving at a rate of only 4.0 percent of disposable personal income, well below the 6.8 percent in the 1990s and the 9.3 percent during the 1980s; moreover, the federal government deficits averaged $305 billion annually between 2002 and 2008, a mere pittance compared with average deficits of $1.3 trillion over the 2009–12 period.

9. See Barry Eichengreen, *Exorbitant Privilege: The Rise and Fall of the Dollar and the Future of the International Financial System* (New York: Oxford University Press, 2011).

10. To my knowledge, the first reference of this literary allusion to the good graces of America's foreign lenders—borrowed from Blanche DuBois in Tennessee Williams's *A Streetcar Named Desire*—came from an exchange between former Senator Paul Sarbanes and former Treasury Secretary Robert Rubin that I observed as one of the witnesses in a Senate hearing on the U.S. trade deficit in 2001; see "Hearing Before the Subcommittee on Economic Policy of the Committee on Banking, Housing, and Urban Affairs of the United States Senate," July 25, 2001.

11. See Paul Krugman, "The Paradox of Thrift—for Real," blog post for *New York Times*, July 7, 2009.

12. Chinese government statisticians have yet to come up with official estimates for economy-wide depreciation allowances—making it difficult to construct a net

saving rate for the nation as a whole. Preliminary efforts are available at the provincial level, putting the depreciation rate at 9.6 percent for the Chinese capital stock which, for a capital stock that is now approximately 65 percent of GDP, would translate into a depreciation share of about 7 percent of GDP. On that basis, China's net saving rate would currently be approximately 42 percent of GDP—in stark contrast with America's zero net national saving rate. See Zhang Jun, Guiying Wu, and Jipeng Zhang, "Compilation of China's Provincial Capital Stock Series Using Perpetual Inventory Method," a paper delivered to the International Workshop on Productivity in China, Tsinghua University, Beijing, January 2007.

13. Germany, with a current account surplus of $219 billion in 2013, has the second-largest current account surplus; see International Monetary Fund, *World Economic Outlook* database, April 2013.

14. See Marcos Chamon, Kai Liu, and Eswar Prasad, "Income Uncertainty and Household Savings in China," IMF working paper 10-289, December 2010.

15. See Nicholas R. Lardy, *Sustaining China's Economic Growth After the Global Financial Crisis* (Washington, D.C.: Peterson Institute for International Economics, 2012).

16. See Eswar S. Prasad, "Rebalancing Growth in Asia," National Bureau of Economic Research working paper 15169, July 2009.

17. See World Bank and the Development Research Center of the State Council, the People's Republic of China, *China 2030: Building a Modern, Harmonious, and Creative High-Income Society* (Washington, D.C.: International Bank for Reconstruction and Development, 2012).

18. See Jason Dedrick, Kenneth L. Kraemer, and Greg Linden, "Who Profits from Innovation in Global Value Chains? A Study of the iPod and Notebook PCs," presented at the Annual Conference of Industry Studies, Alfred P. Sloan Foundation, Boston, May 1–2, 2008.

19. See Dr. Victor Fung, "Global Supply Chains—Past Developments, Emerging Trends," speech before a luncheon meeting of the Century 21 Club, Hong Kong, November 24, 2011.

20. See ibid.

21. See Andreas Maurer and Christophe Degain, "Globalization and Trade Flows: What You See Is Not What You Get!" World Trade Organization staff working paper ERSD-2010-12, 2010.

22. See the joint OECD-WTO note, "Trade in Value Added: Concepts, Methodologies, and Challenges," January 16, 2013.

23. World Trade Organization, International Trade Statistics 2009, 2.

24. Hogan Chen, Matthew Kondratowicz, and Kei-Mu Yi, "Vertical Specialization and Three Facts About U.S. International Trade," *North American Journal of Economics and Finance* 16 (2005), 35–59.

25. Benjamin Bridgman, "The Rise of Vertical Specialization Trade," *Journal of International Economics* 86 (2012), 133.

26. See Robert Koopman, Zhi Wang, and Shang-Jin Wei, "How Much of Chinese Exports Is Really Made in China? Assessing Domestic Value-Added When Processing Trade Is Pervasive," National Bureau of Economic Research working paper 14109, June 2008.

27. Judith M. Dean, K. C. Fung, and Zhi Wang, "Measuring Vertical Specialization: The Case of China," *Review of International Economics* 19 (2011), 609–25, 613.

28. See Koopman, Wang, and Wei, "How Much of Chinese Exports Is Really Made in China?" Hong Kong has long been an important cog in the Chinese export machine as an entrepôt in China's distribution network. For a discussion of this re-export function see Gordon H. Hanson and Robert C. Feenstra, "Intermediaries in Entrepôt Trade: Hong Kong Re-Exports of Chinese Goods," National Bureau of Economic Research working paper 8088, January 2001.

29. These estimates are based on data from the U.S. International Trade Commission, calculated for the year 2004. Earlier research, which focused more directly on Chinese exports to the United States, found that the share traceable to domestic Chinese value added was closer to 40 percent back in 2001, which would suggest an even greater overstatement; see Xikang Chen, Leonard K. Cheng, K.C. Fung, and Lawrence J. Lau, "The Estimation of Domestic Value-Added and Employment Induced by Exports: An Application to Chinese Exports to the United States," presentation, Stanford University, June 2001.

30. TiVA data put the correction of the U.S.-China bilateral trade deficit at 33 percent in 2009; see OECD-WTO, "Trade in Value Added."

31. This calculation is based on U.S. dollar–based average hourly compensation in manufacturing for 2010 as compiled by the U.S. Labor of Statistics and import weights in 2010 for America's no. 2 through no. 9 suppliers taken from the U.S. Department of Commerce. For China, the latest hourly compensation data-point on a comparable BLS basis is $1.36 for 2008; it was extrapolated to an estimate of $2.30 for 2010 based on a 30 percent annual increase—roughly in line with average percentage increases in 2007 and 2008. To be statistically precise, the cost differential between China and the other major trading partners of the United States needs to be adjusted for disparities in productivity levels; while such data are not available on a consistent basis, it is inconceivable that the gap between China and the other trading partners could be reduced by any more than 50 percent by using productivity-adjusted hourly compensation costs—or unit labor costs. That would still place the labor cost disparity at more than fivefold if America's other leading trading partners stepped up and filled the gap left by China—consistent with the basic point in the text.

32. A large body of recent research by Carmen Reinhart and Kenneth Rogoff has focused on the linkages between government debt and economic growth. While this research has stirred up a good deal of controversy in political and policy circles—a controversy exacerbated by the discovery of some data errors in their analysis—there is little reason to dispute their basic finding that eventual pressures might arise from outsize debt burdens. So far that hasn't been the case, but

that doesn't mean it can't happen at some point in the future. While U.S. government debt is now in excess of 100 percent of GDP, America has still managed to sidestep a backup in debt service, or borrowing costs, mainly because of the Fed's zero interest rate policies, in conjunction with foreign buying of Treasuries, led by China. However, in the absence of Chinese purchases, the possibility of a sharp increase in U.S. interest rates can hardly be ruled out. In the face of a major debt overhang, the impacts of such a possibility would obviously be far more acute. See Carmen M. Reinhart and Kenneth S. Rogoff, *This Time Is Different: Eight Centuries of Financial Folly* (Princeton: Princeton University Press, 2009); and Carmen M. Reinhart, Vincent R. Reinhart, and Kenneth S. Rogoff, "Debt Overhangs: Past and Present," NBER working paper 18015, April 2012.

33. See Stephen S. Roach, "America's Renminbi Fixation," *Project Syndicate*, April 2012.

8. The China Gripe

1. See "Reviewing the U.S.-China Strategic and Economic Dialogue," a hearing before the United States Senate Subcommittee on Security and International Trade and Finance of the Committee on Banking, Housing, and Urban Affairs, May 23, 2012.

2. See Jeffrey A. Frankel and Shang-Jin Wei, "Assessing China's Exchange Rate Regime," *Economic Policy*, April 2007.

3. The specific language can be found in Article IV of the IMF's articles of agreement, which states that "each member shall avoid manipulating exchange rates or the international monetary system in order to prevent effective balance of payments adjustment or to gain an unfair competitive advantage over other members." See www.imf.org.

4. This is explicitly stipulated in Section 3005 of the "Omnibus Trade and Competitiveness Act of 1988" (H.R. 3).

5. Some have argued, especially Fred Bergsten, that China's active intervention in foreign exchange markets to sell renminbi and buy dollars—transactions that he estimates average at least $1 billion per day—are prima facie evidence of outright manipulation. Not only is it debatable whether such intervention qualifies as manipulation or active management, Treasury is not legally required to take such intervention into consideration when rendering a manipulation verdict. See C. Fred Bergsten, "Correcting the Chinese Exchange Rate," testimony before the Hearing on China's Exchange Rate Policy for the Committee on Ways and Means of the U.S. House of Representatives, September 15, 2010.

6. See Ronald J. McKinnon, "Why China Shouldn't Float," *International Economy*, Fall 2010.

7. See Eswar Prasad and Lei Ye, *The Renminbi's Role in the Global Monetary System* (Washington, D.C.: Brookings Institution, 2012), and Governor Zhou Xiaochuan's remarks before the Lujiazui Forum in Shanghai on June 28, 2013.

8. It is not just developing countries that have been charged with currency manipulation; a number of developed and newly industrialized Asian economies have also been accused—from Japan, Denmark, and Switzerland to Korea, Hong Kong, and Singapore. See Joseph E. Gagnon, "Combatting Widespread Currency Manipulation," Peterson Institute for International Economics, Policy Brief no. PB12-19, July 2012.

9. See WTO Dispute Settlement database, available at www.wto.org.

10. The remaining WTO cases against China represent complaints brought by the European Union (six), Mexico (four), Canada (two), Japan (one), and Guatemala (one). See *WTO Dispute Settlement: One-Page Case Summaries, 1995–2012,* World Trade Organization, 2012 ed.

11. WTO panels have rendered preliminary findings against China in two other cases: The first is a raw materials export case brought by the United States, Europe, and Mexico in 2009; the second pertains to U.S. objections to countervailing tariffs and antidumping duties imposed by China in 2010 on U.S.-made flat-rolled steel products in response to the "Buy American" provisions of the American Recovery and Reinvestment Act of 2009. In both cases, panel reports are currently being circulated and are still open to appeal. See ibid.

12. In addition to the raw materials export and flat-rolled steel cases cited above, another dispute pertaining to Chinese grants and loans to export-oriented enterprises (as well as related subsidies for agricultural products) was filed by the United States, Mexico, and Guatemala in late 2008 and early 2009 and is still open on the WTO docket. See ibid.

13. See "China—Measures Affecting Imports of Automobile Parts," WTO Dispute Settlement DS339, initially filed in March 2006, available at http://www.wto.org/english/tratop_e/dispu_e/dispu_e.htm.

14. See "China—Value-Added Tax on Integrated Circuits," WTO Dispute Settlement DS309, initially filed in March 2004, ibid.

15. See "China—Measures Affecting the Protection and Enforcement of Intellectual Property Rights," WTO Dispute Settlement DS362, initially filed in April 2007, ibid.

16. See "China—Certain Measures Granting Refunds, Reductions or Exemptions from Taxes and Other Payments," WTO Dispute Settlement DS358, initially filed in February 2007, ibid.

17. See "China—Measures Affecting Financial Information Services and Foreign Financial Information Suppliers," WTO Dispute Settlement DS373, initially filed in March 2008, ibid.

18. See Gary Clyde Hufbauer and Jared C. Woollacott, "Trade Disputes Between China and the United States: Growing Pains so Far, Worse Ahead?" Peterson Institute for International Economics Working Paper WP 10-17, December 2010.

19. These non-WTO actions can be quite significant in terms of the scope of the dispute, as well as the financial compensation of any settlement. The dispute over China's $30 billion of solar panel exports to the West—the largest antidumping

and antisubsidy charges in history—is an important case in point. After long, arduous, and at time contentious negotiations, settlement now appears to be in sight. See Keith Bradsher, "U.S. and Europe Prepare to Settle Chinese Solar Panel Cases," *New York Times,* May 21, 2013, and Robin Emmott and Ben Blanchard, "EU and China Agree Minimum Import Price Near Spot Price," Reuters, July 27, 2013.

20. U.S. President Barack Obama upped the ante on filing WTO complaints against China in 2012, hardly surprising in light of the intense focus on China during the hard-fought presidential election campaign. In March a suit was filed over China's restrictions on the exports of "rare earths," and in July another auto parts complaint was initiated. See www.ustr.gov.

21. See the OECD project on counterfeiting and piracy available at http://www.oecd .org/industry/industryandglobalisation/oecdprojectoncounterfeitingandpiracy .htm.

22. According to the OECD, cumulative inflows of foreign direct investment over the 2003 to 2012 timespan totaled $1.9 trillion for the United States, $1.5 trillion for China, and $0.9 trillion for the United Kingdom, which was in third place; see OECD Foreign Direct Investment Statistics at www.oecd.org/investment/ statistics.

23. See Shenping Yang, "Patent Enforcement in China," *Landslide,* November–December 2011.

24. These figures are taken from the so-called "white book" of *Judicial Protection of Intellectual Property Rights in China,* issued by the Supreme People's Court, April 19, 2011; see Shenping Yang, "Patent Enforcement in China," ibid.

25. See United States International Trade Commission, China: Effects of Intellectual Property Infringement and Indigenous Innovation Policies on the U.S. Economy, Investigation no. 332-519, USITC Publication 4226, May 2011.

26. See Emily Gische, "Repercussions of China's High-Tech Rise: Protection and Enforcement of Intellectual Property Rights in China," *Hastings Law Journal,* June 2012.

27. See World Intellectual Property Organization, *2011 World Intellectual Property Indicators,* WIPO Economics and Statistics Series, 2011.

28. See OECD, "The Economic Impact of Counterfeiting and Piracy," June 2008.

29. For example, the United States did not acknowledge foreign copyrights until 1891 and did not fully conform to the 1886 Berne Convention on international copyright until 1988; see Ha-Joon Chang, "How Important Were Strong Intellectual Property Rights in the Development of Developed Countries?" Technopolicy Brief no. 1, African Technology Policy Studies Network, 2002.

30. See Ha-Joon Chang, "Intellectual Property Rights and Economic Development—Historical Lessons and Emerging Issues," *Journal of Human Development* 2, no. 2 (2001).

31. See Ha-Joon Chang, *Bad Samaritans: Rich Nations, Poor Policies, and the Threat to the Developing World* (London: Random House, 2007).

32. The TRIPS agreement was originally negotiated as part of the 1986–94 Uruguay Round of multilateral trade negotiations under GATT. When GATT evolved into the WTO in 1995, developing economies were granted a "transitional" compliance arrangement with respect to TRIPS that was initially set at five or eleven years based on a nation's degree of development. That transitional period has since been extended until 2013 (2016 for pharmaceutical patents). See www.wto.org.

33. The first general patent law can be traced back to legislation passed by the Venetian Senate in 1474; see Paul A. David, "The Evolution of Intellectual Property Institutions and the Panda's Thumb," paper prepared for the meetings of the International Economics Association in Moscow, August 24–28, 1992.

34. See Akami, *The State of the Internet* 5, no. 4 (2012), and Verizon, "2013 Data Breach Investigations Report," available at http://www.verizonenterprise.com/DBIR/2013/.

35. See David E. Sanger, David Barboza, and Nicole Perlroth, "Chinese Army Unit Is Seen as Tied to Hacking Against U.S.," *New York Times*, February 18, 2013.

36. See Brian Krekel, George Bakos, and Christopher Barnett, "Capability of the People's Republic of China to Conduct Cyber Warfare and Computer Network Exploitation," prepared for the U.S.-China Economic and Security Review Commission by Northrop Grumman Corp., October 9, 2009.

37. See Bryan Krekel, Patton Adams, and George Bakos, "Occupying the Information High Ground: Chinese Capabilities for Computer Network Operations and Cyber Espionage," prepared for the U.S.-China Economic and Security Review Commission by Northrop Grumman Corp., March 7, 2012. See also Dmitri Alperovitch, "Revealed: Operation Shady RAT," McAfee white paper, 2011.

38. See Mandiant, "APT1: Exposing One of China's Cyber Espionage Units," February 2013; and Alperovitch, "Revealed." The importance of the Mandiant investigation is that it addresses the "attribution problem" of cyberterrorism—namely, the identity and location of the attacker. By matching up IP (Internet protocol) machine addresses, Chinese-language keyboard strokes, and physical "hop" points of one persistent threat unit (APT1) over a six-year period, 2006–12, Mandiant's cybersleuths have concluded that this espionage team is most likely a state-sponsored group within the PLA located in Shanghai Pudong.

39. See Office of the Secretary of Defense, Annual Report to Congress: Military and Security Developments Involving the People's Republic of China, 2013, Washington, D.C., 11.

40. Based on data from China's National Computer Network Emergence Response Technical Team (CNCERT), the United States ranked first in foreign attacks on Chinese mainframe computers and websites in the first five months of 2013; see Li Xiaokun, "China Is Victim of Hacking Attacks," *China Daily*, June 5, 2013, and Jason Healey, "China Is Cyber Victim, Too," *Foreign Policy*, April 6, 2013.

41. See Matthew M. Aid, "Inside the NSA's Ultra-Secret Chinese Hacking Group," *Foreign Policy*, June 10, 2013.

42. See Jane Perlez, "U.S. and China Put Focus on Cybersecurity," *New York Times,* April 22, 2013; and S. 884, "The Deter Cyber Theft Act," introduced on May 7, 2013, by Senators Carl Levin (D-Michigan), John McCain (R-Arizona), Jay Rockefeller (D-West Virginia), and Tom Coburn (R-Oklahoma). Ahead of the June 2013 summit between Barack Obama and Xi Jinping, agreement was reached between the United States and China to hold regularly scheduled talks on cybersecurity issues; the first working session took place in Washington, D.C., in July 2013, just before the annual Strategic and Economic Dialogue. And in early August 2013, President Obama announced a sweeping review of U.S. cybersecurity policies. Recommendations for U.S. cyberpolicy initiatives that could shape the agenda for this debate can be found in John D. Negroponte and Samuel J. Palmisano, chairs, "Defending an Open, Global, Secure, and Resilient Internet," Independent Task Force Report No. 70, New York, Council on Foreign Relations, June 2013; Dennis Blair and Jon Huntsman, chairs, "The IP Commission Report: The Report of the Commission on the Theft of American Intellectual Property," National Bureau of Asian Research, May 2013; and Kenneth Lieberthal and Peter W. Singer, *Cybersecurity and U.S.-China Relations* (Washington, D.C.: Brookings Institution, 2012).

43. The Mandiant report accuses a Chinese cyberespionage unit of targeting in its hacking activities toward "at least four of the seven SEIs that China identified in its 12th Five Year Plan"; see Mandiant, "APT1," 24. Mandiant may be overstating these claims; while figure 13 of that report details twenty broad industry groupings (e.g, transportation) that may overlap with China's focus in those areas, it is hard to match them up with precision against China's targeted development plans in narrow subsets of these industries (e.g., electric motor vehicles).

44. See David E. Sanger, "Differences on Cybertheft Complicate China Talks," *New York Times,* July 10, 2013, and Ian Traynor and Dan Robert, "Barack Obama Seeks to Limit EU Fallout over US Spying Claims," *Guardian,* July 1, 2013.

45. See Adam Segal, *Advantage: How American Innovation Can Overcome the Asian Challenge* (New York: Norton, 2011).

46. See Eric Schmidt and Jared Cohen, *The New Digital Age: Reshaping the Future of People, Nations, and Businesses* (New York: Knopf, 2013), 119.

47. See Gordon C. Chang, *The Coming Collapse of China* (New York: Random House, 2001).

48. That quotation can be attributed to James C. Chanos, founder of the "short-selling" hedge fund Kynikos Associates. Chanos's China investment strategy anticipates a collapse in the property market that triggers a hard landing in the Chinese economy; see David Barboza, "Contrarian Investor Sees Economic Crash in China," *New York Times,* January 7, 2010.

49. For example, IMF data show that China's capital stock per worker was only 13 percent of that in the United States and Japan in 2010; see Il Houng Lee, Mur-

taza Syed, and Liu Xueyan, "Is China Over-Investing and Does It Matter?" IMF working paper WP/12/277, November 2012.

50. See Jonathan Woetzel et al., "Preparing for China's Urban Billion," McKinsey Global Institute, March 2009.

51. See Guonan Ma, "Who Pays China's Bank Restructuring Bill?" CEPII working paper 2006-04, February 2006.

52. See the China Banking and Regulatory Commission Annual Report of 2012, Beijing, April 23, 2013.

53. These figures are attributable to several speeches given in 2012 by Liu Mingkang, former chairman of China's Banking and Regulatory Commission, available at www.cbrc.gov.cn; see also Michael F. Martin, "China's Banking System: Issues for Congress," Congressional Research Service, Washington, D.C., CRS Report for Congress, February 20, 2012.

54. See Wen Xiu, "China Regulator Offers Banks Some Breathing Room," Caixin Online, April 9, 2012; see also Daniel J. Arbess, "China Record Boosts Confidence This Is No Bubble," Bloomberg opinion article, October 10, 2011.

55. Jonathan Spence details the collusion between wealthy landholders and clerks in provincial magistrates' offices during the twelve-year reign of Emperor Yongzheng in the early eighteenth century; see chapter 4, "Yongzheng's Authority," in Jonathan D. Spence, The Search for Modern China, 2nd ed. (New York: Norton, 1999).

56. In a signed newspaper article that appeared in the Chinese press in mid-April 2012—a few weeks after the sacking of Chongqing Party Secretary Bo Xilai—Premier Wen underscored the basic principle of "fighting corruption and building clean government" by stressing that the abuses of power can be contained only through effective supervision and immediate responses to reported problems; see Wen Jiabao, "Let the Power Be Exercised Under the Sunshine," in Qiushi (Seeking Truth), April 16, 2012.

57. National Bureau of Statistics of China, China Statistical Yearbook, various issues, 2008–12.

58. See John Garnaut, "Rotting from Within: Investigating the Massive Corruption in the Chinese Military," Foreign Policy, April 16, 2012.

59. See Edward Wong, "New Communist Party Chief in China Denounces Corruption in Speech," New York Times, November 19, 2012.

60. See Zhao Yinan, "Xi Repeats Anti-Graft Message to Top Leaders," China Daily, November 20, 2012; and Alice L. Miller, "The New Party Politburo Leadership," China Leadership Monitor 40 (January 2013).

61. The Corruptions Perception Index is based on a combination of polls and survey data that measure perceived levels of public sector corruption in a population that numbered 176 countries and territories around the world in 2012. The composite index draws on seventeen pieces of source data from thirteen institutions and basically aims at assessing the abuse of public power; it is based on specific

assessments of "bribery of public officials, kickbacks in government procurement, embezzlement of public funds, and on questions that probe the strength
and effectiveness of government anti-corruption efforts." See Transparency
International: The Global Coalition Against Corruption, at: www.transparency
.org.

9. Imbalances and the Great Crisis

1. See, among others, Nouriel Roubini, "The Risk of a U.S. Hard Landing and
   Implications for the Global Economy and Financial Markets," speech at the In-
   ternational Monetary Fund, Washington, D.C., September 13, 2007; Raghuram
   G. Rajan, "The Greenspan Era: Lessons for the Future," paper presented at a
   symposium sponsored by the Federal Reserve Bank of Kansas City (Jackson
   Hole, Wyo.), August 27, 2005; Robert J. Shiller, *Irrational Exuberance*, 2nd ed.
   (Princeton: Princeton University Press, 2005); and Stephen S. Roach, "A Subprime Outlook for the Global Economy," speech before the World Knowledge
   Forum, Seoul, South Korea, October 17, 2007.
2. Source: Bureau of Economic Analysis, U.S. Department of Commerce, July 31,
   2013.
3. See Carmen M. Reinhart and Kenneth S. Rogoff, *This Time Is Different: Eight
   Centuries of Financial Folly* (Princeton: Princeton University Press, 2009).
4. Nomura economist Richard Koo has interpreted the "lost decades" of the Japanese economy through the lens of the balance sheet recession hitting Japan's
   business sector; see Richard C. Koo, *The Holy Grail of Macro Economics: Lessons
   from Japan's Great Recession* (Singapore: John Wiley and Sons [Asia], 2008). It is
   hardly a stretch to apply that analytical framework to a balance sheet recession
   bearing down on America's consumers.
5. Federal Reserve and U.S. Commerce Department data underscore the snail's
   pace of balance sheet repair for the American consumer. Household sector debt
   stood at 116 percent of disposable personal income in early 2013—down from record highs of 132 percent in 2008, but still more than 70 percentage points above
   the 43 percent norm of the last three decades of the twentieth century. Similarly,
   the personal saving rate, at just 4.2 percent in the first half of 2013, was less than
   half the 9.3 percent average of 1970–99.
6. See International Monetary Fund, *World Economic Outlook*, online database,
   April 2013, at www.imf.org.
7. See United Nations Statistics Division, "Historical Data 1900–1960 on International Merchandise Trade Statistics," April 28, 2009, at http://unstats.un.org
   /unsd/trade/imts/historical_data.htm.
8. See J. Ahn, M. Amiti, and D. Weinstein, "Trade Finance and the Great Trade Collapse," *American Economic Review: Papers and Proceedings*, May 2011.
9. That's not to say the financial crisis was irrelevant to trade flows. The liquidity
   pressures in 2008–9 were most acute on financial transactions that involved an

assessment of counterparty risk—essentially bets made by one financial institution on the solvency of others. The sudden demise of Lehman Brothers gave new and urgent meaning to counterparty risk—especially for cross-border transactions involving different regulatory regimes and accounting standards. The heightened risk aversion that followed Lehman's failure affected many of the linchpin markets of global finance—especially interest rate swaps, credit-default swaps, syndicated loans, and trade finance. There was a sharp widening of credit spreads in all of these market segments, as the cost of borrowing embedded in these riskier assets moved up sharply relative to borrowing costs incurred by the U.S. Treasury for so-called riskless assets. That certainly had a material bearing on both the price and availability of trade finance—and the volume of exports and imports that such finance supported.

10. IMF surveys suggest that bank-intermediated trade finance—especially so-called letters of credit and export credit insurance—held up considerably better than that which could be obtained in capital markets, where the liquidity pressures were most acute; see I. Asmundson, T. Dorsey, A. Khachatryan, I. Niculcea, and M. Saito, "Trade and Trade Finance in the 2008–09 Financial Crisis," IMF working paper 11/16, January 2011.

11. See B. Coulibaly, H. Sapriza, and A. Zlate, "Trade Credit and International Trade during the 2008–09 Global Financial Crisis," Board of Governors of the Federal Reserve System, *International Finance Discussion Papers*, No. 1020, June 2011.

12. This calculation is based on a subset of Asia's fourteen largest developing economies as extracted from the broader IMF universe: China, India, Indonesia, the Philippines, Malaysia, Vietnam, Thailand, Bangladesh, Pakistan, and Myanmar, as well as the so-called newly industrialized economies of South Korea, Taiwan, Hong Kong, and Singapore; see International Monetary Fund, *World Economic Outlook*, various issues.

13. World Bank researchers put the crisis-related job loss of Chinese migrant workers in the range of twenty million to thirty-six million during 2008–9; see John Giles, Albert Park, Fang Cao, and Yang Du, "Weathering a Storm: Survey-Based Perspectives on Employment in China in the Aftermath of the Global Financial Crisis," World Bank Development Research Group policy research working paper 5984, March 2012.

14. The four trillion renminbi headline figure announced for the late 2008 stimulus was to be spread out through 2010; the total also included about one trillion renminbi that had previously been earmarked for reconstruction in earthquake-devastated Sichuan province and also included accelerated expenditures for many high-speed rail projects that had long been on the drawing boards. See Barry Naughton, "Understanding the Chinese Stimulus Package," *China Leadership Monitor* 28 (May 2009).

15. See the European Commission, *Quarterly Report on the Euro Area* 11, no. 3 (2012).

16. By now, there is a voluminous literature on the debate over the design and sustainability of the European Monetary Union. Two well-known opposing views

can be found in Alberto Alesina and Francesco Giavazzi, *The Future of Europe: Reform or Decline* (Cambridge: MIT Press, 2006); and Otmar Issing, *The Birth of the Euro* (Cambridge: Cambridge University Press, 2008).

17. See speech by Mario Draghi, President of the European Central Bank, at the Global Investment Conference in London, July 26, 2012, available at www.ecb .int/press.

18. See Reinhart and Rogoff, *This Time Is Different*.

19. A good discussion of the pros and cons of this debate can be found in "The Good, the Bad, and the Ugly: 100 Years of Dealing with Public Debt Overhangs," chapter 3 of the IMF's October 2012 *World Economic Outlook*. The austerity debate itself became something of a cause célèbre in early 2013 as economists from the University of Massachusetts uncovered some data errors in the Reinhart and Rogoff spreadsheets; see Thomas Herndon, Michael Ash, and Robert Pollin, "Does High Public Debt Consistently Stifle Economic Growth? A Critique of Reinhart and Rogoff," University of Massachusetts Amherst Political Economy Research Institute, April 15, 2013. While the Herndon, Ash, and Pollin critique does raise some serious questions about the validity of the notorious 90 percent debt-to-GDP threshold that has been featured prominently in many of Reinhart and Rogoff's papers, it does not disprove the notion that high sovereign debt burdens have long been associated with weaker output growth; see Carmen Reinhart and Kenneth Rogoff, "Debt, Growth, and the Austerity Debate," op-ed, *New York Times*, April 25, 2013.

20. This has been dubbed the "CRIC cycle" by Morgan Stanley's Tokyo-based economist Robert Feldman, who has long argued that Japan's lost decade(s) can be broken down into distinct phases of Crisis, Response, Improvement, and Complacency—with the final phase of complacency invariably setting the stage for the next crisis; see Robert Alan Feldman, "Cobwebs and CRICs," Morgan Stanley Dean Witter Equity Research, April 4, 2001.

21. The events surrounding the enactment of Dodd-Frank financial reform legislation in the United States were a classic case in point. The U.S. Congress empowered a special commission to get to the bottom of the Great Crisis and make recommendations on appropriate policy and regulatory remedies. There were ten commissioners, who along with an investigatory staff of eighty-seven professionals reviewed millions of pages of documents, held nineteen days of public hearings, and interviewed more than seven hundred witnesses. Yet under intense political pressure, Congress couldn't wait for the report from its own commission and enacted the sweeping Dodd-Frank legislation in July 2010, six months *before* the commission published its findings; see *The Financial Crisis Inquiry Report* submitted by the Financial Crisis Inquiry Commission Pursuant to Public Law 111-21 (Washington, D.C.: U.S. Government Printing Office, 2011).

22. Not surprisingly, former Fed Chairman Greenspan was a leading voice in characterizing the Great Crisis as "the hundred-year flood"; see Alan Greenspan, "The Crisis," *Brookings Papers on Economic Activity*, Spring 2010.

23. See Carmen M. Reinhart, Vincent R. Reinhart, and Kenneth S. Rogoff, "Debt Overhangs: Past and Present," NBER working paper 18015, April 2012.

24. Based on an IMF tabulation of global current account balances, the arithmetic sum of surpluses and deficits rose from about 1 percent of world GDP in 1996 to nearly 6 percent in 2006; the IMF projects that this gauge will level out at around 4 percent of world GDP over the 2012–15 period—down from the precrisis peak but still about four times the magnitude of those prevailing in the mid-1990s. See Stephen S. Roach, "Now or Never for Global Rebalancing," speech before the Institute for Global Economics, Seoul, South Korea, May 2012.

25. Even former Fed Chairman Paul Volcker conceded in Senate testimony back in 2001 that it all "seemed, for the time being, a benign process: For the United States, a current account deficit without tears." See Volcker's testimony before the Subcommittee on Economic Policy of the Committee on Banking, Housing, and Urban Affairs of the United States Senate, July 25, 2001.

26. In 2006, the IMF implemented its first formal multilateral surveillance and consultations framework in an effort to deal with global imbalances; five economies were involved—those of the United States, China, the euro area, Japan, and Saudi Arabia. After one round of multilateral consultations in 2007, the effort lost momentum, only to be restarted after the Great Crisis of 2008–9. Analytical support to this process has been more promising, underscored by publication of a series of "spillover reports" for the five economies accounting for the greatest sources of systemic risk in the global economy—those of the United States, China, Japan, Europe, and the United Kingdom; for a summary of these efforts, see International Monetary Fund, *Consolidated Spillover Report: Implications for the Analysis of the Systemic-5*, July 11, 2011.

10. Smoot-Hawley Redux

1. See Douglas A. Irwin, *Peddling Protectionism: Smoot-Hawley and the Great Depression* (Princeton: Princeton University Press, 2011).

2. Press statement of Senator Charles Schumer, "Schumer, Graham Urge Action Against China's Unfair Currency Manipulation," May 17, 2005, available at www.schumer.senate.gov.

3. Comments to the author over breakfast at the St. Regis Hotel in Beijing on March 20, 2006.

4. The U.S.-China Business Council keeps a running tab on all China-related legislation introduced by the U.S. Congress; see www.uschina.org.

5. The House bill (H.R. 2378) was sponsored by Representative Tim Ryan (D-Ohio), along with 159 cosponsors in the 111th Congress (2009–10).

6. The Senate bill (S. 1619) was sponsored by Senator Sherrod Brown (D-Ohio), along with 22 cosponsors, including Senators Schumer and Graham, in the 112th Congress (2011–12).

7. Legislation is required to be passed by both houses of the U.S. Congress during

the same session before it can be submitted for presidential approval. The House bill was passed in the 111th Congress, whereas the Senate bill was passed in the 112th.

8. China, of course, could also fire the first shot. For that to occur, there needs to be a credible motive. For reasons noted in the text, the interplay between economic and political circumstances in the United States lend themselves particularly well to the Washington itchy–trigger finger syndrome. In a China-induced scenario, I suspect the primary motivation would have to come from intensified frictions over a foreign policy issue, possibly a spillover effect from an outbreak of hostilities with Japan. In my view, the odds of the U.S. first shot over economic concerns would be a good deal higher than a Chinese first shot over geopolitical tensions.

9. Ironically, this fictional account of President Obama's action fits all too well with the explicit promise that former Governor Mitt Romney made during the presidential campaign of 2012 to issue just such an edict on January 20, 2013, the day he would have been sworn into office had he won the election; see Stephen S. Roach, "How Governor Romney Could Go Wrong From Day One," *Financial Times,* August 28, 2012.

10. On April 15, 1929, President Hoover called Congress into special session to deal with the problems in the agricultural sector and to focus on tariff-related remedies to this problem; see Irwin, *Peddling Protectionism.*

11. See Charles E. Schumer, *Positively American: Winning Back the Middle-Class Majority One Family at a Time* (New York: Rodale, 2007).

12. While there is a compelling argument that it would probably take a good deal of time for the dollar to lose its special status, that development could be hastened by economic and financial management mistakes of U.S. policy makers; see Barry Eichengreen, *Exorbitant Privilege: The Rise and Fall of the Dollar and the Future of the International Financial System* (New York: Oxford University Press, 2011).

13. See Irwin, *Peddling Protectionism.*

14. *New York Times,* November 4, 1928, cited ibid.

15. Ibid.

16. See Irwin, *Peddling Protectionism.*

17. Ibid.

18. See Ben S. Bernanke, "Deflation: Making Sure 'It' Doesn't Happen Here," remarks before the National Economists Club, Washington, D.C., November 21, 2002.

19. In U.S. dollar terms, world GDP increased from $32.1 trillion in 2001 to $61.2 trillion in 2008. Over the same period, world exports surged from $7.6 trillion in 2001 to $19.8 trillion in 2008, an increase of $12.2 trillion that accounted for 41.8 percent of the $29 trillion expansion of world GDP over this seven-year interval. Source: International Monetary Fund, *World Economic Outlook* database, 2012.

20. See also Carmen M. Reinhart and Kenneth S. Rogoff, *This Time Is Different: Eight Centuries of Financial Folly* (Princeton: Princeton University Press, 2009).

21. See Gary Clyde Hufbauer and Jared C. Woollacott, "Trade Disputes Between China and the United States: Growing Pains so Far, Worse Ahead?" Peterson Institute for International Economics working paper WP 10-17, December 2010.

22. The original exposition of the prisoner's dilemma, which is attributed to Merrill Flood and Melvin Dresher, two game theorists working at the RAND Corporation in the 1950s, was later formalized by Albert Tucker of Princeton. See Robert Axelrod, *The Evolution of Cooperation* (New York: Basic, 1984); and William Poundstone, *Prisoner's Dilemma* (New York: Doubleday, 1992).

23. Professor Yiping Huang of the China Center for Economic Research at Peking University has also argued that the United States and China are trapped in a prisoner's dilemma over trade and renminbi-related frictions; see Yiping Huang, "Krugman's Chinese Renminbi Fallacy," *VOX*, March 26, 2010, available at www.VoxEU.org.

11. Rebalancing

1. See Clay Chandler, Heang Chhor, and Brian Salsberg, eds., *Reimagining Japan: The Quest for a Future that Works* (San Francisco: McKinsey, 2011); also see Stephen S. Roach, "Shinzo Abe's Monetary Policy Delusions," *Project Syndicate*, December 28, 2012.

2. For an interesting discussion of the psychological aspects of America's excess consumption disorder, see Peter C. Whybrow, *American Mania: When More Is Not Enough* (New York: Norton, 2005).

3. See John Kenneth Galbraith, *The Affluent Society* (Boston: Houghton Mifflin, 1958).

4. For the full Chinese-language text of the Twelfth Five-Year Plan, see "Guomin jingji he shehui fazhan dishier ge wunian guihua gangyao" (People's Economy and Social Development Twelfth Five-Year Plan Outline), Zhonghua Renmin Gongheguo Zhongyang Renmin Zhengfu (Central People's Government), http://www.gov.cn/2011lh/content_1825838.htm; for an excellent English-language summary, see Joseph Casey and Katherine Koleski, "Backgrounder: China's 12th Five-Year Plan," U.S.-China Economic and Security Review Commission, Washington, D.C., June 24, 2011.

5. See Wayne M. Morrison, "China's Economic Rise: History, Trends, Challenges, and Implications for the United States," Congressional Research Service, Washington, D.C.: CRS Report for Congress, March 4, 2013. U.S. calculation is based on "National Income and Product Accounts Tables," Bureau of Economic Analysis, U.S. Department of Commerce.

6. National Bureau of Statistics, *China Statistical Yearbook 2012*.

7. In 2011, the ratio of tertiary (services) sector employment to tertiary GDP in China was 0.1331, or 30.1 percent greater than the 0.1023 job-to-output ratio in

the secondary (manufacturing and construction) sector; source: author's calculations based on National Bureau of Statistics, *China Statistical Yearbook 2012*.

8. See "Current Employment Statistics" of the U.S. Bureau of Labor Statistics and *China Statistical Yearbook: 2012*.

9. The theory hasn't always worked perfectly, especially for many high-wage developed economies in recent years. Starting in the 1990s, the pressures of globalization, new technologies, and outsourcing strategies have driven a wedge between marginal productivity gains and real wages. Theory would argue that this is a temporary wedge; that remains to be seen. See Stephen S. Roach, "The Hollow Ring of the Productivity Revival," *Harvard Business Review*, November–December 1996.

10. See U.S. Bureau of Labor Statistics, "International Comparisons of Hourly Compensation Costs in Manufacturing, 2010," December 21, 2011.

11. See Stephen S. Roach, "China's 12th Five-Year Plan: Strategy vs. Tactics," paper prepared for the twelfth annual China Development Forum, Beijing, March 20–21, 2011.

12. See Organization for Economic Cooperation and Development, *Rural Policy Review: China* (Paris: OECD, 2009); and *OECD Economic Surveys: China* (Paris: OECD, 2010).

13. See *China in Focus: Lessons and Challenges* (Paris: OECD, 2012).

14. In 2011, with the urban share of the Chinese population at 51 percent and urban per capita incomes at 3.2 times those of rural incomes, the disposable personal income share of the Chinese GDP was 45 percent. If the OECD migration extrapolations come to pass and the urban share of the Chinese population rises to 67 percent by 2030 (with workers accounting for 60 percent of that increase), and the urban-rural income differential holds at 3.1, the disposable personal income share of the Chinese GDP could hit 57 percent by 2030. Source: author's estimate.

15. See Nicholas R. Lardy, "Financial Repression in China," Peterson Institute for International Economics, Policy Brief no. PB08-8, September 2008.

16. See Marcos Chamon, Kai Liu, and Eswar Prasad, "Income Uncertainty and Household Savings in China," IMF working paper 10-289, December 2010.

17. 2012 Review of the National Council for Social Security Fund, People's Republic of China, available at www.ssf.gov.cn/Eng_Introduction/201206.

18. Converting total retirement assets under management of RMB2669 in 2010–11 by the RMB-dollar exchange rate of 6.1415 in May 2013 works out to about USD $435 billion. There were approximately 257 million participants covered by China's urban basic old-age insurance system at the end of 2010; see International Social Security Administration, *Social Security Coverage Extension in the BRICS* (Geneva: ISSA, 2013), chapter 4, "Towards Universal Social Security Coverage in China."

19. In July 2012, Lei Haichao, deputy director of the Beijing Health Bureau, confirmed the findings of a report issued by the Healthcare Reform Office in China, which indicated that the government was considering additional reforms to its

nationwide healthcare system; see Laurie Burkitt, "China Calls for Health System Overhaul," *Wall Street Journal*, July 25, 2012.

20. According to RealtyTrac, 1,319,516 homes were in foreclosure in June 2013, well below peak rates of 3.6 million in early 2010 but still above the precrisis average of 900,000 in 2005–6. See http://www.realtytrac.com/statsandtrends.

21. See Congressional Budget Office, "Final Sequestration Report for Fiscal Year 2013," Washington, D.C., March 2013.

22. See Klaus Schwab and Xavier Sala-i-Martin, eds., *The Global Competitiveness Report: 2012–2013* (Geneva: World Economic Forum, 2012).

23. See Suzanne Berger and the MIT Industrial Performance Center, *How We Compete: What Companies Around the World Are Doing to Make It in Today's Global Economy* (New York: Currency Doubleday, 2005).

24. See Charles Duhigg and Keith Bradsher, "How the U.S. Lost Out on iPhone Work," *New York Times*, January 21, 2012.

25. See Stephen S. Roach, "America's Savings Imperative," *The American*, American Enterprise Institute Online Magazine, October 1, 2011.

26. As noted in Chapter 4, Fed Chairman Bernanke has been very clear in stressing the distinction between monetary policy and other measures (i.e., macroprudential tools) that should be used to deal with stability risks; see Ben S. Bernanke, "Some Reflections on the Crisis and the Policy Response," speech before the Russell Foundation and the Century Foundation Conference on "Rethinking Finance," New York, April 13, 2012. More recently, Bernanke conceded, "Financial stability is also linked to monetary policy, although those links are not fully understood." See Ben S. Bernanke, "The First 100 Years of the Federal Reserve: The Policy Record, Lessons Learned, and Prospects for the Future," remarks before a conference sponsored by the National Bureau of Economic Research, Cambridge, July 10, 2013.

27. See Stephen Roach, "Time to Revamp the Fed's Flawed Mandate," op-ed, *Financial Times*, November 22, 2010.

12. The Next America Meets the Next China

1. Source: U.S. Department of Commerce and U.S. International Trade Commission.

2. Source: U.S. Census Bureau of the U.S. Department of Commerce.

3. See Stephen S. Roach, "Rethinking the U.S.-China Economic Agenda," testimony before the Subcommittee on Security and International Trade and Finance, U.S. Senate Committee on Banking, Housing, and Urban Affairs, Washington, D.C., May 23, 2012.

4. The American Recovery and Reinvestment Act of 2009 (Public Law 111-5) contained a controversial "Buy American" provision (Section 1605) that required any public building or public works project funded by the stimulus to use only iron, steel, and other manufactured goods that are produced in the United States.

5. In 2010, China countered the U.S. "Buy American" campaign by imposing countervailing and antidumping duties on U.S. exports of grain-oriented flat-rolled electrical steel products. The United States initiated a formal complaint with

the WTO over this action in September 2010; in July 2012, a WTO panel ruled largely in favor of the U.S. position, although the Chinese have appealed and the case still remains open. The details on Dispute DS5414 can be found on the Dispute Settlement database of the WTO at www.wto.org.

6. See Joseph Casey and Katherine Koleski, "Backgrounder: China's 12th Five-Year Plan," U.S.-China Economic and Security Review Commission, Washington, D.C., June 24, 2011.

7. See Yuval Atsmon, Vinay Dixit, and Cathy Wu, "Tapping China's Luxury-Goods Market," *McKinsey Quarterly,* April 2011.

8. See Michael E. Porter, *The Competitive Advantage of Nations* (New York: Free Press, 1990).

9. See Stephen S. Roach, "Services Under Siege—The Restructuring Imperative," *Harvard Business Review,* September–October 1991.

10. The trade deficit of China's uncompetitive services sector has widened from $8.8 billion in 2006 to $55.3 billion in 2011; see Long Guoqiang, "China's Trade Deficit in Services: Structural Evolution and Future Strategy," *China Development Review* 14, no. 4 (2012).

11. In 1988, the United States accounted for fully 48 percent of total G-7 outlays on services; see ibid. OECD data suggest the U.S. share of G-7 services spending has been roughly stable in the 45–50 percent range through 2010.

12. See International Monetary Fund, World Economic Outlook database, April 2013.

13. The deceleration of nominal Chinese growth built into the extrapolation exercise would have been more pronounced were it not for the offsetting assumption of steady renminbi currency appreciation of about 1 percent per year versus the U.S. dollar that we have also built into these calculations.

14. This final leg of the extrapolation exercise is based on the combination of sustained annual growth of nominal GDP of 5.25 percent in the United States and 8.5 percent in China over the 2026–30 time period. Under those assumptions, the Chinese economy would finally surpass the U.S. economy as the largest economy in the world in 2028. Reflecting the two countries' vast disparities of population, convergence in per capita GDP would not occur for several more decades, at the soonest.

15. See Ingo Borchert, Batshur Gootiiz, and Aaditya Mattoo, "Guide to the Services Trade Restrictions Database," World Bank policy research working paper 6018, June 2012.

16. See J. Bradford Jensen, *Global Trade in Services: Fear, Fact, and Offshoring* (Washington, D.C.: Peterson Institute for International Economics, 2011).

17. Productivity growth makes it a stretch to use labor shares to draw inferences on the allocation of output for any economy. It turns out, however, that this is less of a leap of faith in labor-intensive services, where productivity levels tend to be lower and productivity growth considerably slower than in manufacturing.

18. See U.S. International Trade Commission, *Recent Trends in U.S. Services Trade: 2011 Annual Report,* publication no. 4243, July 2011.

19. See Yuval Atsmon, Max Magni, Linha Li, and Wenkan Liao, "Meet the 2020 Chinese Consumer," *McKinsey Consumer and Shopper Insights,* March 2012.

20. In China, the ratio of those sixty-five years and older to the working-age population (nineteen to sixty-four) is set to more than triple over the next thirty years—rising from 11 percent in 2012 to 35 percent by 2042. Source: United Nations World Population Prospects: The 2008 Revision; medium variant available at www.un.org/esa/population/.

21. In the interest of full disclosure, the author was a member of the Board of Directors of China International Capital Corporation from 2007 to 2010.

22. Not all Chinese services need to follow the foreign partnership approach. The example of Ctrip, China's leading domestic travel and hotel booking service, is a case in point—although the business was built by Chinese entrepreneurs who had extensive prior experience in Silicon Valley and international markets.

23. This generational nomenclature of the PRC's leadership progression was first articulated by Jiang Zemin. He depicted himself as being at the "core of the third generation of leaders." The first generation, of course, was Mao, followed by Deng (second), Jiang (third), Hu Jintao (fourth), and now Xi Jinping (fifth). See Cheng Li, *China's Leaders: The New Generation* (Lanham, Md.: Rowman and Littlefield, 2001).

24. China's new premier, Li Keqiang, appears to have an especially deep understanding of both the challenges to and the blueprint for a consumer-led rebalancing of the Chinese economy. Under his oversight, a large team of researchers from China's Development Research Center, the think tank of the State Council, collaborated with an equally large team from the World Bank in producing a monumental report on the restructuring of the Chinese economy. See The World Bank and the Development Research Center of the State Council, the People's Republic of China, *China 2030: Building a Modern, Harmonious, and Creative High-Income Society* (Washington, D.C.: International Bank for Reconstruction and Development, 2012); see also Stephen S. Roach, "The Slow Boat from China," *Foreign Policy,* July 9, 2013.

13. Codependency, the Internet, and a Dual Identity Crisis

1. Asthenic personality disorder is the formal nomenclature for the dependent personality disorder (DPD). The *Diagnostic and Statistical Manual of Mental Disorders* (5th ed., DSM-IV-TR), published by the American Psychiatric Association in 2013, lists dependence as a personality disorder (diagnostic code: 301.6); the *International Statistical Classification of Diseases and Related Health Problems* (ICD-10), endorsed by the World Health Organization in 1990, also classifies dependency as a personality disorder (diagnostic code: F60.7). Codependency has been applied to the psychological disorder that arises from an unhealthy close relationship between two dependent individuals. See Douglas J. Scaturo, Timothy Hayes, David Sagula, and Todd Walter, "The Concept of Co-Dependency and Its

Context Within Family Systems Theory," *Family Therapy* 27, no. 2 (2000), 63–70; Douglas J. Scaturo, *Clinical Dilemmas in Psychotherapy: A Trans-Theoretical Approach to Psychotherapy Integration* (Washington, D.C.: American Psychological Association, 2005); Theodore Milton, Carrie Milton, Seth Grossman, Sarah Meagher, and Rowena Ramnath, *Personality Disorders in Modern Life* (New York: John Wiley and Sons, 2004); and Melody Beattie, *Codependent No More* (Minneapolis: Hazelden Foundation, 1986).

2. The exact language in the ICD-10's diagnostic code F60.7: "there is often a tendency to transfer responsibility to others."

3. See Jonathan D. Spence, *The Chan's Great Continent: China in Western Minds* (New York: Norton, 1998).

4. This potential escalation of our economic version of dependence and codependency is also grounded in the scale that psychologists use to rank the severity of defense mechanisms that are associated with personality disorders. The "Defensive Functioning Scale" is calibrated in seven levels, from manageable and sustainable to unmanageable and unsustainable: (1) high adaptive level; (2) mental inhibitions (compromise formation) level; (3) minor image-distorting level; (4) disavowal level; (5) major image-distorting level; (6) action level; and (7) level of defensive dysregulation. See Appendix B of the fourth edition of *Diagnostics and Statistical Manual of Mental Health Disorders* (2000), 807–9.

5. Source: Internet World Stats: Usage and Population Statistics, available at www.internetworldstats.com/stats3.htm.

6. See China Internet Network Information Center, *31st Statistical Report on Internet Development in China*, January 15, 2013.

7. See Stephen S. Roach, "China's Connectivity Revolution," *Project Syndicate*, January 26, 2012.

8. This late 2011 survey is based on a sample of fifty-seven hundred Chinese Internet users from both large and small cities. See Cindy Chiu, Davis Lin, and Ari Silverman, "China's Social-Media Boom," McKinsey, April 2012.

9. See China Internet Network Information Center, *31st Statistical Report on Internet Development in China*.

10. Source: Bureau of Economic Analysis, U.S. Department of Commerce.

11. The economic growth literature is voluminous. For a good summary of the history of the debate, see David Warsh, *Knowledge and the Wealth of Nations: A Story of Economic Discovery* (New York: Norton, 2006); among the leading expositions of the growth debate, see Robert M. Solow, *Learning from "Learning by Doing": Lessons for Economic Growth* (Stanford: Stanford University Press, 1997); Robert E. Lucas, Jr., *Lectures on Economic Growth* (Cambridge: Harvard University Press, 2002); and Robert J. Barro, *Determinants of Economic Growth: A Cross-Country Empirical Study* (Cambridge: MIT Press, 1997).

12. See Jonathan D. Spence, *The Search for Modern China*, 2nd ed. (New York: Norton, 1999).

13. See ibid.

14. These fears were conceptualized around the construct of a "Jasmine Revolution"—named after the early 2011 upheaval in Tunisia. See Ian Johnson, "Calls for a 'Jasmine Revolution' in China Persist," *New York Times,* February 21, 2011.

15. See Seymour M. Lipset, "Some Social Requisites of Democracy: Economic Development and Political Legitimacy," *American Political Science Review,* 1959.

16. See Daron Acemoglu, Simon Johnson, James A. Robinson, and Pierre Yared, "Income and Democracy," *American Economic Review,* June 2008.

17. These same researchers also find that unique country-specific factors, such as religion, population density, and diverging development paths, also contribute to the spurious correlation between democracy and development. Ibid.

18. See Ann Florini, Hairong Lai, and Yeling Tan, *China Experiments: From Local Innovations to National Reform* (Washington, D.C.: Brookings Institution Press, 2012).

19. See Thomas Lum, "China and Falun Gong," *Congressional Research Service Report for Congress,* May 25, 2006.

20. See Cheng Li, "The End of the CCP's Resilient Authoritarianism? A Tripartite Assessment of Shifting Power in China," *China Quarterly,* no. 211 (September 2012). While Li is particularly concerned about the sustainability of China's current political system in the aftermath of the Bo Xilai scandal, at a January 2013 seminar at Yale Law School he stated categorically that he would still attach an 85 percent probability to China's successful transition to democracy in the next ten years.

21. China's so-called "SkyNet" team (rumored to number more than thirty thousand) is the world's largest paid and volunteer cyberpolice force; moreover, that figure understates the resources dedicated to the effort, as many Internet portals conduct their own independent filtering of restricted and borderline content. See Wilfred Yang Wang, "Who's Blocking the Chinese Internet?" *Journal of Contemporary Criminal Justice* 26, no. 1 (2010); and Constance Bitso, Ina Fourie, and Theo Bothma, "Trends in Transition from Classical Censorship to Internet Censorship: Selected Country Overviews," *FAIFE Spotlight,* October 2012.

22. See Chiu, Lin, and Silverman, "China's Social-Media Boom."

23. See Florini, Lai, and Tan, *China Experiments.*

24. See ibid.

25. See Jinglian Wu, *Understanding and Interpreting Chinese Economic Reform* (Mason, Ohio: Thomson/South-Western, 2005).

26. See Zheng Bijian, *Peaceful Rise—China's New Road to Development* (Beijing: Central Party School Publishing House, 2005).

27. See Francis Fukuyama, *The Origins of Political Power: From Prehuman Times to the French Revolution* (New York: Farrar, Straus and Giroux, 2011).

28. See He Weifang, *In the Name of Justice: Striving for the Rule of Law in China* (Washington, D.C.: Brookings Institution Press, 2012); Minxin Pei, *China's Trapped Transition: The Limits of Developmental Autocracy* (Cambridge: Harvard University Press, 2006); and John L. Thornton, "China's Leadership Gap," *Foreign Affairs,* November–December 2006.

29. McLuhan's seemingly radical pre-IT insight, "the medium is the message," has

been validated by the ubiquitous Internet; fully thirty years before the launch of the Internet, McLuhan provided an extremely prescient vision into the roles of media and communications in society. See Marshall McLuhan, *Understanding Media: The Extensions of Man* (New York: McGraw-Hill, 1964).

30. See Florini, Lai, and Tan, *China Experiments*.

31. Taken from Churchill's speech before the House of Commons, November 11, 1947; see Robert Rhodes James, ed., *Winston S. Churchill: His Complete Speeches, 1897–1963* (New York: Chelsea House, 1974), 7: 7566.

32. According to Netcraft's "Web Server Survey," there were 629 million websites in January 2013. See http://news.netcraft.com/archives/category/web-server -survey/.

33. By contrast, the same poll found that 30 percent of the U.S. user community felt that the Internet acted to temper political extremism; see Aaron Smith, "The Internet and Campaign 2010," *Pew Internet*, a project of Pew Research Center, March 17, 2011.

34. Radio-delivered extremism is an especially important aspect of this problem. According to Arbitron's RADAR report, the national radio audience in the United States totaled 241 million listeners in December 2012, or 92 percent of the population; see http://arbitron.mediaroom.com/index.php?s=43&item=849. At the same time, according to press reports, estimates of the listening audience for Rush Limbaugh, host of America's most listened to radio talk show and the country's most well-known right-wing political commentator, have ranged between 20 and 30 million; http://www.washingtonpost.com/wp-dyn/content/ article/2009/03/06/AR2009030603435.html. With radio's penetration rate of 92 percent higher than the 78 percent Internet penetration rate, the impact of extremism through this delivery channel should hardly be minimized.

35. As noted in Chapter 5, the metrics of American political polarization are at their highest levels since 1879; see Nolan McCarty, Keith Poole, and Howard Rosenthal, "Polarized America," at www.voteview.com/polarized_america.

36. See Stephen S. Roach, "The Slow Boat from China," *Foreign Policy*, July 9, 2013.

ACKNOWLEDGMENTS

This book continues a journey that began for me in the late 1990s. Back then, as the chief economist and head of Morgan Stanley's highly regarded global economics team, I was acutely embarrassed by a wrenching crisis—the Asian financial crisis—that had left our forecast in shambles. Determined to figure out what those events meant for Asia and the rest of the world, and operating under nothing more than a hunch that China held the key to the endgame of that crisis, I tore up my travel schedule and shuttled back and forth to Beijing every other month in late 1997 and 1998.

It quickly became evident to me that China was different. Seared by tough memories of centuries of instability—to say nothing of the more recent Cultural Revolution—I saw a modern Chinese leadership that was utterly determined to dodge the pan-regional crisis that was raging on its borders. It had both the commitment and the wherewithal to pull it off, to separate itself from the rest of Asia's crisis-torn pack. That was my personal aha moment. It didn't take long for me to get hooked on the Chinese development miracle and start to ponder what that meant for the rest of us. And the more I pondered, the more it turned into a puzzle—centered on an increasingly complex economic relationship between the United States and China.

The past three years at Yale have enriched this journey tremendously, offering the privilege of the classroom laboratory to try out many of the ideas and concepts developed in this book. I am especially appreciative of Rick

Levin's warm and welcome offer to join the faculty of Yale's new Jackson Institute for Global Affairs. I am also indebted to Jim Levinsohn, director of the Jackson Institute, for providing me with the latitude and support to design new courses to fit my interests and passion. And a special note of gratitude to my good friend and teaching partner Jeff Garten, who made the Yale connection possible from the start.

Several Yale students helped in the research for this book. Thanks to Nataliya Langburd, Michael Love, Molly Ma, and Rich Tao for their most supportive efforts. Thanks also to the more than 750 students who have now taken my "Next China" course, offering insightful feedback, fascinating research papers, and challenging questions along the way. And I have gained much from constructive dialogue on U.S.-China issues with my new colleagues on the Yale faculty, including Jonathan Spence (who opened my eyes to a very different perspective on China with his amazing 1999 book, *The Chan's Great Continent*), Ian Shapiro, Paul Gewirtz, Aleh Tsyvinski, Zhiwei Chen, Amy Chua, Deborah Davis, Stan McChrystal, Peter Schott, and Jessica Weiss.

This book attempts to give equal weight to the Chinese and American perspectives of their codependent relationship. I am deeply indebted to good friends in China, in the United States, and around the world for sharing their thoughts, insights, and feedback on many of the issues that I raise in these pages. On the Chinese side, they include Dai Xianglong, Gao Xiqing, Guo Shuqing, Hu Xiaolin, Li Ruogu, Liu Mingkang, Lou Jiwei, Lu Mai, Helen Qiao, Xiang Huaicheng, Andy Xie, Yin Yong, Yu Yongding, Zhou Xiaochuan, Zhu Guangyao, and Zhu Min. From the United States and elsewhere, I am grateful to Fred Bergsten, Lael Brainard, Jim Chanos, Henry Kissinger, Nick Lardy, Ken Lieberthal, Rakesh Mohan, Peter Nolan, Eswar Prasad, Sandy Randt, Markus Rodlauer, Stapleton Roy, Hal Scott, and Laura Tyson. My appreciation for their wise and patient counsel in no way implicates any of them in the analyses, ideas, and conclusions of this book.

The editors at Yale University Press were superb—fair, tough, and insightful from the inception to the end of this project. Bill Frucht challenged me both on the structure and clarity of my thinking (imagine that!)—and forced me to ponder the imbalances in my original portrayal of *Unbalanced*. Dan Heaton left no stone unturned as the ever-tenacious quality cop throughout the editorial process. I am immensely grateful to both of them for raising the bar on this book.

Last, and of course not least, my wonderful family has once again delivered the ultimate these past couple of years—to say nothing of the decades that preceded this project—as I disappeared for seemingly endless stretches of time to write, travel, teach, and speak on U.S.-China issues. This book would not have come together were it not for the unflinching support and understanding of my special partner, Katie, and our extraordinary six girls. *Fēi cháng gan xie!*

Final Word. I have made every effort to ground the themes and arguments in this book in up-to-date fact-based analytics. But in a world of rapidly unfolding events and ever shifting data trends, that is much easier said than done. As I signed off on the final proofs of this book in early August 2013, the U.S. and Chinese economies, to say nothing of the global economy, were in a state of great flux. The debate over the China slowdown and the U.S. recovery was intensifying. Charges and countercharges were flying on cyberhacking and trade issues. And to cap it off, a major multi-decade recasting of the statistical underpinnings of the U.S. economy was released by the Commerce Department on July 31. While the data and the events that form the foundation for this book have, I hope, been synced with these latest developments, there will undoubtedly be new twists before the publication process is complete. While this book attempts to take a clear view on what is admittedly an uncertain future, there is, of course, no telling what lies ahead for the Next America, the Next China, and the fascinating relationship between them.

INDEX